D1527475

# The
# EMBATTLED
# NORTHEAST

# The
# Northeastern Algonkian

Montagnais – Nascapi

Quebec

Maliseet

Abenaki

Androscoggins

Kennebecs

Penobscots

Wawenocks  Passamaquoddies

Micmac

Sacos

Boston

*The*

# EMBATTLED

# NORTHEAST

———————◆———————

## THE ELUSIVE IDEAL OF ALLIANCE IN

## ABENAKI-EURAMERICAN RELATIONS

*Kenneth M. Morrison*

UNIVERSITY OF CALIFORNIA PRESS   BERKELEY   LOS ANGELES   LONDON

UNIVERSITY OF CALIFORNIA PRESS
BERKELEY AND LOS ANGELES, CALIFORNIA

UNIVERSITY OF CALIFORNIA PRESS, LTD.
LONDON, ENGLAND

COPYRIGHT © 1984 BY THE REGENTS OF THE UNIVERSITY OF CALIFORNIA
LIBRARY OF CONGRESS CATALOGING IN PUBLICATION DATA

Morrison, Kenneth M.
  The embattled Northeast.

  Includes bibliographical references.
  1. Abenaki Indians—Government relations—To 1789.    2. Indians of North America—
Government relations—To 1789.    3. Abenaki Indians—History—Colonial period, ca. 1600–1775.
4. New England—Canada—History—Colonial period, ca. 1600–1775.    I. Title.
E99.A13M67    1984        305'.897        83-18002
ISBN 0-520-05126-2

PRINTED IN THE UNITED STATES OF AMERICA

1 2 3 4 5 6 7 8 9

For lessons learned and taught

—For the Old Man and Old Lady

# CONTENTS

# ACKNOWLEDGMENTS

My debts are enormous and they begin with the many institutions that provided access to the documents this study uses. First among them is the Public Archives of Canada, where a researcher is made at home as nowhere else. I also found hospitality at the Folger Library of the University of Maine at Orono, the Maine Historical Society, the Massachusetts State Archives, the Massachusetts Historical Society, the American Indian Studies Center at UCLA, and especially the Center for the History of the American Indian at the Newberry Library. My fellowship year at the Newberry was nothing short of a scholar's dream. Since Abenaki documents are scattered in many places, I worked for varying lengths of time at the New York Public Library, the Boston Public Library, the New Brunswick Museum, the Peabody Museum of Salem, Massachusetts, and the Maine State Library. I wish to acknowledge the University of Maine at Orono, the Newberry Library, and the University of California, Los Angeles, for generous grants that facilitated my research by giving me time to travel and write.

I found a permanent home in an isolated cabin in the Maine woods, the ideal place for concentrated thought and writing. Blueberry Cove has been a haven I could not have enjoyed without the tremendous assistance of my parents, Percy and Lucille Stewart, and my friend Pat Welch. So many other friends have given me support that I could not thank them all, but among them Robert Gerrity and Richard Hunt stand out for sharing their special knowledge of colonial Maine. Similarly, my students at UCLA played a special role in the writing of this book. In a very real sense a community emerged from our discussion of the challenge of American Indian history. For their critical responses, encouragement, and crucial research assistance, I want to thank Margaret Beemer, Roger Bowerman, Ann Brooks, Michael DiRosario, Robert Funsten, Cass Johnson, Susan Kenney, and Rebecca Kugel.

Scholarship is always collaborative and a number of colleagues contributed substantially to my study. Alfonso Ortiz shared his vision and from our first meeting encouraged me to pursue American Indian history. Kees Bolle, Richard Hecht, Francis Jennings, Karen Kupperman, Neal Salisbury, and Alice R. Stewart have each helped to keep me honest. I am especially grateful to Gary B. Nash, who in his extensive comments on several drafts of the manuscript showed me the reality of collegiality. I also want to thank my editor, Amanda Clark Frost, for the careful attention she gave this book. Andrea and Darryl Nicholas, Dr. Eunice B. Nelson, and Dr. Peter Paul lifted my spirits when I felt most discouraged. Singly and together they reminded me that this book is far more than a scholarly exercise in that it continues the dialogue between Abenaki and Euramericans which began at first contact. From them I learned again the power of alliance.

Finally, my greatest intellectual and literary debt is owed to my editors, Kate Vozoff and Max Benavidez. In sharing the agony of the writing, they transformed pain into quiet joy.

Blueberry Cove—                                    Kenneth M. Morrison
toward the head of
North Twin Lake, Maine

# CHRONOLOGY

| | |
|---|---|
| 1480−1600 | Fishing, trading, and exploration |
| 1604 | Founding of Acadia |
| 1607−1608 | Popham Colony |
| 1608 | Founding of New France |
| 1620 | Founding of Plymouth Colony |
| 1630 | Founding of Massachusetts Bay |
| 1646−1652 | First Abenaki mission |
| 1675−1678 | First Abenaki-English war and migration to the Jesuit mission at Sillery |
| 1688 | Outbreak of second Abenaki-English war |
| 1693 | Governor Phip's Treaty renewed |
| 1703 | Outbreak of third Abenaki-English war |
| 1713 | Treaty of Portsmouth |
| 1717 | Governor Shute's Treaty |
| 1722 | Outbreak of Dummer's War |
| 1724 | Attack on Norridgewock |
| 1727 | Dummer's Treaty |

Acadia

Port
Royal

Mt. Desert Island

Province of Maine

Penobscot R.

Kennebec R.

Monhegan

Pemaquid

Androscoggin
R.

Ft. Popham

York

Discovery/Contact
Sites

# INTRODUCTION

## *The Comparative Challenge of Indian-White Relations*

Although I began this study with only general impressions of my future work, my curiosity was deeply rooted in local tradition and family lore. I was born in a small Maine town on the Kennebec River—a place that had once been home to the Norridgewock Abenaki who play a central role in this book. Among my earliest recollections are family excursions on Memorial Day to Old Point cemetery where my immigrant ancestors rest in what once had been the fields of Norridgewock. A weathered stone obelisk standing among the pines commemorates the ancient importance of this place. Ironically, the monument eulogizes a French missionary, Sebastien Racle, rather than the Indian people with whom he worked. As a child I did not perceive this oversight, but the granite shaft near the river captured my imagination.

In my teens I read local history and learned that Norridgewock represents passionately contested ideals, political infamy, and the enduring hatred of religious fervor. There, on a quiet August afternoon in 1724, a small English force sought to revenge the wartime wounds of half a century. They left Norridgewock a smouldering ruin, its people killed or dispersed, and its old French priest dead among his people.

I learned my historical craft by coming to grips with the issues Norridgewock raised. For three hundred years American and Canadian historians have returned to the memory of Norridgewock only to amplify the nationalistic and religious prejudices that the village once evoked. Since historians have typically written about Norridgewock from either an English or a French perspective, I had to combine two apparently incompatible interpretations. In the early stages of serious study I gathered French and English documents that located the village's significance in the tragic history of the Canadian-American Northeast. I recorded a brutal story. All parties to the conflict had ample cause for frustration, anger, and bitterness. In fact, as I discovered, their inability to ease those tense emotions led again and again to open blows. Conspiracy, treachery, and animosity had been the order of the day.[1]

My investigation first focused almost exclusively on the Europeans who attempted to influence the Abenaki peoples holding the balance of power. Much of this early work therefore centered on a diplomatic history of the Northeast, particularly the region now included within the state of Maine and the province of New Brunswick. I followed well-developed paths. Historians had shown that French and English fought for control over Abenaki lands lying between their colonies. It was also clear that religious animosities carried from Europe fueled intercolonial disagreements. Both levels of this conflict caught the Abenaki between New England and New France. From 1675 to 1760 the Abenaki waged six major wars against the English. In most of these conflicts the tribes allied themselves with the French. Although the imperial context of this Abenaki-European struggle has dominated historical attention, colonial power politics was only one aspect of the conflict.

After several years I realized that confrontation and accommodation were defined not only in Boston and Quebec but in Abenaki villages as well. Caught between belligerent Europeans who were painfully becoming Americans, the Abenaki did their best to remain aloof from foreign quarrels. They almost always warred for their own reasons, a political independence that the French and English found hard to fathom. The Abenaki invariably sought their own domestic and diplomatic goals. As a result, my study of imperial diplomacy became a tribal history that placed intercolonial relations in an unexpected light. Abenaki relations with Europeans were rooted in a social philosophy that combined religion with politics. In affirming their alliance with the French, even while seeking peace with the English, the Abenaki steadfastly asserted self-determination. The tribes' enduring relationship with the French expressed a carefully considered preference. The first purpose of this book is therefore to examine the criteria by which the Abenaki assessed Europeans and to reconstruct their historical relations accordingly.[2]

I assumed that the passage of time separating the present from the events of the era of early Abenaki-Euramerican contact would make objectivity possible. But the task was not so easy. How could I understand each people on their own terms? The antipathy the Abenaki, French, and English felt for one another derived from great cultural differences. The three peoples perceived the world in fundamentally conflicting ways. Initially, they shared little common ground. And time did not help. By the eighteenth century little real communication had been achieved. Hence, a fair-minded, comparative approach to Indian-white relations had to become the second purpose of this book.[3]

I gained assurance in learning techniques to read the documentary record for Abenaki voices. Once I understood Abenaki traditions and their place in the colonial world, I could ask comparative questions about French and English diplomacy from the tribes' point of view. I joined other historians in examining ethnological studies for the information they could provide. Along with many of these scholars I learned that it was necessary to overcome widely accepted but ethnocentric estimations of Indian character. If colonials tended to condemn Indians as culturally "savage," their descendants have been reluctant to question that judgment. This misinterpretation has been as much a failure of thought as of imagination. In recent years historians and anthropologists have frankly admitted that American Indian history poses difficult intellectual issues. Scholars of Indian history now discuss not only what they study but how they study it. In the process many are gaining new insights from an interdisciplinary view of the social character of Indian-white relations. Indian history has not only to seek an Indian perspective, it must also explain the factors that affected intercultural communications. My real work started when I realized the exciting possibilities of that ethnohistorical collaboration.[4]

These challenges define the special concerns of ethnohistory, which is at once a cultural and a historical approach to the study of social interaction. My anthropological studies outlined a model for an ethnohistorical methodology and defined the critical factors requiring attention. As an ethnohistorian I have analyzed each people's cultural organization, religious and social values, and specific historical behavior. Since I am first a historian, it has seemed natural to assess how all three of these categories affected one another and changed over time. The French, English, and Abenaki all experienced momentous upheaval throughout the colonial period, and all were changed by the manner of their communication.

History is the study of unique events, and with other historians I find it necessary to emphasize the behavioral level of Indian-white interaction. My purpose is to examine northeastern peoples' willingness to deal fairly and directly with one another. As the book evolved, it became apparent that culture change and adaptation involved mutual scrutiny, defensive negotiation, constructive compromise, and violent rejection. Anthropology has identified a simple but major distinction that directs my interpretation of these complex interactions: Cultures do not meet, but people who are culture bearers do. In a fundamental sense, then, this book applies an ethnohistorical methodology to the ways in which Indians, French, and English struggled to find common ground and to take responsibility for their lives. Through consensus and conflict, they each created the separate realities in which they lived. And in the need to interpret these reconstructed interactions, another level of my study emerged.[5]

It has been equally vital to estimate the motives of French, English, and Abenaki as they attempted to communicate. Here again I have benefited from interdisciplinary studies that show that social values are at the heart of cultural order. The three peoples had strong opinions about what was right and wrong and about what made individuals trustworthy or treacherous. These opinions organized their societies internally and, as important, oriented each people to outsiders. Basic assumptions about personal and social identity were intrinsic to every discussion between the Abenaki and their colonial neighbors. The three peoples attempted to establish political influence over one another, but, more important, they each called on seemingly indisputable values to justify their actions.[6]

The final element of my ethnohistorical orientation recognizes the subtle influences of culture. Briefly put, I have viewed Abenaki, French, and English cultures from the perspective of social anthropology. The study of economic, political, and religious institutions provides a framework within which social values and historical behavior can be understood. Among both Indians and colonials, institutionalized activities reflected the ways in which these peoples met communal needs for security and solidarity. Since personal identity is more or less a socialized adjustment to group life, particular cultures represent intersubjective agreements about the nature of reality. While I disagree with those who claim that culture determines personal behavior, I do recognize that culture exerts regular, considerable, and discernable influence on how people behave. I have tried to consider the ways that ecological adjustment, social organization, and characteristic technologies tempered the internal and external social orientations of each people.[7]

Although I am concerned with French and English culture and values, every level of my historical investigation is based on an ethnographic study of Indian life. The Abenaki were tiny groups of related tribes that in turn were a small part of the Algonkian-speaking peoples of the Northeast. As used in this book, Abenaki refers to the various tribes that inhabited the river basins of New Hampshire, Maine, and New Brunswick. From west to east these peoples were the Pennacook, Saco, Androscoggin, Kennebec, Wawenock, Penobscot, Passamaquoddy, and Maliseet. When appropriate, especially in the early chapters, I have drawn on the experience of the other Algonkian (especially the Micmac and Montagnais-Naskapi) to illustrate the forces that affected the Abenaki as a whole. This technique was necessary since the sources are rich but uneven.[8]

According to English documents, the westernmost Abenaki—Pennacook, Saco, and Androscoggin—bore the brunt of the first war with New England and their self-defense ignited the second. After that, little is known about them. During the third war most migrated to Canadian mission villages or went to live with eastern neighbors. After 1689 the Kennebec Abenaki from Norridgewock led an effort to deal with New England. The Penobscot and Maliseet were also confederates in these Kennebec affairs, but distance made them much less visible to the English. That situation changed after 1724. With the destruction of Norridgewock during the fourth war the Penobscots emerged as leaders of a new intertribal alliance, and the English in turn gave them primary attention. Except for brief mention in the records of the early settlement period, the Passamaquoddy are all but invisible before 1760.

Spotty as the record may be, English documents do note significant intertribal differences. Prior to 1724 the Abenaki tribes were far from single-minded. They often disagreed among themselves and responded to Europeans independently. Their political identity was restricted to family bands of ten to thirty people and to those bands related through intermarriage and common history. Although French Catholicism and war with the English gradually drew them together, political self-reliance and independence remained an essential feature of their social structure. As initial misunderstandings hardened into bitter resentments against Europeans, tribal autonomy began to feel like weakness. In this light it becomes clear why the Abenaki adapted to Europeans by strengthening intertribal relations. They pursued alliance with Europeans as one way of fostering unity among themselves.[9]

As I reflected on how the tribes responded diplomatically to Europeans, I came to appreciate that the Abenaki were far from culturally simple. It is true that they did not have technologies based on metals, lacked political unity, and practiced what appears to have been an individualistic religion. Nevertheless, I found that even under the disruptive conditions of contact the Abenaki shared with Europeans a driving need to maintain social order. This study thus joins others in affirming the qualitative complexity of Indian life and the thoughtfulness of Indian adaptation. Throughout the colonial period the Abenaki continued to skillfully exploit the seasonal resources of their territories, successfully struggled to achieve agreement among themselves, and reinterpreted their religious world view. On all these levels similarities between the tribes and their European neighbors outweighed cultural differences.

I joined other ethnohistorians in asking interdisciplinary questions about Indian-white relations and learned from the Abenaki themselves how best to answer them. While I often wished for more information about the Abenaki point of view, ethnohistory pointed me in a new direction. In particular, I found Abenaki mythology and folklore to be a rich resource expressing the basic principles of Indian religion and cultural life. Since I had already determined that a discussion of comparative social values was essential to my study, the subjective character of the recorded oral traditions offered me just the motivational data I required. If ethnohistory is an experimental approach to comparative history, then the study of oral tradition offers one major perspective for establishing Indian motivations.[10]

While mythological and folkloric sources rarely tell us what individuals experienced at particular times and offer virtually no details for understanding discrete events, they do cast important light on general attitudes and values. In their educational role oral traditions were face-to-face speech events that embodied Abenaki history. For example, stories of Gluskap, the Abenaki and Micmac culture hero, myths about the formation of social structure, and tales about the character of cannibal giants express the basic religious and cognitive orientations of Abenaki life.

Anthropologists, folklorists, and historians of religion have discussed the critical techniques that make it possible to interpret such material. Oral traditions can be studied for thematic consistency and for variation in detail; they can also be compared intertribally. The causal effects of religious power among Algonkian tribes are well known. In the Abenaki case Gluskap's power of *Kta'hando* is pervasive throughout the written stories and demonstrates how power actually operated in social life. The same critical perspective can be applied to the character of Gluskap himself. Examples of culture heroes are found all over North America, and wherever they appear they cast the world into its present physical and moral condition. It is exactly this symbolic uniformity that is present in traditions about cannibal giants. Among the Algonkian from Nova Scotia to western Lake Superior these beings pose an ethical challenge to the order-giving function of the culture hero.[11]

A commonly used ethnohistorical technique, the direct historical approach, provides another tool for analyzing tradition. In this case the evidence is read from present to past. Oral accounts from the nineteenth and twentieth centuries are corroborated with ethnological information about Abenaki and other Algonkian peoples and with evidence from colonial observers in order to trace cultural continuity and change. Having functioned since the beginning to define social order, Abenaki myth had elasticity enough to encompass shifting realities. Myth itself adapted to renew the Abenaki's sense of self.[12]

Myth and folklore, when understood as unique records of tribal values, expose the Abenaki's idea of dynamic historical change. Unlike Euramerican documents, these oral accounts do not hide subjectivity behind supposed fact. Nevertheless, they do stem from a special and useful bias. While historians attempt to separate truth from fiction, folk memory delves deeper. Written history too often inquires only about what happened. Myth explains why events occurred as folklore remembers. Such comparison shows that Abenaki traditions are remarkably consistent over time. For all northeastern peoples—Indian and European alike—myth endures in the very fact that it embodies historical change.[13]

In juxtaposing these oral, written, and ethnographic sources I have come to understand that while cultural destruction has been a prominent feature of northeastern Indian-white relations, it was not the only outcome, or even the most important. This is why I attempt to ask my questions from an Abenaki perspective. On one level I assess the disruptive effects of European contact. On a more important level I recognize that Abenaki history is one of survival and cultural persistence. The tribes grappled with unrelenting crises because contact undermined their communal values. They often responded with personal creativity and collective flexibility. Interpersonal harmony was for them nothing short of a prime directive. Without this mythologically rooted ideal the Abenaki would have succumbed to external forces and drawn destruction upon themselves. In other words, this book examines the social history that the Abenaki themselves remember. The theme of alliance which dominated Abenaki interests poses new answers to old questions about Indian history.

In particular, a comparison of Abenaki and European religious orientations led me to reassess the role material factors played in contact interactions. Historians have typically assumed that American Indians and Europeans were on a collision course because their material cultures were incompatible. It seems that European technology and markets threatened to make Indian subsistence practices and redistributive economies obsolete. After all, Europeans themselves asserted that this cultural revolution was their first mission in America. Only economic and political transformation could prepare Indians for a meaningful role in Christian history. Abenaki myth questions this theme of technological progress and spiritual conversion.[14]

Historians commonly accept a multileveled, functional explanation of the way in which Europeans influenced contact and directed cultural change. For most scholars European dominance has seemed unquestionable. Europeans had the advantages of mobility, technologies based on metal, and capitalist expertise. Since American Indians had not developed such capabilities, their response to an increasingly subordinate situation has seemed a mere reflex of self-interest. It has been supposed that Indians either clung to a dying culture or struggled to replace lost territory and resources by accommodating themselves to European market economies. Self-interest in these terms would also explain the historical pattern of political and military alliances by which native peoples played Europeans against one another to maintain their own independence.

One widely accepted functional approach attempts to explain comparative French and English relations with Indians. This interpretation claims that two simple facts account for positive Indian estimations of the French. First, New France had just 3,000 inhabitants in 1663. A full century later its population had grown to only 60,000. According to functionalists, these few people did not compete for land, and Indians therefore saw Canadian intentions as benign. Second, the French created a symbiotic economic relationship with Indians. Canada so depended on the fur trade, functionalist historians assert, that government officials responded cautiously to Indian demands. Apparently, then, converging self-interests bonded French and Indians in unusual ways. A parallel argument tries to explain why Indians did not respond as well to the English. A burgeoning population, interested mostly in farming, dictated inevitable war.

While such functional interpretations of Indian-white relations can be compelling, they remain partial explanations because they are insensitive to the changing motives of both Indians and colonials. Furthermore, such interpretations make inappropriate historical generalizations. As Abenaki efforts to ally themselves with the French and English would indicate, human relations involve more than economic or political motives. At best, functional analysis isolates situations— commercial, military, political, and even religious—in which the Abenaki and Europeans attempted to communicate. In a broader view it can be seen that such situations did channel intercultural contact. But they never determined its outcome. At the very least, self-interest meant different things to English, French, and Indians. What is more, each of these people disagreed among themselves.

The history of Abenaki-European alliance reveals how material factors structured interaction. Differences in social scale did affect the three peoples' ability to communicate. They reacted to one another across a great cultural divide. The theoretical literature has by no means resolved the comparative issues that separate urban and nonurban peoples, but it does suggest that large-scale societies skew human intercourse. Social scale implies a good deal more than demographic and institutional complexity. While such factors obviously point out that people living in large-scale societies require highly developed social organizations, these factors are too general to encompass the diverse interactions of Indian and European peoples. In fact, a wide range of cultural characteristics channeled the particular effects of scale on social consciousness in the Northeast.[15]

Literacy is one major example of how scale affected all northeastern people. The written word made communication with Europe's metropolitan centers possible, affected the political and religious evolution of both New England and New France, and, in making economic and diplomatic development possible, complicated Indian-white alliances. Print minimized the cultural adjustments that Europeans had to make to the northeastern environment, although it could not prevent the formation of distinct regional identities. Literacy reminded Europeans of their past and called them to their destiny. Without the written word neither French nor English could have maintained an ideology of religious and technological progress. In these ways print inevitably made the small-scale oral cultures of the Abenaki seem underdeveloped.[16]

Keeping such distinctions in mind, it is possible to appreciate the distance between Europeans' pretensions to just empire and their often unethical actions. In his study of the seventeenth-century American conquest, Francis Jennings exposes the cant of English expansionism and reexamines the concepts of savagery and civilization. He asserts that both are moral judgments with little significance as objective descriptions of real people. Put this way, any comparison of Abenaki or European humanity must recognize that colonials used contradictory moral and intellectual criteria to distinguish their character from that of Indian people. At base, Europeans in general were unable to see that the Abenaki were also ethically motivated to make sense of cultural differences.[17]

The two peoples nonetheless had much in common. Both Indians and Europeans, for example, deplored the competition that resulted from the sixteenth- and seventeenth-century fur trade. Economic conflict flouted each people's social ideal of cooperative alliance. Europeans saw trade as one way to revitalize their sense of community, and so the settlement of the Northeast opened an intense period of social experimentation. While Europeans tried to create viable societies in spite of the competition fostered by their economic and political institutions, the Abenaki tried to ease commercial discord and extend friendship to their new neighbors. For colonials, contact evoked a similar challenge of extending community, life-style, and values beyond narrow national confines. In attempting their own cultural revitalization, Europeans defied the social imperatives of their economic and political institutions no less than did Indians. All northeastern peoples expected conflict but shared haunting visions of harmony.[18]

The social experiments of contact could only proceed within the parameters of European and Indian cultures. Culture, as a moral foundation, defines commonsense notions about how the world is constituted and how it operates. For the Abenaki, French, and English ethical codes reflected particular social organizations that oriented persons to one another and to the practical tasks of survival. But culture encompasses more than these functional concerns. As a lived experience, it also embodies mythic assumptions about how the world ought to be. Northeastern Indian-white relations threw such beliefs into confusion.[19]

By the second quarter of the eighteenth century several generations of Abenaki and Europeans-become-Americans had struggled with the problems and possibilities of contact. The challenge of constructive association constantly changed but invariably evoked unconscious fears and fed self-indulgent anger. Only sometimes did it nurture alliance. In each generation pessimists and bigots predominated, but always a few optimists embraced tolerance and followed the call of some far vision. Their attempts to achieve the elusive ideal of mutuality makes the seventeenth- and eighteenth-century Northeast an important scene in North American social history. All arenas of contact—religious, economic, political, and military—elicited experiments in communication and compromise. These efforts reveal a vital dimension of Indian-white relations then and now.

# 1

# FISH, FUR, AND DISCORD

## *The Struggle toward Alliance*

Uncertainty and competitive violence structured the formative period of Indian-white relations. Exploration of America's northeastern coasts is usually seen as a bold, aggressive beginning. Actually, it accelerated long-standing European conflicts that had just reached the point of takeoff. In the sixteenth century newly vigorous European states vied with one another for overseas ventures. Nevertheless, England and France were slow to grasp the possibilities of colonialism. Left in the hands of vigorous individuals, with occasional official voyages, a full one hundred years of reconnaissance produced little continuity of personnel or organization.

Instead, Europeans embarked into the unknown single-mindedly seeking profits. Initially, technological innovations slowly drew American Indians and Europeans together. Codfish first attracted the attention of independent fishermen and unexpected revenues whet entrepreneurial appetites. Although fishing elicited adapted forms of European commercial organization and technology, American Indian furs soon broadened the search for other sources of wealth. Together, fish and furs stimulated international competition, making the Northeast a major arena in which England and France fought for economic supremacy.

The early fishing voyages to the Grand Banks off Newfoundland rarely touched shore. Codfish were caught, dressed, and packed in salt for rapid transit back to Europe. Wet cod fishing efficiently produced a palatable product. In time, however, a new fishing technology made a land base essential to European enterprise: the French were the first to learn that codfish were ideal for drying in the sun. Dried cod were light, imperishable, and more delicious than the wet variety. Gradually this innovation pushed the fishing fleet toward sunny shores. Once aground, regular European and American Indian contact began.[1]

The Algonkian-speaking tribes living on northeastern coasts also confronted attractions that expanded their world. Throughout the sixteenth century they reacted cautiously, watching the newcomers' behavior for signs of hostility or fellowship. Before 1550 the dressed skins and furs they bartered provided incidental profits for themselves and for fishermen whose attention remained unwaveringly on cod. Eventually, European demand for furs and fish drew eastern and western Atlantic peoples into permanent, mutually profitable, frequently abrasive, and always dynamic contact. For better or worse, commerce defined the first level of social struggle between Indians and Europeans.

The intersection of European and Algonkian economies poses special challenges for historical interpretation. First, the surviving documents are few and far between. Historians have used these sources to reconstruct European reconnaissance of the Northeast's resources and peoples, but the explorers' accounts do not do justice to the complexity of Indian response. According to European testimony, sixteenth- and seventeenth-century encounters had but a single theme. As a result, many historians argue that the commercially sophisticated Europeans overawed the northeastern Algonkian who naively exchanged valuable furs for worthless trinkets.

This view is ethnocentric. Ethnohistorical studies have shown that commercial exchange was regulated as much by Indian economic organization as by European trade expectations. At the outset we have only to recognize that Algonkian peoples posed as much of a challenge to Europeans as the Indians themselves confronted. Ethnohistorians realize that even such a simple reorientation changes the way in which we understand Indian-white relations. It is safe to say that before Indian experience can be appreciated most ideas about the comparative vigor of Indian civilization and our own must be abandoned. In contradiction to once widely held convictions, it is now clear that Indians were active participants in their own history.

It is apparent that the destructive nature of Indian-white relations has made students of American Indian history unduly concerned with the effects of tragedy. The small-scale character of Indian societies has made them seem vulnerable to change. Fundamentally challenged and abruptly uprooted, Indian cultures may seem to have been vanquished or internally collapsed. Certainly, this theme of doom runs through many accounts of Indian history. Heated scholarly arguments over the morality of cross-cultural associations, efforts to assign blame and absolve guilt, along with attempts to balance Euramerican duplicity against the vitality of tribal resistance—all derive from a kindred fixation. While substantial evidence suggests that cultural change is seldom so quick or so far-reaching, devastation has become one of the central themes of Indian history.[2]

In fact, concepts of social disorganization and cultural decline do not describe the early effects of contact between the northeastern Algonkian and Europeans. The first of the Algonkian to experience contact— Montagnais, Micmac, and Abenaki—were as ingenious in responding to new and advantageous trade associations as were the venturing Europeans. Whatever the long-range implications for their continued cultural integrity, the Algonkian seized these economic opportunities with an assurance that belies the prevalent assumption that Europeans were technologically superior.

The sixteenth and early seventeenth centuries were a time of mutual discovery, and at least until the Northeast was extensively settled, Algonkian societies regulated the course of their economic and political adaptation. The fur trade provided them with an expanded repertoire of techniques as metal amplified both domestic arts and subsistence tasks. These were substantial modifications to the Algonkian's material culture, but each tribe reacted to change in ways that complemented traditional social values. Alterations in material culture created a florescence rather than a decline of Algonkian cultures.

In a much more basic way trade created enduring problems of association between Algonkian fur producers and European purveyors of metal products. Constructive economic contact challenged both peoples to recognize a shared humanity. Seen from an ethnohistorical perspective, this process of discovery was fraught with difficulty. Trade required that both come to grips with differences and similarities in economic and political organization. Discussion of these comparative issues dominated the exploratory exchanges, and commercial contact became the initial context for accommodation and conflict. While these issues had not been resolved by the beginning of the seventeenth century, significant common interests had emerged.[3]

INITIAL PROBES

Throughout the first half of the sixteenth century the northeastern Algonkian remained a minor concern to most Europeans. Cod fishing and the fur trade essentially defined the perimeters of European fascination with these people and their resources. Nonetheless, despite the fact that fish and fur provided the basis of early and subsequent contact, a more definitive transaction was evolving. Each time a fur was traded or a metal good exchanged, something subtle happened. Europeans and American Indians began learning how to think about and react to one another.

Initially, Indians had only brief glimpses of European fishermen and for a time treated them in a fairly openhanded manner. Europeans chose a rather different approach and before long Indians regretted even limited encounters. When Gaspar Corte Real returned home from his 1501 voyage to Newfoundland, he brought with him fifty-seven Beothuk captives. Many Indians became European slaves or curiosities in the sixteenth century, but the Beothuk and the Micmac absorbed the first shock of contact. The Beothuk's defensive withdrawal from European aggression hides their eventual extermination. The Micmac, however, resisted. In the 1520s João Alvares Fagundes of Portugal established a fishing station on Cape Breton Island, but hostilities with the local Micmac and competing fishermen soon closed it. Except for the Beothuk and the Micmac, few tribes had more than glimpses of the strange men sailing the North Atlantic and the brevity of contact handicapped most Indians in gauging European character.[4]

It was not long before Indians had seen enough to make them cautious. A 1524 French voyage under the command of Giovanni da Verrazano found evidence of previous European visits to the Northeast. North of Cape Cod, the explorer came on Abenaki whose behavior indicated that the Beothuk were not the only tribe to regret the European acquaintance. Verrazano declared that the Abenaki "were full of crudity and vices, and were so barbarous that we could never make any communication with them, however many signs we made to them." In fact, the Abenaki were wary rather than dumb. Graphically expressing familiarity with aggressive European trading habits, the Abenaki gave Verrazano a nonverbal message that he recorded in his journal:

> If we wanted to trade with them for some of their things, they would come to the sea shore on some rocks where the breakers were most violent, while we remained in the little boat, and they sent us what they wanted to give on a rope, continually shouting to us not to approach the land; they gave us the barter quickly, and would take in exchange only knives, hooks for fishing, and sharp metal.

Such obvious calculation offended Verrazano. "We found no courtesy in them," he complained, "and when we had nothing more to exchange and left them, the men made all the signs of scorn and shame that any brute creature would make."[5]

The Abenaki had ample grounds for caution. Apparently unaware of the disparity between his words and behavior, Verrazano wrote: "Against their wishes, we penetrated two or three leagues inland with XXV men, and when we disembarked on the shore, they shot at us with their bows and uttered loud cries before fleeing into the woods." It was precisely this European insolence that led to violent episodes throughout the early contact period. Estevão Gomes, a Portuguese explorer, returned home in 1525, as Verrazano had before him, with Algonkian captives to mark his passage.[6]

Another French voyage, this one under the command of Jacques Cartier in 1534, met other Indian people who were aware of the possibilities for trade. In searching for a western passage through the continent Cartier inspected the Gulf of St. Lawrence and the east coast of New Brunswick. While surveying the Bay of Chaleur, he observed Micmac behavior suggesting that private enterprise had again preceded official voyages of discovery. The Indians, said Cartier, made "signs to us that they had come to barter with us; and held up some furs of small value, with which they clothe themselves." Moreover, they "bartered all they had to such an extent that all went back naked without anything on them; and they made signs to us that they would return on the morrow with more furs." Unlike Fagundes, Verrazano, and Gomes, whose actions had provoked a defensive response from Indians, Cartier left the Micmac expecting continued peaceful commerce.[7]

Sailing north, Cartier may have been the first European to meet Iroquoian-speaking people. Although their home base at Stadacona was much farther up the St. Lawrence River, the Iroquoians were on one of their regular fishing trips to the gulf. These people were far more wary than the Micmac had been, but they were also intrigued. "When they had mixed with us a little on shore," Cartier wrote, "they came freely in their canoes to the sides of our vessels. We gave them knives, glass beads, combs and other trinkets of small value, at which they showed many signs of joy, lifting up their hands to heaven and singing and dancing in their canoes." Cartier did not trade extensively at that time, but he promised to return with ample goods for trade. Unlike the Micmac at the Bay of St. Chaleur, however, the Iroquoians learned to view the French with suspicion: Cartier captured two of their party.[8]

Having found in the St. Lawrence River a possible water route into the heart of the continent, Cartier turned toward France. Following the northern coast, he encountered the Montagnais, another Algonkian-speaking group. Obviously comfortable with Europeans, twelve Montagnais "came as freely on board our vessels as if they had been Frenchmen." They communicated that they had recently met fishing vessels in the Gulf of St. Lawrence.[9]

Official voyages on this and other occasions merely confirmed a knowledge of the region already held by the numerous fishermen who dried their catch on shores adjacent to Newfoundland. It may be that members of Cartier's crew knew these waters well, that they had more experience than their commander, and that they returned to the Gulf of St. Lawrence with personal profit in mind. Although Cartier wintered twice in Canada, official attempts to exploit northeastern North America lagged behind a driving, individualistic commercialism. Fishing was the first profit link between the two Atlantic coasts. But as resourceful fishermen met Indians willing and even eager to trade furs, European interest in the Northeast broadened.

The profits fishermen made from even casual fur trading soon drew the avid interest of French investors. The first recorded voyage exclusively for furs occurred in 1569. In 1581 merchants of St. Malo, Rouen, and Dieppe organized an extremely lucrative voyage to the St. Lawrence River. A second ship, dispatched secretly in 1582, found a seemingly limitless supply of furs. The following year French merchants sent three ships, and a fleet of five followed in 1584. A Rouen merchant, Étienne Bellenger, sailed to Nova Scotia and Maine in 1583 to establish a trading colony and missionary post. Although he ultimately abandoned the enterprise, he returned to France with furs that brought a neat 1,000 percent profit. Shrewd entrepreneurs that they were, other merchants rushed ten ships to Canada in 1585. The results surpassed their wildest dreams: the expedition produced profits as high as 1,400 percent.[10]

Richard Hakluyt, an Englishman aware of French maritime exploits in the Northeast, enviously observed 20,000 crowns of fur in Paris in 1583. Knowing that England had not yet entered the race for New World profits, Hakluyt prodded national pride. Practical men responded. The English fishing fleet, which in the 1570s still consisted of only four "small barkes," began to grow dramatically. One Englishman, Anthony Parkhurst, urged his countrymen to outstrip foreigners by settling Newfoundland, contending that " 'peopled and well fortified . . . we shall bee lordes of the whole fishing in small time.' " When Parkhurst numbered the English fleet at forty or fifty ships in 1578, he realized that the English conquest of the fisheries was well under way.[11]

Although the English faced stiff competition—100 Spanish, 50 Portuguese, and 150 French ships visited the Grand Banks in 1578— they prevailed against all rivals. Determined to wrest a place for themselves, various influential Englishmen supported the nation's bid for hegemony in Atlantic waters. With more bravado than real impact, Humphrey Gilbert took ceremonial and temporary possession of Newfoundland for the British crown in 1583. English privateering had begun the year before, and Bernard Drake attacked twenty Portuguese vessels in 1585, taking ten as a war prize. Conflicts over the fisheries won the English all that they desired and produced something more: French and Basque fishermen abandoned eastern Newfoundland and joined the already numerous trading vessels in direct contact with the American mainland. As a result, English aggression in the last quarter of the sixteenth century concentrated European and Algonkian contact in two areas: Tadoussac on the north shore of the Gulf of St. Lawrence and the islands adjacent to the continent.[12]

Tadoussac, a site at the mouth of the Saguenay River, commanded both the northern hinterland of present-day Quebec and the St. Lawrence interior. Here both Indians and Europeans gathered to fish and to capture sea mammals, especially seals and whales. The fur trade can be positively dated at Tadoussac from the 1550s, but it may well have had a longer history. Whatever the exact date of its origin, the site typified the process of commercial development: sealing, fishing, and incidental fur trading grew rapidly as the English drove their European rivals west, away from Newfoundland.[13]

Tadoussac also localized early competition between Frenchmen. By the late 1580s immense and easily achieved profits led to violent confrontations between French traders. In 1587 two Frenchmen, Jean and Michel Noel, lost four small trading vessels, probably to French rivals. To secure protected access to fur trade profits, the Noels' father Jacques requested and received from the French crown monopoly rights to the St. Lawrence region. In return Noel agreed to colonize the territory. He soon faced outraged opposition from the merchants of St. Malo, who wanted the trade to remain unregulated and opposed permanent settlement. For the time being, business superseded King Henri III's strategic interest in colonization.[14]

The second area of intense contact bordered the western side of the Gulf of St. Lawrence. European exploitation of this region's maritime resources followed a pattern similar to that established at Tadoussac. Throughout the 1580s, 200 vessels a year visited Prince Edward Island alone. While domestic rivalries continued, commercial conflict in the gulf rapidly became international. In 1591 Englishmen captured a French and a Basque ship, both of which were returning from the Magdalen Islands. The French vessel carried valuable walrus tusks, leather, and oil while the Basques had a cargo "of Riche Fures as beavers, martrenes otters and many other Sortes." With the aid of Stevan de Bocall—a renegade Basque pilot willing to sell his expert knowledge of gulf fisheries, fur trading, and Indian relations—the English also began to move beyond Newfoundland. They were especially drawn to the Magdalen Islands, where summering Micmac seem to have developed positive ties with the French and Basques. When Englishmen attacked French and Basque ships in 1597, three hundred Micmac opposed the aggression.[15]

This fracas on the Magdalens provides a glimpse of the intergroup dynamics that channeled the developing trade. Since fishermen and traders concentrated on the maritime regions of the Northeast and since national and international competition was prevalent in this era, Algonkian contact with European merchants involved a dangerous flirtation with violence. But the Micmac and Montagnais had had ample opportunity to gauge European character. It would appear then that the Micmac who repulsed English aggressions in the summer of 1597 expressed a critical preference. Friendship fostered trade.

TOWARD SETTLEMENT

Until the opening of the seventeenth century Europeans seldom visited the shores west of the Nova Scotian peninsula. In 1579–80 an

English expedition to the Penobscot River in Maine failed to find anything that could substantiate rumors of a wealthy city called Norumbega where people adorned themselves with gold, silver, and pearls. The explorers did report favorably on the temperate climate and the Penobscot's suitability for settlement. In 1583 Étienne Bellenger traded within the Gulf of Maine and he commented on people who were still "gentle and tractable." Such a remark suggests that few Europeans had reached the Abenaki. Beyond these voyages there is only a hint of Basques quietly entering the Bay of Fundy in the last quarter of the century. Still, trade developed. The French later reported, though with exaggeration, that the western Micmac spoke a language that was "half Basque."[16]

Whatever the Basques may have contributed to developing trade relations, the French had a greater impact on the entire Northeast. As the sixteenth century closed, the French consolidated what they had learned of American Indians and tried again to centralize trading arrangements. In 1600 Pierre de Chauvin de Tonnetuit received from King Henri IV commercial control of the St. Lawrence fur trade. Although Chauvin agreed to establish 500 settlers in Canada over a ten-year period, he obviously preferred trade to colonization. For two years he profited from the trade without fulfilling the terms of his monopoly. His French competitors resented their exclusion, but Henri IV initially resisted merchant complaints against Chauvin. Once again, however, persistent commercial opposition confounded royal resolve, and two other merchant groups were admitted as equals to Chauvin's privilege and responsibility.[17]

The expanded Chauvin monopoly not only helped restrain commercial conflict but trained Frenchmen in Indian diplomacy. These men eventually combined trade and colonization successfully. Pierre de Gua, the Sieur de Monts, and Samuel de Champlain, founders of the first seventeenth-century French colony, learned their profession alongside Chauvin at Tadoussac. They mastered new commercial techniques: even as early as 1600, the Canadian fur trade had become an amalgam of Indian and French customs. Champlain's 1603 book *Of Savages* documents the interpersonal character of the commercial alliance. Unlike most traders, who interacted with Indians only as a casual sideline to fishing, the French merchants sought a more enduring relationship. Two Montagnais who journeyed to France with Chauvin expressed the unfolding accommodation. According to Champlain, with whom they returned to Tadoussac in 1603, they told their people "of the good reception that the king had given them, and of the good entertainment they had received in France, and that they might feel assured His Majesty wished them well, and desired to people their country, and to make peace with their enemies (who are the Iroquois) or send forces to vanquish them." In effect, the Montagnais who visited France became cultural go-betweens, as did the French who wintered in America.[18]

Mutual hospitality formed the bedrock of the early alliance. When in Canada, the French were also richly feted. Champlain describes the *tabagie*, a feast that ritualized relations. The Montagnais sachem Anadabijou received the French respectfully and in the time-honored manner. Seating them at his side, the headman "began to smoke tobacco," Champlain wrote, "and to pass on his pipe to Monsieur du Pont-Gravé of St. Malo, and to me, and to certain other Sagamores who were near him." Then Anadabijou welcomed the French "with gravity" and affirmed their friendship. The tabagie followed immediately and everyone feasted on ten kettles of moose, bear, seal, beaver, and wildfowl.[19]

Pragmatic concerns underlay the form of the *tabagie* and gave it substance. Anadabijou identified the grist of the 1603 alliance, saying that "he was well content that His said Majesty should people their country, and make war on their enemies." Anadabijou also savored the "advantages and profit" the Montagnais and their allies would reap. These words were more than calculated rhetoric. One thousand allied Algonkian—Montagnais, Abenaki, and Algonkin—were at that time celebrating their recent victory over the Iroquois.[20]

The Algonkian who gathered annually at Tadoussac were the first American Indians to experience the long-term cultural impact of the fur trade. European metal goods, such as axes and kettles, created a steady market. The coastal peoples, especially Montagnais and Micmac, enjoyed advantages in the developing trade. Precontact trading patterns intensified as the eastern Algonkian traded metal for furs with more isolated Indian tribes. As Anadabijou stated, war with the Iroquois was a direct result of this increased trade. Commercial rivalries amplified traditional conflict because the tribes vied for the furs of the St. Lawrence and its tributaries. The eastern Algonkian needed exclusive access to French traders if they were to maintain their advantageous position. By 1603 the Montagnais had organized a trading network that included many of the tribes of northern Quebec.[21]

Because the French gave these intertribal trading patterns careful attention, they established a premier role for themselves in northeastern trade. While it is true that most Frenchmen remained obsessed with free-wheeling commerce, a few entrepreneurs aimed to combine profit with permanent settlement in what is now Maine, New Brunswick, and Nova Scotia. Their ultimate dominance came not from numerical superiority but from a recognition that Indians were crucial to the developing trade. The founders of Acadia—the Sieur de Monts, Samuel de Champlain, and Jean de Biencourt de Poutrincourt—inherited the experience of fifty years of commercial contact. They still had much to learn about the Algonkian Northeast, but by 1600 the French generally understood Indian peoples' temperament, alliances, and trading customs.

Lack of experience worked against the English when they began to challenge the French. In search of knowledge, wealth, and possible settlement sites in Abenaki country, three English voyages pushed beyond the Nova Scotian peninsula between 1602 and 1605. These explorers expected favorable trade, but their commercial strategies were cautious. It is not surprising that their uneasiness fostered disdain. As John Brereton noted in 1602, the Abenaki were of "broad and grim visage, of a blacke swart complexion, their eiebrowes painted white." The Abenaki felt English contempt in 1603 when Martin Pring set dogs upon them. The French also approached unknown Indians gingerly. Sometimes hostilities occurred, but seasoned French traders were less inclined to see danger where there was none. Unlike the inexperienced English, the French had begun to temper fear with open-mindedness. [22]

The English invariably treated the Abenaki contemptuously, especially when trading. "We used them kindly," Pring reported, but he gave the Abenaki "divers sorts of our meanest Merchandise." Captain George Waymouth's party was as calculating in 1605. When the Abenaki offered to barter fish for sea biscuit, the English refused. "In maner of exchange," Waymouth's scribe James Rosier explained, "I would alwayes make the greatest esteeme I could of our commodities whatsoever." Even when the Abenaki ritually offered tobacco, their gift was rebuffed. "We would not receive anything from them without remuneration," Rosier wrote. Aboard ship, however, Waymouth was always generous to the Indians "to the end we might allure them still to frequent us." Rosier explained his captain's deliberate reaction to the Abenaki: Waymouth wished to impress on the Abenaki that English power exceeded the bounds of trade. He magnetized a sword "to cause them to imagine some great power in us; and for that to love and feare us." [23]

Such calculation created difficulty. George Waymouth alienated the Abenaki and undercut any possibility for peaceful coexistence. While the English suspected the Abenaki of planning some attack, Waymouth took the initiative. Rosier later noted that Waymouth had intended all along to take Abenaki captives. Three were taken when they visited Waymouth's ship, including the "one we most desired to bring with us into England." This man "received exceeding kind usage at our hands, and was therefore delighted in our company." Others were captured on shore, although not without resistance. Waymouth set the precedent for a long heritage of contempt and violence between English and Abenaki, and his captives hoodwinked gullible Englishmen at every opportunity. [24]

These Abenaki were the first Indians seen in western England and they caused nothing short of a sensation. Sir Ferdinando Gorges and another eager Englishman, George Popham, scrutinized the captives with mounting enthusiasm. "And the longer I conversed with them," Gorges wrote, "the better hope they gave me of those parts where they did inhabit, as proper to our uses, especially when I found what goodly Rivers, stately Islands and safe harbours those parts abounded with." Backed by popular sentiment and prominent supporters, Gorges and Popham obtained a royal charter in April 1606 for two colonization corporations: the Virginia companies of London and Plymouth. While the London Company turned its attention south, Plymouth concerned itself with northern Virginia, later called New England. Although members of the Plymouth company were more interested in fishing than in settlement, Gorges and Popham overrode their reluctance. [25]

The Plymouth company's experiment in colonization was disastrous. Gorges and Popham had hoped that commercial relations with the Abenaki would smooth the path of settlement, and it may well have been that the Indian captives deliberately encouraged them with enticing stories. In fact, two of Waymouth's captives actively discouraged Abenaki aid to the would-be colonists. The first, Nahanada, returned to his home in 1606 and undoubtedly told the Abenaki ugly tales of English people. When Popham arrived in Maine the following year with the second captive, Skidwarres, he was coolly received by a defensive Indian people. Highly suspicious of English intent, the Abenaki armed themselves but then fled from the Popham party. Perhaps to regain credibility—the English had forced Skidwarres to lead them to Nahanada—they released their second captive. Now abandoned by their supposed Abenaki friends and still believing that Indian aid would be forthcoming, the Popham colonists found their way alone to the lower Kennebec River.[26]

Although inadequate planning, factionalism, and weak leadership doomed the Popham colony to failure, poor Indian relations also contributed substantially to its demise. Nahanada and Skidwarres remained aloof, and the Abenaki of the Kennebec River came to view the settlement suspiciously. A French Jesuit, Pierre Biard, learned the Abenaki's reaction to the colony in 1611 when the Kennebec told him that they admired George Popham, who "got along remarkably well" with them. Nonetheless, the Androscoggin Abenaki disliked him and claimed credit when he died in February 1608. "These people make a practice of killing by magic," Biard observed dryly.[27]

After Popham's death, the colonists began to abuse the Abenaki: "They drove the Salvages [sic] away without ceremony; they beat, mal-treated and misused them outrageously and without restraint," Biard reported. The Abenaki waited for their chance and killed eleven of the colonists while they were fishing. An English document supports Biard's account of the violence. Gorges himself acknowledged that the root cause of the colony's collapse lay in Nahanada's and Skidwarres's hostility: "They shew themselves exceeding subtill and conninge, concealing from us the places, wheare they have the commodityes wee seake for, and if they finde any, that hath promised to bring us to it, those that came out of England instantly carry them away, and will not suffer them to com neere us any more."[28]

The French experienced far less trouble during the same period, although they too had difficulties. In 1604 the Sieur de Monts received a trade monopoly covering the St. Lawrence River and Algonkian territory to the south. Hoping to avoid the arduous winters of Tadoussac and intrigued by reports of mineral resources, de Monts first settled among the Passamaquoddy Abenaki. After a difficult winter in 1604–05, he moved the colony to Port Royal on the western coast of Nova Scotia and began to recoup his losses. Trading profits were high despite stiff competition from French and Basque interlopers. Acadia turned out to be far less attractive than de Monts and his associate Champlain had supposed.[29]

Still, the western Micmac and their Abenaki neighbors were congenial and eager to trade. In fact, the tribes were even prepared to make peace with each other in order to foster a closer French association. In 1604 Champlain used the skills he had learned at Tadoussac to mediate between the tribes. The Penobscot welcomed his overtures on behalf of the Micmac and promised to "hunt the beaver more than they had ever done, and barter these beaver with us in exchange for things necessary for their usage."[30]

While the French savored such assurances, they nonetheless explored Acadian coasts for another vital advantage. Their experience at Tadoussac and on the St. Lawrence had taught them the ideal conditions for a trading colony. To receive large quantities of furs, the French needed Indian allies to act as distributive agents throughout an extensive hinterland. Acadian Indians did have considerable supplies of furs, but none of their rivers offered access to inland Indian tribes who might be induced to trade. These conditions suggested to de Monts's associates that the St. Lawrence and its tributaries were more promising than Acadia, but another event forestalled their initial venture. In 1607 de Monts's monopoly was abolished. With de Monts's support Champlain established a permanent post at Quebec on the St. Lawrence in 1608 and became the founder of New France.

Other Frenchmen remained in Acadia and continued to trade with the Algonkian. Jean de Poutrincourt received a grant from de Monts for the settlement at Port Royal and the king confirmed this limited concession. With free trade reestablished in 1609, merchants rushed to Acadia, but they ignored Poutrincourt's right to one-fifth of all furs. That very summer Henry Hudson observed two French ships trading furs with the Penobscot Abenaki "for red cassocks, knives, hatchets, copper kettles, trevits, beades and other trifles." Hudson's behavior also cast new light on the Penobscot's developing relationship with the French. For after observing the Indians for five days the English explorer suddenly "drove the savages from their houses and tooke the spoyle of them." Although other Englishmen fished and traded among the Abenaki, they usually noted that the Indians were decided Francophiles. "We ranged the coast both East and West much further," John Smith said of his 1614 voyage, "but our Commodities were not esteemed, they were so neere the French who afforded them better, with whom the Salvages [sic] had such commerce that only by trade they make exceeding great voyages."[31]

The French and English shared similar goals in this early period, but the French had one outstanding advantage: they knew that regular and intimate contact facilitated trade. The French applied the lesson well and added a noncommercial dimension to their trade alliance with the Algonkian. Priests of the Society of Jesus traveled in the company of fur traders, seizing every chance to know Indians firsthand. Father Pierre Biard, for example, introduced himself to Maliseet, Penobscot, and Kennebec peoples as well as to the Micmac, who commanded the priests' primary attention.

The Jesuits were initially pleased to discover that the Algonkian felt that baptism symbolically allied them with the French, but the priests soon adopted a more cautious approach. They faced monumental obstacles: language differences, conflict with the Sieur de Poutrincourt at Port Royal, and their own unrealistic expectations. The priests felt encouraged, nevertheless, because the Algonkian recognized that the missionaries' interests transcended the commercial objectives of other Europeans. The tribes saw the Jesuits as ritualistic specialists comparable to their own shamans. In fact, the priests had earned a reputation as healers even before they met some Abenaki groups.[32]

Despite Indian interest, other Frenchmen threatened the Jesuit mission. The priests were unpopular in France and knew they would have to become Poutrincourt's financial partners in order to begin their mission. This arrangement contained the seeds of conflict because Poutrincourt greatly resented Pierre Biard's active interference in the colony's civil affairs. With the support of individuals prominent in court circles, especially the Marquise de Guercheville, the Society of Jesus began an independent mission in Acadia. In May 1613 the Jesuits left Port Royal and created the mission of Saint Sauveur near Mt. Desert Island in the Gulf of Maine. The mission was short-lived. Early in July Samuel Argall, acting on behalf of the Virginia Company of London, attacked the mission. After an ineffectual resistance, the Jesuits succumbed and temporarily left North America.[33]

The abrupt termination of Saint Saveur and the subsequent destruction of French settlements at Saint Croix and Port Royal had both an immediate and a long-term impact on the Abenaki. First, the attack brought home again the implications of alliance with Europeans. The eastern Abenaki learned that if they sided with the French, they would have to contend with English hostility. Second, the mission's ruin confirmed the eastern Abenaki's preference for the French despite the dangers involved. A French trading post among the Maliseet on the St. John River survived Argall's attack unharmed. Charles de Biencourt, Poutrincourt's heir in Acadia, also constructed a similar fort on the lower Penobscot River and profited substantially until Plymouth Colony seized the post in 1626.[34]

ALGONKIAN CULTURE CHANGE

The Algonkian did not passively observe these early contact events. Like Europeans, Indians experienced an expanding world and they adapted to new technological and social horizons. It is frequently argued that the fur trade reoriented American Indian cultures, but such views typically emphasize the negative aspects of commercial exchange while they minimize Indian efforts to regularize the trade and apply metal goods to the improvement of their lives. Hindsight is dangerous because it reads later economic crises into the earlier time. The formative period of European-Algonkian relations was mutually profitable, invigorating, and only sometimes destructive.[35]

The effects of contact rumbled throughout the Algonkian world, but the immediate impact of the trade was moderate. The Micmac and the Abenaki altered their hunting, gathering, fishing, and domestic technologies with no idea of remaking themselves culturally. They only sought greater efficiency in those tasks. Judging by frequent French assertions that Indians were lazy, and devoted as the tribes were to the pleasures of social life, the Algonkian probably did wish to enhance their leisure activities. Metal and cloth replaced fur, bone, wood, and stone as raw materials, but Europeans also adopted new technologies to exploit the Northeast.

Metal products played a role in the Micmac and Abenaki economies analogous to the role fish and furs played in Europe. The Algonkian sometimes used metal products as Europeans had intended, but often they did not. The Algonkian sought metal for their own purposes and used finished metal goods to meet traditional needs. When an object served their purpose, it was adopted with no cultural disorientation. If the artifact did not seem useful, they adapted it to other ends. Copper pots, for example, were a major innovation in Algonkian life and were used for more than cooking. Once flattened and cut to create distinctive ornaments, kettles did not differ materially from the copper the Algonkian had long used. Products that retained European functions—including kettles, hatchets, fish hooks, and needles—made traditional activities more efficient without altering their nature. Whether used in ceremonies such as funeral feasts, in hunting, fishing, and warfare, or in the labors of domestic life, metal goods redefined long-established interests.[36]

Early European observers noted these adaptations as well as the seasonal mobility that continued to produce a varied diet. Abundant plant, animal, fish, and shellfish resources provided the Algonkian a lavish living—all without work, the missionary Pierre Biard complained. Their extensive use of maritime foods especially struck Europeans. Before trade influenced subsistence activities, the Abenaki, Micmac, and Montagnais depended heavily on the sea and summered on the coast. One hundred years later they still lived on the coast, taking sea mammals, fish, shellfish, and innumerable kinds of shore birds.[37]

Biard detailed the seasonal activities that led the Micmac and the Abenaki up the bays, rivers, and lakes to family hunting territories. Isolated from their fellows for much of the year, the Algonkian exploited beaver, caribou, moose, and bear. Spring found them together, feasting on fish—smelt, herring, sturgeon, salmon. Migratory wildfowl arrived soon after. "These then, but in still greater number, are the revenues and incomes of our Savages," Biard exclaimed; "such, their table and living, all prepared and assigned, everything in its proper place and quarter."[38]

In time the archaeological record may show that the fur trade changed an older cycle of this winter/spring, inland/coast orientation. Some evidence already hints that the precontact Passamaquoddy had a different seasonal mobility pattern than that described in European documents. Still, evidence throughout the colonial period indicates that the fur trade did not significantly alter the tribes' relationship to the land. The fur trade placed a premium on hunting and trapping skills, and it is likely that the previously established family hunting territories became more formalized Abenaki institutions after regular commerce began. For both the Micmac and the Abenaki the expansion of a trapping economy did not displace traditional economic resources.[39]

This is not to say that commercial contact had no impact on the Abenaki. From a functional point of view, the fur trade had similar implications for both sides of the Atlantic: it benefited both Europeans and Indians to organize the trade. Individualized contact between fishermen and Indians provided too convenient an opportunity for trading abuses and violence. To avoid friction Europeans and the Algonkian hoped to regulate trade. Nevertheless, they understood this challenge in very different ways.

In the European context economic activities were highly individualistic. Economic life depended on specialists who were rewarded variously for their services to the overall enterprise. Financiers who accumulated and used working capital made corporate ventures possible. As we have seen, this capitalist structure increasingly typified sixteenth- and seventeenth-century fishing and trading. Although these large-scale organizations made European expansion possible, their cooperative features were in fact functionally individualistic, for profits were not shared equally. Instead, after capital gain and loss were balanced, net profits were divided either in proportion to the initial investment or according to the expertise contributed.

Europeans expected that trade would conform to this economic system, and the formal features of Algonkian economics did encourage their erroneous assumptions about Indian motivations. For example, Indians asserted and traders recognized tribal or national status as the cornerstone of commercial contact. Since trade involved the free movement of goods and people, the Algonkian envisioned structured relations with European merchants. They accorded diplomatic status to some foreigners, exchanged spokesmen, and ritualized gift-giving between political officials. Pierre Biard described the complicated cultural factors that governed Algonkian trade:

> You may be sure they understand how to make themselves courted. They set themselves up for brothers of the King, and it is not expected that they will withdraw from the least from the whole farce. Gifts must be presented and speeches made to them, before they condescend to trade; this done, they must have Tabagie, i.e. the Banquet. Then they will dance, make speeches and sing *Adesquidex, Adesquidex*, that is that they are good friends, allies, associates, confederates, and comrades of the King and of the French. . . .[40]

These role patterns imply that the Algonkian strove to draw Europeans into an economic ideology based on reciprocal exchange between allies. The Algonkian did not divide profits according to energy expended or expertise applied or even according to the proportional surplus individuals produced. They rewarded productivity with status and responsibility, not with goods, money, or any other abstract measure of value. In their cultures individuals won social acclaim only if they freely distributed profits among the people. The Algonkian valued productive persons and assessed and honored their significance directly. They were not interested in capital formation for its own sake. Rather, they recognized economic success in terms of the security achieved for the community as a whole. The sachems, generally the most successful providers, acted as redistributive agents. They not only created a surplus but assured its fair division. Pierre Biard noticed how the system worked: "Now all that the young men capture belongs to the Sagamore; but the married ones give him only a part, and if these leave him, as they often do for the sake of the chase and supplies, returning afterwards they pay their dues and homage in skins and like gifts."[41]

The fur trade challenged this redistributive imperative and made the ideal more difficult to achieve. It had the same impact on Europeans. In emphasizing economic individualism, trade created a broader field for social struggle and, if anything, intensified connections between economic production and political status. Biard observed ambitious men causing "quarrels and jealousies." Some sachems, like Membertou, attached themselves to the French to ensure their position and influence. Marc Lescarbot said of Membertou that "rumour runs that he has many enemies, and is well content to keep close to the French, in order to live in safety." Europeans also treated headmen with greater respect and that practice confirmed the status gradations within Algonkian societies. In 1624, for example, an English fur trader, Christopher Levett, noted the potential for vanity: "The *Sagamores* will scarce speake to an ordinary man, but will point to their men, and say *Sanops*, must speake to *Sanops*, and *Sagamors* to *Sagamors*."[42]

Such character traits found new avenues for expression in European company, but traditional social mores continued to direct Indian behavior. The Waymouth expedition, for instance, observed typical group behavior. The English tantalized some of the Abenaki with brandy, candy, and raisins and marveled that "some of every thing they would reserve to carry to their company." The Abenaki's concern for one another impressed other Englishmen. James Rosier noted that if one Indian was given anything, "he will distribute part to every one of the rest." Sharing trade goods was typical. When Poutrincourt gave Marchin knives, hatchets, and other items, the sachem passed them out immediately among his people.[43]

Intertribal relations were not so amicable, and at that level trade had profound social implications. Violent as the repercussions of commercial contact could be among the tribes, European trade did not suddenly pit the northeastern Algonkian against one another. Instead, trade exacerbated quarrels already entrenched in Algonkian life. Indian societies were extremely small, even among the populous agricultural tribes south of the Kennebec River. Tribal allegiances—which were defined among the Abenaki by their territorial orientation to particular watersheds—divided as much as united them.

Primary social identifications adhered to the kinship relations within individual hunting groups. Any larger social order stemmed from the intermarriages that alone linked these family bands. Bands of a single river drew together to discuss issues of common concern. Sometimes they acted with a single purpose. Band organization nevertheless dictated the extent of effective solidarity: social distance divided. Because hunting bands were related, neighboring groups consulted one another on issues of war and peace. They were much less inclined to confer with strangers. For all the Algonkian, familiarity fostered alliance and remoteness bred contempt.[44]

Nonetheless, trade had always provided the otherwise isolated tribes a limited context for constructive meetings. European influence began to realign these exchange networks, inflame old animosities, and amplify the divisiveness of the Algonkian's small-scale political institutions. Although other produce and crafts were exchanged, the original intertribal trade had concentrated on two items, corn and wampum. Both flowed from the New England Algonkian to Nova Scotia, and the direction of the trade was in itself cause for considerable resentment.

Furthermore, traders met ingrained social prejudice that as often as not obstructed even traditional exchange. Roger Williams observed that trade among the Narragansett aroused suspicions: "Who ever deale or trade with them had need of Wisedome, Patience and Faithfulnesse in dealing for they frequently say Cuppannawen, you lye, Cutlassokakomme, you deceive." Since the Micmacs were the easternmost of the Algonkian, their unfavorable position in the traditional trade certainly convinced them that the southern Algonkian were exploitative. Without a commercial system to regulate the relative value of corn, wampum, and furs, every exchange held the potential of triggering hostilities. Since the Micmac did not practice agriculture, corn was obviously important, but Micmac women also prized the white and blue-black wampum beads that the Wampanoag and the Narragansett skillfully manufactured. They used the shell beads for highly developed crafts, including intricate collars, bracelets, and belts. French traders early recognized the demand for produce and wampum—and exchanged food and glass beads, partially alleviating Micmac dependence on the southern Algonkian—but the traders could not overcome Indians' preference for traditional shell.[45]

Wampum was expensive, so the Micmac tried to use French goods to change trade patterns to their own advantage. For a number of reasons their efforts failed. Micmac demand for European goods exceeded the supply and it is likely that any surplus of metal products was small. The Micmac did slowly transmit metal goods south, but it is certain that stone tools remained in use. Champlain noted that the Algonkian in Massachusetts still used stone hatchets, except for a few metal tools received "from the Indians of the Acadian coast, with whom they are bartered for furs." Nevertheless, the Micmac remained disadvantaged because the relative value of corn and wampum remained high, probably much higher than they liked. John Smith described the southern Algonkian's dominance: "In the north (as I have said) they begunne to plant corne, whereof the South part hath such plentie, as they have what they will from them of the North. . . ."[46]

Ancient hostilities also impeded trade. Marc Lescarbot noted that the Algonkian had always warred among themselves and that raiding for agricultural produce caused intertribal tensions. Champlain learned that the people at the mouth of the Kennebec River no longer attempted to grow corn "on account of the war they used to wage with others who came and seized it." The "others" were either Micmac or their eastern Abenaki allies, the Passamaquoddy and the Maliseet. When Champlain made this remark, he had just concluded a peace agreement between the Penobscot and the Micmac, but his new allies refused to accompany him to the Kennebec because their "great enemies" lived there. Champlain suggests that raiding was widespread and that all the Algonkian fortified their villages.[47]

To improve their trading position the Micmac needed to resolve these quarrels with the western Abenaki. They had to meet French expectations as well. The French mediated between the tribes, hoping that the Micmac would become traders carrying metal products south and transporting furs back to Port Royal. They thought, in short, that the Micmac would conform to earlier precedent and trade along the coast as did the Montagnais beyond Tadoussac. Champlain expressed French intentions in 1604: "In course of time we hoped to pacify them, and to put an end to the wars which they wage against one another, in order that in the future we might derive service from them, and convert them to the Christian faith." In turn, their alliance with the French suggested, at least to some Micmac, the utility of intertribal harmony.[48]

In July 1605 a Micmac sachem and apprentice trader, Panounias, went with Champlain to explore the coast south of the Penobscot River. They soon discovered, however, that their hope for a commercial alliance with the agricultural Algonkian was premature. Champlain notes that Panounias faced a limited market. He attempted commerce with Abenaki on the Saco River, "but they possessed only their clothes, which they bartered; for they make no provision of furs except to clothe themselves." Farther south the Algonkian were even more disappointing. "They bartered their bows, arrows, and quivers for pins and buttons, and had they possessed anything better would have done the same with it." Only a few Abenaki encouraged French plans. On the return voyage Champlain and Panounias met Marchin, the Androscoggin sachem, who eagerly sought an alliance and released an eastern Abenaki captive to confirm his good will. Sasinou, of the upper Kennebec River, also wished to return two prisoners, but the French could not wait to meet him.[49]

Despite this inauspicious beginning, the Micmac and eastern Abenaki seized these overtures with French approval. In the fall of 1606 the Sieur de Poutrincourt, along with a Micmac and a Maliseet, attempted to establish peace with the western Abenaki. At Saco they met Marchin and Olmechin, the local sachem, who heartened them by surrendering yet another Micmac captive. Messamouet and Secoudon, the two Indian diplomats, "had much merchandise gained by barter with the French which they came hither to sell—to wit, kettles, large, medium and small, hatchets, knives, dresses, capes, red jackets, pease, beans, biscuits, and other such things." Champlain later wrote that both wished for more than simple profit: they wanted to "make an alliance with those of that country by offering them sundry presents."[50]

Messamouet explained the benefits of alliance. He reminded the western Abenaki how "they had often had friendly intercourse together, and that they could easily overcome their enemies if they would come to terms, and make use of the friendship of the French whom they saw there present exploring their country, in order in the future to bring merchandise to them and to aid them with their resources." Arguing his case for nearly an hour, Messamouet reinforced his eloquence with substantial presents: "he flung into the canoe of Olmechin all his merchandise, which in those parts was worth more than three hundred crowns in cash, as though making him present thereof in sign of the friendship which he wished to show him."[51]

The western Abenaki seemed uninterested in any association. Olmechin offended Messamouet when he did not acknowledge the proffered gifts and alliance. Lescarbot asserted that "from this day Messamouet considered how he might make war upon Olmechin." Actually, a more serious problem irritated the Micmac: when Olmechin did reciprocate, his presents were exclusively agricultural products—corn, tobacco, beans, and pumpkins. Even though this produce was the currency of intertribal trade and war, the Micmac had other requirements. To become traders of European goods they needed furs to pay the French. As Champlain expressed it, Olmechin's gifts "did not altogether satisfy Messamouet, who departed much displeased because he had not been suitably repaid for what he had given them."[52]

This commercial confrontation should be understood within the context of established Algonkian relations. While European trade aggravated intertribal hostilities, it did not alter traditional motives for war. It is often argued that the fur trade gave Indians new reasons for conflict and that warfare changed as the tribes sought to control and even eliminate competition. Such views, whatever their application elsewhere, do not apply to the early seventeenth-century Northeast. European commerce affected intertribal relations, but the Algonkian consistently subordinated economic issues to older disagreements. Hostilities troubled Indian-Indian relations and were not much changed by the Micmac's bid for commercial leadership within a refurbished intertribal alliance. The Micmac and the eastern Abenaki had long been enemies of the Indians west of the Penobscot River. Olmechin only confirmed this age-old antipathy when he repudiated the offer of an alliance.

This disagreement was not the direct cause of an intertribal war that broke out in 1607. Late the year before a war party led by Iouaniscou, probably a Micmac, attacked the western Abenaki for unknown reasons. Champlain reported all that is known about the raid: "Iouaniscou and his companions had killed some other Indians and carried off some women prisoners, and that near Mount Desert Island they had put these to death." The western Abenaki immediately retaliated by killing the Micmac Panounias on Penobscot territory. His body was carried to his father-in-law, Membertou, along with an anxious apology from the Penobscot sachem, Bessabes. The sachem said that "he was very sorry for Panonias' death. . . that it was without his knowledge that Panonias had been killed, and that since it was not his fault. . . he hoped they would remain friends as heretofore."[53]

As Micmac law required, and ignoring Iouaniscou's provocation, Membertou vowed revenge for his son-in-law's death. He spent the winter of 1606—07 creating a wartime alliance of Micmac, Montagnais, Maliseet, and Passamaquoddy. Under his leadership the allies attacked the Sacos on their home territory and killed ten people. "This whole war," Champlain thought, "was solely on account of Panonias, one of our Indian friends, who. . . had been killed at Norumbega [Penobscot] by the said Onemechin's and Marchin's people." Thus, while there seems to be evidence of the commercial causes of the war—Panounias was a trader—circumstances also show that revenge remained a major cause of conflict.[54]

There is difficulty in explaining these events beyond the antipathy Messamouet, Secoudon, and Iouaniscou kindled individually. At Panounias's death feast, Membertou cursed the "subjects of Bessabes" responsible for the murder. His words imply two things. First, they suggest that Bessabes's people may have killed Panounias without their sachem's knowledge. This explanation is easily rejected because Champlain specifically named western Abenaki sachems Olmechin and Marchin as the offenders. Second, Membertou's words may also indicate that Olmechin and Marchin were tributary sachems in an alliance led by Bessabes. Perhaps the Penobscot had been associated with the western Abenaki before 1604, but the evidence is weak. The Penobscot were then at war with the Micmac, but Champlain also said that they and the western Abenaki were enemies. In any case, Bessabes flatly denied any affiliation with Olmechin and Marchin when he apologized to Membertou in 1606. Such facts contradict even the English belief that an Abenaki confederacy existed under Bessabes's leadership.[55]

To suppose that Olmechin and Marchin were Bessabes's confederates wrongly interprets the Algonkian in another way. Such political associations did not exist beyond temporary cooperation. According to Pierre Biard, Algonkian societies hardly extended past the influence of a single sachem. The Jesuit observed meetings in the summer when "several Sagamores come together and consult among themselves about peace and war, treaties of friendship and treaties for the common good." But he also noted the limitations of alliance. It happens, Biard declared, that without order and subordination among themselves, the sachems "frequently depart more confused and disunited than when they came."[56]

It is therefore not surprising that intertribal war continued long after 1607. The Penobscot again came to blows with the Micmac after 1613, and John Smith described the two peoples as "mortall enemies." In 1615 Sir Richard Hawkins, president of Plymouth Company, came on such intense Indian warfare that he sailed farther south. The Micmac

slew Bessabes, and Sir Ferdinando Gorges relates that the other sachems
"fell at variance among themselves, spoiled and destroyed each others
people and provisions, and famine took hould of many."[57]

The intertribal wars of 1607—15 played a central role in postcontact
Abenaki history. The conflicts demonstrate the way in which Abenaki
social organization continued to channel the impact of commercial
contact with Europeans. While the fur trade did not radically affect the
tribes' internal economies, it did expose a fundamental political weakness that these peoples would have to resolve. The extremely small-scale
character of their political organization meant that the Algonkian were
not prepared to deal with regular and intense contact among themselves. Pierre Biard noted that political alliances in the Northeast
usually united linguistically related peoples. Nevertheless, he observed
that "the confederation often extends farther than the language does and
war sometimes arises against those who have the same language." Such,
in effect, were the diplomatic and cultural confusions that commerce
intensified.[58]

### TREACHERY AND INTERCULTURAL DISCORD

Trade had other social implications that troubled the Algonkian and
Europeans. The first hundred years of contact was characterized by
intercultural violence that made mutual flexibility imperative. Commerce called for formal associations that could resolve disagreements as
they arose. Both groups assumed that intercultural trust would be
possible only if there were effective political arrangements for easing
disputes. Moreover, before the Algonkian or Europeans could approach
each other with any assurance, they first had to resolve civil strife. It
turned out that Europeans, especially the English, were even more
quarrelsome among themselves than the Algonkian.

Intertribal disagreements were far less vicious than English clashes on
the maritime and trading frontiers. The Gulf of Maine's gradual integration into a transatlantic economy repeated among the English what
had been international contests on the sixteenth-century Laurentian
frontier. English nationalism provided no more unity of purpose than
did Algonkian tribalism. If the English were to develop profitable
alliances with Indians, they had first to govern themselves. In the first
quarter of the seventeenth century the task proved impossible.

Much of the violence stemmed from the individualistic nature of the
English advance. After the premature Popham effort to colonize the

Kennebec River, the English fell back and concentrated on maritime resources near Abenaki shores. In 1605 Captain Waymouth discovered Georges Bank, one of the world's great fishing grounds, just off the Maine coast. The English at once concluded that fishing alone warranted voyages to northeastern waters. Georges Bank promised "a more profitable returne. . . than from Newfoundland" and therefore provided economic inducements necessary to finance the region's eventual settlement.[59]

Captain John Smith spurred this move toward the Northeast. In his 1616 *Description of New England* he detailed the commercial goals that produced competition between the English and the Algonkian. For example, Smith found Georges Bank especially attractive because of its proximity to shore where cod could be dried. Likewise, he anticipated the advantages the Algonkian peoples offered: "Now, Young boyes and girles Salvages, or any other, be they never such idlers, may turne, carry, and return fish, without either shame, or any great paine: hee is very idle that is past twelve yeares of age and cannot doe so much: and she is very olde, that cannot spin a thred to make engines to catch them." How Smith proposed to accomplish this exploitation is unclear, but he did insist on the pivotal role of effective force. An experienced leader with the aid of thirty or forty men could "subject the Salvages, and feed daily two or three hundred men."[60]

Focusing always on the profits to be won, Smith's prognostications involved Indians in other competitive ventures. He declared that the English could expect 6,000 or 7,000 furs annually. If French traders could be ousted, an additional 25,000 could be gathered. While he shrewdly offered to protect the western Abenaki from the Micmac and their French allies, he knew that such interventions were hazardous. As historian Karen Ordahl Kupperman has argued, violence was so pervasive that Englishmen like Smith could only bluster to hide their actual vulnerability. On two occasions in 1614 his party skirmished with Indians and Smith responded with prudent admiration: "We found the people in those parts verie kinde, but in their furie no lesse valiant." Such bold resistance proved to him the reality of Indian humanity because they seemed to act like Europeans.[61]

Smith also regretted the problems domestic violence created. Before his 1614 voyage was over, both Smith and the Algonkian regretted the acquaintance of Thomas Hunt, captain of a companion vessel. Smith claimed that Hunt slandered his efforts, stole his ideas, and abandoned him on a desolate island. All of this led Smith to rue "the ingratitude of some, the malicious slanders of others, the falsenesse of friendes, the treachery of cowards, and slownesse of adventurers." Hunt, for one, seized his own advantage. He captured twenty Indians, sold them into Spanish slavery, and created an enduring Algonkian distrust of the English. Smith deplored the maltreatment of these "poore, innocent soules," but Hunt's heavy-handed actions stemmed logically from the pragmatic view of the Indians that Smith advocated. In fact, rivalry among English fishermen and traders went hand in hand with exploitation of the Algonkian.[62]

Even Sir Ferdinando Gorges, who exemplified English determination to create stable colonies in the Northeast, decried the competitive individualism of his countrymen. Gorges recognized free-wheeling self-interest as the root of destructive relations with Indian peoples. Castigating fishermen for being "worse than the very Savages," Gorges asserted that they raped Abenaki women and plied the men with hard liquor. He wrote that the Indians, when drunk, "fall together by the eares, thereby giving them occasion to seek revenge." Gorges accused transient fishermen of constantly abusing Indians in trade. Worse, they sold firearms to the Abenaki, "wherewith the Savages slew many of those Fisher-Men, and are growne so able, & apt, as they become most dangerous to the Planters." These men, said Gorges, contribute "to the overthrow of our trade and the dishonour of the Government." In 1623 Gorges sent his son Robert to rectify these disorders. Ill equipped for the enormous task, the younger Gorges achieved little in the way of reform and the situation deteriorated. The Abenaki killed "the master of a ship of Plymouth with eighteen of his company" in the early 1620s.[63]

Gorges remained frustrated, but one of his counselors, Christopher Levett, grappled more successfully with the problem. Levett, more than anyone, plumbed the violence that troubled the English and disrupted their relations with the Algonkian. In 1623–24 Levett sailed along the Maine coast on a personal voyage of discovery to locate a site for a 6,000-acre grant he had received from the Council of New England. In this adventurous pursuit of property he was not unusual, but the manner of his reconnaissance repudiated the violent ways of other Englishmen fishing and trading in Maine waters.[64]

While he favored exploitation of the Northeast for England's public good, Levett argued that relations with the Abenaki would have to be tempered with justice. He was relieved when the sachem of Casco and Quack invited him to build a trading post on tribal lands. He said that Indian peoples had "a naturall right of inheritance, as they are the

Sonnes of Noah." This admission was far from a radical acknowledgment of Indian property rights, since Levett also believed that New England could be had "for little or nothing." A cool pragmatist, Levett thought that Indian title should be purchased so as to bridle their hostility. Candidly stating his purpose, Levett found "it fit to carry things very fairly without compulsion (if it be possible) for avoyding of treacherie." He differed from his fellows, then, only in his willingness to ease the Indians' dispossession. He remained typical by anticipating that New England would be developed with or without Indian cooperation.

Levett did reject the methods used by other Englishmen. He found that fishermen and casual traders were as heedless of English as they were of Indian rights. One sea captain warned Levett that "he cared not for any authorities in that place and though he was forbid to trucke yet he would have all [the furs] he could get." And who "should say the contrary," Levett exclaimed in acquiescing to the force of arms. The renegade had "a great Ship with 17. peeces of Ordinance and 50. men." With Levett helplessly looking on, the pirate seized Abenaki furs with impunity. The Indians scorned the "Roague," and Levett said that "he and his company fell upon them & beate them." This and similar incidents impressed on Levett that treachery could be expected everywhere, especially in the absence of effective government. He could only advise Gorges that unless malefactors were punished either "for disobedience, or contempt of authority," they would incite the Indians against the English. Abuse of authority, Levett claimed, "is the way to cause all Planters to have their throats cut."

Levett's attitude toward Indians mirrored his advice for the control of uncivil Englishmen: they should be treated with aloof kindness or with blunt authority. Levett's own behavior, unlike his compatriots, replaced brash demands with quiet diplomacy. Refusing gifts of furs with which the Abenaki sweetened trade, undoubtedly a significant source of profit for avaricious traders, Levett affirmed Abenaki values. He told them "it was not the fashion of English Captaines alwaies to be taking." Since the Abenaki admired magnanimous men, his methods were profitable.

Levett's opinions were based on his experience with unruly Englishmen, but his caution with the Abenaki also throws light on Algonkian disputes. He was not disturbed that the western Abenaki remained at war with the Micmac further east. Levett told the Indians "that they should kill all the TARRANTENS [Micmac] they should see (being

enimies to them) and with whom the English have no commarsse."
Although Levett found intertribal wars useful, purely tribal disputes
made him uneasy. While he recognized that the Abenaki had learned to
curse interlopers in the English tongue, Levett could not appreciate the
subtle impact that intercultural violence had on Indian peoples.

Unwittingly, Levett provided evidence that as a direct result of
English example the Abenaki had begun to use strong-armed tactics
among themselves. He could see "no Government or Law amongst them
but Club Law: and they call Masters of Shippes SAGAMORE, or any
other man, that they see have a commaund of men." He also claimed
that the Abenaki's calculated relations with foreigners matched their
treatment of one another: "They are very bloudy minded and full of
Tracherie amongst themselves, one will kill another for their wives, and
he that hath the most wives is the bravest fellow. . . ."[65]

Ironically, the Abenaki thought better of Levett than he did of them.
Their gift-giving does not support Levett's contention that they reacted
with guile. Rather, it suggests that the Abenaki extended the privi-
leges of their domestic economy to embrace otherwise contemptible
strangers. Levett adjusted his own behavior to suit Abenaki norms, but
he did so without appreciating their unique values. Still, Levett's
testimony should not be dismissed because the social disagreements he
witnessed were one result of commercial contact.

What emerges from Levett's description then are the divisive conditions that challenged Abenaki and Europeans alike. By the second
quarter of the seventeenth century violence overwhelmed the Atlantic
frontiers. Levett realized that if New England was to be established, the
pacification of all maritime and trading contenders was necessary—
through persuasion or force. Attracted first by fish, Englishmen soon
grasped the lucrative potential of the fur trade. Because profits were
limited, Indian furs forced the English into an individualistic competition that thwarted the corporations favoring settlement. Levett's experience proved the need for strong government. Moreover, by 1624
New England had squabbling sovereignties. The Council of New
England had authorized a separatist colony of pilgrims as well as other
fledgling settlements. France was temporarily out of the contest, her
budding empire in the hands of English developers. Some abandoned
Acadians sought accommodation with Sir William Alexander's short-
lived government of Nova Scotia, as he had renamed the territory.
When Acadia was returned to France in 1632, international disagree-

ments began in earnest. Acadians and New Englanders continued to possess and repossess the region throughout the colonial period.[66]

These economic and territorial rivalries were only indirectly related to intercultural contact. Europeans were forced not only to grapple with issues posed by Indian peoples but to resolve national and international differences. In the Northeast, France and England confronted each other directly. Although disagreements were often felt as clashing religious conviction, the two nations also eyed the rich resources of the region. Even as early as 1610 the Acadian battle with New England had become a localized, Euramerican contest. Entirely apart from their national governments, settlers quickly developed their own disagreements and confronted rivals independently. In fact, French and English fought as vehemently among themselves as with each other.

Cultural pluralism did not come easily to the Northeast, and rivalry soon became the hallmark of contact. Destructive quarrels thwarted Indian and European efforts to deal constructively with the changes that economic relations produced. Abenaki attempts to regulate relations failed because there was little personal continuity in their meetings with English fishermen and traders. As in the sixteenth century the English presence remained transient. In this way the Abenaki came to distrust the English, met force with force, and slowly realized that intertribal unity was necessary for their own defense. Increasingly, throughout the seventeenth century the tribes drew together around anti-European sentiments. Similarly, even after settlement began, the English failed to govern themselves. Indian hostility increased the need for strong civil authority. And Abenaki resistance confirmed English expectations that Indians could not be trusted. The net result of all this discord was ideological polarization. Economic competition, it turned out, was only the outword manifestation of far deeper differences.

# 2

## THE SACRED AND THE PROFANE

*The Social Ideologies of Contact*

A new arena for long-standing European conflicts had emerged in the Northeast. Beyond the struggle for political and economic control of the region, religious discord divided French and English colonials. While both peoples agreed that Christ expressed himself in everyday life, they differed about his purpose. Specifically, the French and English disagreed about the relationship of religion to social life. And since Europeans could not resolve their own religious quarrels, it became all the more difficult for them to comprehend American Indian religious and social life.

In Europe an old world of localized folk communities was fighting for survival against an emerging impersonal urban order. Change was inevitable and threatened older forms of community life. Even in the Middle Ages Europe had cities that gave it the potential for large-scale social consciousness. Most important, the Continent had a small group of literate religious leaders who were committed to the creation of a common European creed at the expense of folk belief.[1]

Medieval Europe had inherited the idea of centralized political authority from Rome. In governing itself through the principles of Roman law, the Catholic church gave Europe a continent-wide coherence. Slowly ecclesiastical law transcended the customs of the little community. Local political units shared the same expansionistic goal. All of

Europe had, or developed, technologies that made it possible to create regional and then national economies. Given these urban characteristics, it was only a matter of time until folk communities became centralized nation-states.[2]

For Europeans civilization and urbanization were synonymous, and as modes of association, cities eroded the folk allegiances of the small communities. By the sixteenth century cities and states organized the European landscape, although neither had achieved dominance. On one hand, post-Renaissance people implemented political and economic centralization, asserted administrative order, and sought social efficiency. On the other, they everywhere confronted resistance to large-scale social controls. Both English and French kings increased their authority, but not without great effort.[3]

Cities did unite distant communities, but the cities were not yet in administrative or economic control of their hinterlands. England and France were lands of great social extremes. Feudal and capitalist manors, great wealth and grueling poverty, pretentious social hierarchies and disorderly poor constituted the frontiers of European societies. Extended families disintegrated in the cities. Neighborliness and reciprocal deference were becoming ideals largely honored in the breach. Carl Bridenbaugh's observation about English social change applies equally well to French life: "People retreated to anonymity, and impersonality prevailed in human relations. . . . Gradually a cosmopolitan spirit pervaded men's minds; the countryman became a citizen."[4]

The urbanization of Europe coincided with a turbulent shift in social consciousness. City dwellers asserted superiority over their rural cousins and directed toward them the same terminology they would later use to condemn Indian character. It augured poorly for European-Indian relations that propertied city folk judged their inferiors "rude (almost) as the crudest Savages." Francis Bacon not only reckoned rural Englishmen as "savage men" but warned against using the "scum of people" as colonists. The language of disdain was remarkably uniform. Women, said one French adage, are imperfect beasts "without faith, without law, without fear, without constancy." Grain rioters in Lyon roused the same response: they were " 'the dregs of the populace, with no order, no rein, no leader . . . a beast of many heads . . . an insane rabble.' " In effect, the upper classes claimed that the lower classes were no better than rustics.[5]

Greater literacy—itself the hallmark of civility—also strained social relations. Citizens asserted that the traditional world was the source of much contemporary disorder and their view enjoyed wide intellectual credibility. While scholars were discovering that European vernacular languages possessed an admirable vitality, the folk were condemned as quickly as they came to literate consciousness. Study of rural oral traditions led to efforts to eradicate vulgar speech. Linguistic reform was particularly pronounced in France, which had almost as many dialects as localities. Marking the extension of royal authority, courtly French became the model. Similarly, scholars began to see in popular proverbs deplorable remnants from the world of ancient Celtic barbarians. Printed collections of proverbs proved that the folk were backward and prompted demands for vigorous cultural change. French theologians led the way with lists of popular "superstitions" requiring correction.[6]

City people attempted to reorient the moral character of the lower classes but were far from successful. Surviving European tribal peoples, peasants, rustics, the urban poor, and eventually American Indians all challenged civility. These were outsiders who threatened the established order. As potential rebels, they were feared and scorned because urban values were not nearly so universal as citizens claimed. At least some of the entrenched upper classes knew that it was possible to reassess urban Europe by rural or even "savage" standards. In 1515 country folk welcomed the count of Flanders, asserting that they rather than the people of nearby Bruges were "the true inheritors of the Golden Age." Urban claims of superiority often rang hollow. Michel Montaigne wrote: "What truth is that, which these Mountaines bound, and is a lie in the world beyond them." Europeans were confused. They could not comprehend their own character.[7]

In this way what became the European mission in America reflected an unconscious social crisis. Europeans had emerged from the politically fragmented Middle Ages with greater unity only to find folk solidarity an impediment to national order. Wherever the folk survived, church and state worked to assimilate them. This internal colonialism expressed a paradox that Europeans carried with them wherever they ventured. Educated and wealthy Europeans thought that they alone possessed a coherent social order. Forgetting that Christian civilization was only an ideal, colonials responded to American Indians as if the myth were actual. The opinion makers of the colonial period hid their own differences behind a vision of moral progress.

In effect, Europeans came to America with contradictory purposes. The deeply religious colonials were men who sought to create godly societies. At the same time they were businessmen and believed that God rewarded diligent Christians with worldly riches. Christ himself called for European expansion into the American forests. He had ordained that piety and profits were to work hand in hand. In fact, God and money strove toward different goals. Commercial competition was the source of national and international conflict. Because the pursuit of profit and the resulting frontier violence did not accord well with any European ideal, merchants and missionaries agreed on the need for law and order, but they did not examine the real cause of conflict as it emerged in their economic endeavors. The way to resolve discord thus also escaped understanding.

Inconsistent European ideas about Christianity's effect on social behavior conditioned reactions to American Indians. Historians have studied the way that Europeans clung tenaciously to the preconception "We are civilized and they are savage." Such extreme ideas about morality and civil order were first applied among Europeans themselves. They had no need to develop a special ideology to justify their exploitation and dispossession of American Indians.

### CIVILITY AND SAVAGERY

French and English assessments of Indian cultures were inaccurate. All literate Europeans believed in an overidealized sense of social order. They thought that church and state worked together to achieve common welfare. The reality was not so simple. Both the forces of urbanization and American colonization contradicted these ideological assumptions. Europeans hoped that colonization would ease proliferating domestic social problems, and it struck them that American Indians had paradoxically achieved what was beyond their own grasp. Europeans expected to meet savages, but Indians confounded all presumptions.

Sir Thomas More in his searching *Utopia* wondered aloud at the sudden, unflattering light America cast across early modern Europe. How would it be, More inquired, to have communities untrammeled by the cultural baggage of laws, religion, and property? Using only their natural but virtuously developed intellectual faculties, Utopians avoided the evils of European civilization. They rejected economic, political, and religious tyranny. More perused the possibilities and his religious yearnings brought Europeans directly to grips with their own limitations. Europe attempted to fulfill its destiny in the New World, but from the beginning of contact America unflatteringly mirrored a deep-seated social crisis.[8]

Thomas More was only one of many Christian humanists calling for European renewal. And, as it turned out, his defense of a revitalized Catholic civilization contributed to a growing controversy. Europeans became painfully divided in coming to grips with the forces transforming their societies. The very meaning of life had become elusive, and in an effort to define the moral challenge they faced, a growing middle class lashed out at Catholic corruption. In both England and France this new elite demanded secular and religious reform. The Protestant Reformation and the Catholic Counter-Reformation signaled an era of tumultuous change. As historian Peter Laslett has put it, Europeans searched for a world they had lost.[9]

The English experience of this social paradox best illustrates the ideological differences that polarized French and English colonials. The two peoples thought about the world in radically different terms. While Protestants came to reject the secular world as debased, Catholics increasingly embraced a moderate tradition of reform. These religious dissensions profoundly affected Indian-white relations. French Catholics' acceptance of folk religious practices gave them a far more tolerant perspective on American Indian cultures. The tremendous cultural and linguistic diversity within France may also have fostered cultural relativism. English and French may have agreed on their Christian mission to American Indians, but they were preconditioned to quarrel about the task.

History itself became subject to ideological disagreement in the sixteenth century. As a result, the English were driven toward a new vision of man's relationship to God. The Gutenberg revolution unleashed broad forces of change. Printed texts brought the past closer than it had ever been before. In particular, a widely available vernacular Bible popularized Protestant rejection of papal authority. The Anglican separation from Rome expressed a deep conviction: the English believed that they had always had a special calling. After all, had not the reign of Tiberius, the emperor who killed Christ, also seen the preaching of the Gospel in Britain? It was time to perfect that ancient beginning.[10]

As England separated from the Roman Catholic church, the English-language Bible defined an altogether new sense of historical process. Its discovery as a literal, personal guide to daily living gave every individual an ominous responsibility to further God's design. An emerging and vital sense of English nationalism owes much to this individualized, Christian sense of history. The English Bible suggested that cultural uniformity was a sure sign of God's favor, just as the new secular politics implemented a large-scale social order.[11]

Already preconditioned to think of contemporary events as the visible workings of divine will, the English learned from the Bible of the cosmic historical combat between the purified city of God and the corrupt city of man. Since daily events were emblematic of the continuing war between Christ and Satan, the sixteenth-century English discovered how their past had been the crucial battleground between good and evil. When they rejected Roman Catholicism, the English necessarily abjured much of their pre-Roman and medieval history. They therefore maligned the moral character of their forebears. Their Saxon ancestors, the English knew, had been "great Idolaters, worshipping trees, and fountains of water." Time had brought little improvement. [12]

Biblical reasoning affirmed the civilization and Christianization of Celtic Britain. It also condemned pagan rituals that had survived in Catholic dogma and worship. Early missionaries to Celtic heathens had accepted gradual change. Appreciating the stubborn tenacity of local religions, Pope Gregory the Great had urged a broad tolerance. Insofar as possible Gregory directed his missionaries to subsume heathen rituals within Christian word and practice. As a result, Celtic Christianity united the cultures of successive foreign invaders into a vigorous amalgam tied to local religious traditions.

According to biblically inspired reformers, English Catholicism was actually an instrument for the jubilant forces of Satan. Local cults of the saints and Christ's Virgin Mother, miraculous springs, holy shrines, and relics drawing pilgrims from afar were all ancient delusions nourished by the Roman Catholic church. The Bible condemned such practices. Thus, the war between Satan and Christ during the Middle Ages became in the sixteenth century a controversy over the nature of God's activity in the world. Catholics held that God's intervention was largely sacramental but included a number of rituals that Christ had given to the Roman church to use in his behalf. Protestants, however, had little use for what they considered the superstitions through which the church controlled human beings in the service of anti-Christ. They claimed that Rome's doctrine of good works deluded people into thinking that they might win salvation from Christ. Calvinist Protestants rejected Catholic dogma. Instead, they believed in God's arbitrary election of a few saints and his terrifying punishment of the unregenerate masses. [13]

The English Reformation unleashed complex political forces. On one level, the English became intensely nationalistic and, on another, dedicated themselves to a moral reordering of decadent society. But yearnings for godly reform could not produce a consensus on the kind of society England ought to be. A bitter, backward-looking Catholic minority retreated underground. Many more English remained conservative, indifferent even to the moderate reforms of the Anglican state church. Increasingly, Anglicans met resistance. Experimental forms of Protestantism criticized the immorality of both church and state.[14]

Other intellectual issues were directly related to these disagreements about man's relationship to God. The French and the English had also to explain their new awareness of cultural diversity. A widespread belief that some Europeans—and all American Indians—were morally degenerate expressed more than cultural and religious prejudice. Such attitudes reveal the uncertainties of contemporary European anthropology. Europeans thought that humans came in three distinct types: natural, civil, and spiritual. They themselves had progressed to the third and final stage. Discovering tribal peoples in Africa and America, as well as confronting ethnic groups that still survived in Europe itself, provoked a reexamination of these basic anthropological ideas.[15]

The ensuing discussion was urgent and speculative. Europeans had always pretended "civil" superiority over their "barbarian" neighbors, but Christian reformers held deeper convictions. They contended that unless members of civil societies were also godly, they were as morally wicked as savages. This belief became a vigorous imperial tool. Both civil and religious reformers could easily condemn natural peoples. Without civil governments to enforce domestic security and to ensure unfettered communication between distant places, natural peoples were believed to be treacherous among themselves and especially dangerous to strangers. "Natural" social organization not only defied the superiority of urban civilization but also opposed Europeans' vision of universal history. Such thinking had ominous implications for colonial assessments of American Indian life. European anthropology made the wealthy and powerful urban upper classes the social norm of excellence. Both their material culture and religious ideology ensured dominance.[16]

Christopher Columbus established the formula in America when he described Indians as "a people very deficient in everything" because they had neither iron, religion, nor law. Soon thereafter Amerigo Vespucci asserted that New World peoples lived without benefit "of law, religion, rulers, immortality of the soul, and private property." Both explorers projected onto Indians urban social expectations. In effect, their thinking reflected the dominant cultural structures of European life.[17]

The opposing concepts of civilization and savagery recognized both the structural and moral elements of culture, but European logic juxtaposed those ideas uneasily. Columbus and Vespucci assumed that civil institutions were necessarily related to the religious values that ostensibly regulated them. Urban social structure and Christian ethics appeared mutually indispensable. The concepts actually declared the extreme ethnocentrism of European self-esteem: condemnation of American social life required that Indian societies be structurally simple and morally anarchistic. Since European civilization was in crisis, harmonious but "savage" sociality confounded their judgments. "Your Highnesses may believe," Columbus affirmed with no sense of irony, "that in all the world there cannot be a people better or more gentle."[18]

The earliest explorers of the Northeast exemplify this intellectual confusion. They suggested that American Indians possessed no culture at all and that their rudimentary humanity had not yet emerged from its natural environment. They "were clothed in Beestes skynnes and ete raw ffleshe, and were rude in their demeanure as Beestes." Gaspar de Corte Reale said that Indians "live like the ancient fauns and satyrs"; they had the form but not the substance of men and women. Other Europeans glimpsed a truer but similarly paradoxical humanity in Corte Reale's captives. "They may appear mere savages," commented the Venetian ambassador to Spain, "yet they are gentle, and have a strong sense of shame." Another observer agreed with this favorable judgment. "I have seen, touched, and examined these people," Alberto Cantino wrote. "Their manners and gestures are most gentle; they laugh considerably and manifest the greatest pleasure."[19]

English assessments of Indian peoples conformed to these ambivalent perceptions. Their thinking illustrates the cognitive and ethical complexities of contact which derived from the Protestant Reformation. More often than not, early observers noted the Indians' admirable humanity and sophisticated technologies. They even surpassed the English in efficient hunting, fishing, and agriculture. The English had expected lawlessness, but found instead signs of civility in Indians' limited governments and in tribal status distinctions. These were not the communist anarchies European anthropology premised.

Additionally, it appeared that Indians had only a few laws because their amiable nature valued generosity and shunned aggressive discourse. "As their evill courses come short of many other Nations," observed William Wood, "so they have not so many Lawes, though they be not without some." In short, Indians' trustworthiness indicated a suitable accord between their personalities and social structures. At least in the early years of contact the English did not begrudge Indians their due as consciously ethical persons. Both their languages and religious rituals suggested that Indians had descended from Adam— although they seemed to have been derived more immediately from lost Hebrew tribes.[20]

Remarkable as these departures from cultural prejudice may have been, even they did not ease English doubts. In the end Indians were not viewed as fully human. They may have been praiseworthy for adapting to the American environment, but since the English intended to remake the land to fit their own economic organization, Indians would have to submit and conform. Similarly, while Indians may have had some feeble notions about God, such ethical "footsteps" did not make them trustworthy. English thinking concluded not only that Indians lived in sorry spiritual ignorance but that they were Satan's associates in his intensifying war against Christian order. Although Thomas Morton generally admired Indian character, even he remained convinced that Satan controlled Indian life through the machinations of their powwows, as he called their religious leaders: "They may be rather accompted to live richly wanting nothing that is needful; and to be commended for leading a contented life, the younger being ruled by the Elder, and the Elder ruled by the Powahs, and the Powahs are ruled by the Devill, and then you may imagin what good rule is like to be amongst them." Roger Williams was only somewhat more sympathetic. He asserted that ungodly English people were no less degraded than Indian heathens.[21]

The paradox of "savage civility" could not be resolved within European intellectual traditions. Irreconcilable images of bestial and noble savages persisted as versatile justifications for English and French visions of empire. Until colonials confronted the root causes of their own social conflict, they could have no assurance of Indian humanity. Before and after contact Europeans attempted to explain social imperfections by theological arguments. Human beings and their works were, within the Christian tradition, profane and capable of only limited social good. Sacred intervention alone gave merit to human affairs. Created in God's image, people remained degenerate until godliness transformed their lives.

In the sixteenth and seventeenth centuries Europeans had only just begun to question how secular and religious institutions affected the quality of their social life. They might revolt against the worldly authority of the medieval church, but their optimism did not lead them to a clear view of how culture itself affected human behavior and solidarity. Europeans knew that their driving impulse toward social reform derived from religious principle. They were less sure of how to begin civil reorganization.[22]

## RELIGIOUS PARADOX AND FRENCH RECONNAISSANCE

The French represent a special case of these intellectual and ethical troubles. English settlers for their part, confronted the agricultural Algonkian, who had village societies and relatively complex political systems. The French, however, tested preconceptions against smaller tribes that were only marginally agricultural and more mobile in their subsistence activities. For all Europeans these Micmac and the Abenaki peoples epitomized the savage. Therefore French efforts to understand and communicate with these tribes most clearly expose the ideological challenge and the potential for constructive alliance in Indian-white relations.

Three men exemplify the French attempt to bridge the cultural gulf. *Marc Lescarbot*, a lawyer and *bon vivant*, spent slightly more than a year in Acadia. A Jesuit priest, *Pierre Biard*, had two years to plumb the theological implications of Algonkian ethics. *Chretien LeClercq*, a Recollect priest, worked among the Micmac for twelve years at the end of the seventeenth century. All three had preconceived notions about the sublime and brutish in human affairs. They found that those assumptions cut two ways. Lescarbot, Biard, and LeClercq soon realized that they could not accurately assess Micmac and Abenaki cultures without examining their own. While most eighteenth-century French-men exaggerated Indian nobility, these three men recognized both the virtues and vices of Algonkian humanity. That French ideologues later used their published observations to criticize French society should not distort the honest efforts these men made to meet the Algonkian directly.

Marc Lescarbot shared with other scholars of his time historical insights derived from the diligent reconstruction of classical and bib-lical texts produced during the Renaissance. These books offered startling views of Greco-Roman customs and unsettling accounts of the tribal cultures of northern Europe. Lescarbot differed from most thinkers in his broad cultural relativism. He understood that these descriptions could throw new light on contemporary cultures—Euro-pean and Indian. It had become commonplace to dismiss American

Indians by associating their character with that of tribal Europeans and their rustic descendants. Lescarbot refused to play on such emotions. To avoid prejudice he searched classical antiquity, European folk traditions, and descriptions of North and South American Indians to find analogies to the Micmac culture he observed.

Lescarbot drew these strands together by continually referring to the cultural behavior of his readers. He asked them to evaluate Algonkian social customs but insisted that they could do so only if they took a critical look at their way of life. In brief, Lescarbot asked fundamental questions about intercultural dialogue and offered a new, systematic way to compare and contrast various cultural traditions. As a result, he tendered bold answers and castigated French notions of self-respect. Judged against the anthropological standards of his own day, Lescarbot forwarded innovative, if ultimately frustrated, ideas.[23]

The lawyer did not accept the theory that civilization adhered exclusively to particular institutions and religious beliefs. "God delights in diversity," he asserted, "and in human diversity most of all." Positing a universal human nature, he quoted *Ecclesiastes*: "All men have a like entrance into the world, and the like going out." Lescarbot immediately added that "each nation hath added some ceremonies." For him Algonkians shared a troubled human condition, and their unique struggle warranted close attention. Lescarbot found that simply to contrast civilization and savagery could not explain either differences or similarities between Algonkians and Europeans. "If we commonly call them Savages," he wrote, "the word is abusive and unmerited, for they are anything but that."[24]

Lescarbot rejected the argument that urban institutions made Europeans superior. On close examination the Micmac, "though naked" and apparently natural people, had ample measure of what he called the four "civil" virtues: fortitude, temperance, generosity, and justice. He did not sentimentalize such character traits. Indian culture struck him as remarkable only to the extent that it defied his expectations. He praised Micmac fortitude because it was behaviorally related to their impulse "to do good by honour." At the same time he chided these Indians for excesses. Lescarbot felt that the warrior's honorable courage often descended into vengeful brutishness. While arguing that the Micmac were admirable, he also insisted that they were not perfect: "The Christian religion alone can bring them to reason, as in some sort it does with us; I say, in some sort, because among us very imperfect men are found as well as among the Savages."[25]

Lescarbot may have expressed the religious paradox of European civilization, but he did not question the application of Christian ethics to all peoples. Abandoning his characteristic flexibility, he insisted that the Micmac had no religion at all. His basis for that judgment is significant. The Micmac were pagans, he asserted, because they had no religious institutions: "I call it not religion unless there be some ritual and divine service." This rigid stance is the more remarkable because Lescarbot admitted the limited efficacy of Christian ethics. As he put it, the Micmac "follow nature; and if we curb anything . . . it is the commandment of God which makes us do so, whereunto many stop their eyes."[26]

It was one thing to document with historical contrasts the positive qualities of "savage civility." It was altogether another to account for the civil savagery of the European world. Lescarbot was intensely aware that Micmac culture did not differ from the persistent forms of European tribalism. Ethnicity made Europe as linguistically and culturally diverse as America. Lescarbot further observed that Micmac beliefs had counterparts in the tribal aspects of Catholic rituals and festivals. What Protestants identified as superstitious figures and idolatrous representations of the saints, Lescarbot considered "books of the unlearned." It is here that he resolved to his own satisfaction the religious authority and mission of the Catholic church. Since the church embraced both illiterate Europeans and American heathens, Lescarbot thought that cultural tolerance ought to ground the religious program of reform:

> You cannot all at once eradicate the deep-rooted customs and habits of any people, whoever they may be. The Apostles did not do it, neither was it done several centuries after them; witness the ceremonies of the candles on Candlemas, the Processions of the Rogation-days, the Bonfires of saint John the Baptist's day, the holy Water, and many other traditions that we have in the Church, which have been introduced for a laudable purpose, to convert to a good usage what had only been abused.[27]

In fact, Lescarbot's unstinting admiration for Micmac communalism belied his avowal that they needed Christianity. "Indeed," he remarked, "I shall say that they have more humanity than many Christians, who for the last one hundred years have . . . committed upon women and children cruelties more than brutish, whereof the histories are full." He acknowledged the Micmac's achievement as instinctive: they had no formal law "but that which nature teaches them, that one must not offend another." That principle seemed to provide adequate moral and civil guidance. In particular, Lescarbot respected the non-materialistic emphasis of tribal social values. He believed that the Micmac's rejection of status distinctions based on property and authority needed no improvement. He found their politics "the most perfect and most worthy of man, seeing that he is a sociable animal." The Micmac had, he claimed, the "life of the ancient golden age, which the holy apostles would fain have restored again." To Lescarbot the poverty and squalor of European cities twisted the "natural humanity" of their peoples. "Which makes me blush for France," he admitted, "wherein our Christianity shows nothing of what was good in our Paganism."[28]

In Lescarbot's comparison of Indian and European cultures, civilization hid a decadence produced by widespread immorality. Lescarbot repeatedly implied that private property created ambition, vain glory, envy, avarice, and luxurious overindulgence. Poor people, he insisted, suffered because of the ungodliness of the wealthy—those "bloodsuckers of the people" or "those rats in the granary." While he insisted that Algonkian societies did not suffer such evils, he could not explain how the Micmac achieved communal order. Lescarbot could not go beyond the condemnation of greedy individuals to an appreciation that French culture itself institutionalized the profane social behavior he so detested. He isolated economic individualism as the central moral sickness in French life, but he apparently could not envision its reform: "In France one must be either hammer or anvil; one must either plague another or be one's self plagued."[29]

Confronted with the Algonkian's small-scale social life, Lescarbot retreated to a naive hope that his countrymen would forsake their evil ways "to recall the golden age, and to take away the misery which we see in the majority of men." With that aspiration, his political thought reached an impasse. He resolved the comparative issue in a contradictory manner: France must recognize its mission to American heathens who existed "without God, without law, without religion, living in pitiable ignorance." For Marc Lescarbot, as for all Europeans, the myth of Christian civilization explained the unthinkable and held moral anarchy at bay.[30]

The Jesuit priest, Pierre Biard, recapitulates Lescarbot's intellectual exploration of the Northeast and further demonstrates the rational impasse of European anthropological and religious thought. Like Lescarbot, the Jesuit initially assumed that civil institutions and Christian morality were inseparable. One month after his arrival in Acadia, Biard harshly described the Micmac:

They are, I say, savage, haunting the woods, ignorant, lawless and rude: they are wanderers, with nothing to attach them to a place, neither homes nor relationship, neither possessions nor love of country; as a people they have bad habits; are extremely lazy, gluttonous, profane, treacherous, cruel in their revenge, and given to all kinds of lewdness, men and women alike. . . .[31]

Biard's contempt originated in his belief that godly culture provided human beings with a sense of identity that they would otherwise lack. This conviction masked an uncertainty that soon emerges in his writings. Every element of Biard's initial assessment can be turned on its head. The mobility the priest deplored, for one example, can also be seen as an emblem of the Algonkian's true civility. Biard himself described the seasonal cycles of Algonkian life and admitted that the Indians had in effect a fundamental attachment to the places where they lived. Biard could not take his observations to their logical conclusion. Rather, he applied rigid institutional criteria to Algonkian culture and ethics, agreeing with Lescarbot that Micmac religiosity was limited to the satanic: "They had no temples, sacred edifices, rites, ceremonies or religious teaching just as they have no laws, arts or government."[32]

Time somewhat tempered Biard's harsh estimation of Algonkian character. By the time the Jesuit returned to France he appreciated that a difference in social scale informed Algonkian life. Since "there can be no more polity than community," the priest reasoned, the Algonkians "cannot have great polity. Yet they cannot do without since they are men and brethren." This comparative insight led Biard to examine analogous political behavior, and he discovered the consensual principles that structured every aspect of Algonkian culture. Biard admired this political felicity and concluded that "the nature of our Savages is in itself generous and not malicious."[33]

Ultimately, the very existence of cultural differences perplexed Biard as much as it did Lescarbot. The priest remained even more culture-bound than the lawyer. Although he favorably contrasted Algonkian economic behavior with the "extreme covetousness" of the French, he insisted that French culture was theologically superior. If Algonkian social life confounded Christian politics, as Lescarbot admitted nervously, Biard showed little such concern. Yet the priest acknowledged the same dilemma: European institutions and the secular behavior they fostered flouted Christian ethics. The French themselves, he observed, "needed instruction scarcely less than the natives."[34]

After two years among the Algonkian, Biard recognized that Indians were fully justified in preferring their own way of life. If, he said, we "compare their good and ill with ours, I do not know but that they, in truth, have some reason to prefer (as they do) their own kind of happiness to ours, at least if we speak of the temporal happiness, which the rich and worldly seek in this life." It seemed to him that the distinguishing features of Algonkian life rested on the scarcity of material pleasures available to them. They were therefore more content than Europeans could imagine.

Biard finally contended that Micmac social harmony could not be attributed to their ethical decision to live in certain ways: "It is true, nevertheless, that they are purely and absolutely wretched, as much because they have no part in the natural happiness which is in the contemplation of God, and in the knowledge of sublime things and in the perfection of the nobler parts of the soul, but chiefly because they are outside the grace of our Lord JESUS CHRIST, and the way of Eternal salvation." Biard claimed that depravity would be their core social attribute as long as the Algonkian remained non-Christian.[35]

Biard used linguistic evidence to prove Algonkian savagery. Since the Indians "have no definite religion, magistracy or government, liberal or mechanical arts, commercial or civil life, they have consequently no words to describe things which they have never seen or even conceived." Biard's observation seems an unusually astute recognition of the linguistic reflections of social organization, but he used it to argue that the Algonkian were mentally deficient. The priest asserted that they could neither understand nor verbally convey abstract or spiritual realities. "It is certain," he insisted, "that these miserable people . . . will always remain in a perpetual infancy as to language and reason."[36]

Biard's thinking shows that the Algonkian remained as much a paradox for the French as for the English. Neither rational nor theological principles could explain tribal social order. Seventeenth-century theological assumptions condemned the Algonkian as ignorant and superstitious. Biard's deprecation of their ethics illustrates the inadequacy of European claims to cultural and moral superiority. All colonials believed that everyday life was subordinate to what might be called otherworldly dimensions of experience. At that level Indians and Europeans were not so different: both felt vulnerable to gods, saints, malevolent beings, and other spirits. Neither Jesuit priest nor Puritan minister doubted that powerful forces existed within American Indian rituals. Indeed, well into the colonial period clergymen feared that Indians were Satan's instruments.[37]

But Europeans claimed that Indian ignorance went beyond spiritual decadence. Urbanized culture gave the French and the English a second reason for righteous dogmatism. While settlers and Indians alike perceived spiritual forces behind the visible world, a secular trend in European thought ensured the eventual separation of their two mentalities. The two peoples eventually came to perceive time and space from different perspectives, a reflection of their small- and large-scale social orientations. In Europe private property, new agricultural technologies, and the development of capitalist economies produced an ever widening series of organizational hierarchies. And as the world became increasingly subordinate to technological manipulation, European intellectual attitudes became despiritualized.[38]

English Protestants and French Catholics assumed that reason and revelation were inseparable because Christ himself worked within European expansion. With the development of widespread literacy, Christianity became a major force of cultural homogeneity. As economic and political technologies extended across the face of Europe, they linked and transformed small communities. Literate Christianity simultaneously crossed political boundaries and amalgamated cultural differences. Christianity attempted to justify urbanization and national centralization. It also worked to create a religiosity based as much on reason as on revelation. This struggle between biblically defined social behavior and the impersonal social imperatives of cities came to characterize Western European social conflict.

French as well as English carried this struggle to the Algonkian Northeast. The widening gulf between Indian and European mentalities can be seen in Father Chretien LeClercq's evaluation of the Micmac. Succeeding Pierre Biard by some seventy years, LeClercq still suffered from the Jesuit's chauvinism, and his bias marred his otherwise rich description of Micmac life. On one hand, he expressed shock at the tribe's social profligacy, claiming that the Indians would eat all the available food, without regard for future needs. On the other hand, he recorded how Micmac women actually dried moose meat against lean times. Simply put, LeClercq held Indian culture in contempt. Unlike Lescarbot and Biard, he could not see why the Algonkian might prefer their own way of life. He failed to comprehend how they were, as he put it, "pleased to live and die in their natural ignorance." The Micmac struck LeClercq as unreasonable rather than mentally deficient. He noted that missionaries had educated a few who in a short time became "philosophers and even pretty good theologians." He added, however, that their intelligence was no cause for optimism: "But, after all, they have ever remained savages, since they have not had the sense to profit by their considerable advantages, of which they have rendered themselves wholly unworthy by leaving their studies in order to dwell with their fellow-countrymen in the woods, preferring, on the basis of a foolish reasoning, the savage to the French life."[39]

LeClercq ascribed gross ignorance to the Micmac because "they do not know how to read nor how to write." He thus added a new level to Biard's argument that the Algonkian were linguistically degenerate. Not only was their language devoid of all spiritual and abstract concepts, they also could not share the civil and religious symbolism that literacy imparted. For this reason, it seemed to LeClercq, the Algonkian remained attached to their own illogical tribal traditions. His distinctions appear more arbitrary than rational; neither distaste nor sympathy could dispel his tenaciously held cultural assumptions. Still, the Micmac continued to draw an admiring but perplexed response from the French: "They preserve among them," LeClercq contended, "the manner of living which was in vogue during the golden age, and those who imagine a Gaspesian [Micmac] as a monster of nature will understand only with difficulty the charity with which they mutually comfort one another."[40]

LeClercq himself found it difficult to comprehend Micmac reality. He ridiculed Algonkian mythological beliefs at the same time as he admitted the effective reality of their religious rituals. Like Father Paul LeJeune, who avowed that spirits actually visited the Montagnais in their shaking tent ritual, LeClercq accepted that Micmac shamans communicated with spirits. "Several of our French have believed, a little too easily," he commented, "that these juggleries are nothing but trifles and child's play." Because the priest acknowledged the actuality of Micmac shamanism and insisted that such powers were not derived from natural causes, he presumed that shamans were in league with the devil. It says everything about the rigidity of the European mind that LeClercq discounted ample evidence of Micmac religious sensibilities. Instead, he applied the same institutional criteria that Lescarbot and Biard had used. He concluded that the Micmac had never known a god "since they have lived down to our day without temples, priests, sacrifices and any indication of religion."[41]

LeClercq grasped only the surface of Micmac reality. The Algonkian believed that all things had souls, even objects that Europeans regarded as manifestly lifeless. "Our Gaspesians," LeClercq explained, "in common with all the other Indians of New France, have believed up to the present that there is in everything, even in such as are inanimate, a particular spirit which follows deceased persons into the other world, in order to render them as much service after death as these had received therefrom during life." These spirits included the souls of moose, beaver, dogs, even canoes, and snowshoes.[42]

In the face of LeClercq's enduring skepticism, the Micmac defended their animate universe. Their beliefs rested on revelation, and they trusted the evidence of their experience. They told the priest that they had learned the true nature of life from "Papkootparout the guardian, the master, the governor, and the ruler of all souls." Several men had gambled with Papkootparout and had not only won from him the gift of life itself but also the blessings of corn and tobacco. They said that Papkootparout "commanded them to plant these in Gaspesia, assuring them that all the nation would receive therefrom an inconceivable advantage."[43]

LeClercq described this mythological explanation as "ridiculous." Both Papkootparout and his blessings of life struck the priest as a "strange" and "foolish fancy." He wrote that "from these false premises, based upon a tradition so fabulous, they have drawn these extravagant conclusions—that everything is animated and that souls are nothing other than the ghost of that which had been animated." He was certain that Catholicism, unlike the Micmac religion, was a true faith. A written testament made Christianity reasonable.[44]

All Christian Europeans relied on the evidence of the Word to support their religious views. It was a powerful argument. Roger Williams, for example, overheard a discussion among Narragansetts who were trying to make sense of his religious advice. Williams had told them that the souls of the dead went either to heaven or hell, not to the southwest, as their oral traditions stated. Forced to admit that neither they themselves, nor Williams, could give a firsthand report of the soul's destination, Miantonomo, the Narragansett sachem, expressed the intellectual assurance that most English, but only some Indians, accepted. Miantonomo said that the minister "hath books and writings, and one which God himself made, concerning mens soules, and therefore may well know more than wee that have none, but take all upon trust from our forefathers."[45]

European confusion about Algonkian humanity reached full development on this issue of religious rationality. Early explorers had expected Indians to be savages, but tribal social behavior confounded that initial judgment. Later observers admitted that Indian societies were as successful as any that they had ever seen. They concluded that American Indians, like Europeans, could be improved. Colonial Europeans varied in their tolerance of cultural differences, but they all championed spiritual and technological progress. Indeed, they insisted that the two went hand in hand. Given such premises, Europeans could only reason that mental deficiency, traditional ignorance, and moral turpitude prevented the institutional, technological, and spiritual advancement of Indians.

MYTH AND ALGONKIAN SOCIALITY

Detailing the Micmac's and Abenaki's affluent subsistence economies and closely observing their social manners and politics, French colonials noted the essential features of Algonkian cultures. They frankly admitted disorientation—a mixture of admiration, dismay, and even disgust—at what they observed. Realizing that the Algonkian were highly moral people, the French became interested in Indian points of view, if only to learn how to convert the tribes. English reactions to the Indians stemmed from the same ambivalence, but French observers exposed what would become long-standing cross-cultural problems.

Centuries of frustrated scrutiny suggest that the Algonkian lived within cultural and moral structures that Euramericans could not fully comprehend. Such intellectual dilemmas troubled Frank G. Speck, a twentieth-century anthropologist who was unusually sympathetic to Indian people. Speck remarked that among the Montagnais-Naskapi of Quebec "a superstition becomes as much a fact as a visual or auditory observation." Their tenacious beliefs disturbed Speck because these "superstitions" existed without the "visual or auditory observation" that scientific knowledge requires. He did not think that Indians actually communicated with otherworldly beings, but he did believe that the Algonkian and Europeans shared the same perceptual processes. He added, however, that the Montagnais-Naskapi insisted on something more. They remained convinced that animals, plants, rocks, and man-made objects had an independent existence, a power of will, and a voice demonstrably like their own. "Such an attitude is as real to him," Speck wrote, "as it is unreal to a sophisticated mind. Beneath the exterior is the inner element which, in the native mind, is the very 'soul' of the thing." Speck joined distinguished company when he judged the "sophisticated mind" superior to the muddled observations of the Montagnais-Naskapi. Nonetheless, he did identify a continuing problem in understanding comparative culture.[46]

One of Speck's students, A. Irving Hallowell, finally broke with Euramerican ethnocentrism. He argued cogently that Western Europeans' cognitive style simply cannot grasp American Indian experience. "It is unfortunate," Hallowell remarked, "that the natural-supernatural dichotomy has been so persistently invoked by many anthropologists in describing the outlook of peoples in cultures other than our own." He succinctly states the dilemma: "If in the world-view of a people, 'persons' as a class include entities other than human beings, then our objective approach is not adequate for presenting an accurate description of the 'way a man, in a particular society, sees himself in relation to all else.' "[47]

Hallowell established that the Algonkian related to the world in a fundamentally different manner from Euramericans. Algonkian languages include an animate category that gives personal status to things Euramericans see only as objects. Hallowell noticed that stones were classified as animate and asked an old Ojibwa man for clarification: "Are *all* the stones we see about us here alive?" The old man pondered the question before replying: "No! But *some* are." Hallowell demonstrated that LeClercq and Speck had underestimated the Algonkian mind. He came to understand that Indians were far from superstitious: "The Ojibwa are not animists in the sense that they dogmatically attribute living souls to inanimate objects such as stones. . . . Whereas we should never expect a stone to manifest animate properties of any kind under any circumstances, the Ojibwa recognize, *a priori*, potentialities for animation in certain classes of objects under certain circumstances." Other anthropologists have observed such heightened social awareness among tribal peoples: to such peoples "the cosmos is personal and humanlike," Robert Redfield noted.[48]

Unlike Europeans, who made themselves the world's only measure, the Algonkian considered themselves to be first among beings who shared personal equality. Their mentality and ethics posited that social relations with other-than-human persons shared the same behavioral rules as human intercourse. They held that such beings lived in societies separate from but like their own. In addition, the Algonkian expected such persons to have a direct impact on human affairs.

The Algonkian did not recognize functional modes of causality. They would not have asked what effect the fur trade had on their lives. In accounting for the trade's impact, which did concern them, their attention concentrated on how people—Indians and Europeans alike— behaved while trading. Hallowell was emphatic: "Above all, any concept of impersonal 'natural' forces is totally foreign" to their thought.

He highlighted the "impersonal" character of European notions of cause and effect. The Algonkian would not recognize the results of techno-logical or even cultural causes. They would not ask *what* caused events. Instead, "Who did it, who is responsible, is always the crucial question to be answered." The Algonkian way of knowing expressed an intense experience of encompassing sociality. The Algonkian embodied that awareness in their cultural organization.[49]

Differences in social scale informed the outward and inward orienta-tions of Indian and Euramerican societies. The Algonkian world was firmly based on the immediate, face-to-face group, and webs of kinship organized their world. The structurally defined civilized-savage typol-ogy of Europeans had little relevance for Algonkian sociology. Their world categorization was socially direct: civilized-savage became kin-folk-strangers in their estimation. Relations of functional status—the roles, economic specializations, and class hierarchies of the European world—were not acknowledged among the Algonkian. Rather, they assessed people in terms of an individual's social consciousness. They lived within a world order given coherence by the good and bad actions of persons. Europeans accepted a similar philosophy of personal respon-sibility but added impersonal concepts of property, law, religious, and political authority.

Indian mythology reveals a sociology quite different from the mythic principles of European life. In the Algonkian's formative age humans and animals were not only amiable but were essentially alike. The Indians had no Adam to name animals and thus to differentiate them from humans. In their primary age humans and animals shared the same nature, lived with and married each other without distinction. Simi-larly, the Algonkian had no belief comparable to the Judeo-Christian fall from grace. Human sin did not shatter the amity of the initial world. For example, the Abenaki culture hero Gluskap shared no character traits with Adam. Gluskap exposed the evil exercise of power for all to see and he established an ethical system that could contain it. Adam did neither.

Gluskap taught the Abenaki and Micmac that evil came from dis-ordered social relations, and their mythology encapsulated that under-standing. Since evil was inherent in the world, it had to be dealt with. In a Passamaquoddy account Gluskap had an evil twin, Malsum, the wolf. Unlike Gluskap, who was born naturally, Malsum thrust himself into the world directly through his mother's flesh, killing her in the process. Gluskap first acted for humankind when he killed his obstreperous brother. In a Penobscot tale he had three jealous siblings, but he vanquished them in games that tested their respective powers.[50]

Even Gluskap had to learn good and evil from his grandmother, Woodchuck, who raised and educated him. He was an exuberant adolescent, well intentioned, but not always conscious of his impact on the world. While he learned easily how to hunt, fish, and make canoes and snowshoes, moral concepts came with more difficulty. To Woodchuck's dismay Gluskap carried his concern for her welfare to extremes. To make food easily available to his grandmother, he seized all animals and trapped all fish behind a huge weir. Woodchuck appreciated help but scolded Gluskap for his excesses. If all the animals and fish are dead, she asked, "What will our descendants do to live?" Gluskap repaired his error and learned the lesson. Woodchuck proudly proclaimed: "He will be a great magician. He will do great wonders for our descendants as he goes on."[51]

Gluskap grew judicious as he matured. The world was full of beings who did as they pleased with no care for people. As one tale says of Lox: "Great magic things he does, but little does he benefit others." Gluskap set about transforming the world, forcing such overbearing persons to conform to human morals. To moderate the wind he cajoled the giant bird Culloo to flap its wings less vigorously. Gluskap stole tobacco from Grasshopper when he refused to share it. With Summer's help Gluskap overcame the worst effects of Winter. He examined animals so they could not take unfair advantage of people. Some of them, like Squirrel and Beaver, were too large and the culture hero reduced them to their present size. In all that he accomplished Gluskap modified the world for human welfare.[52]

Gluskap did a great deal more. To ensure his people's happiness he showed them proper moral conduct, teaching them the rules that ought to govern relations with other-than-human persons and with one another. As one myth shows, Gluskap taught magnanimity as the source of ethics. Seven of his neighbors, including Crow, Sable, and Partridge, kidnapped his grandfather and abandoned Gluskap to die. Determined on revenge, Gluskap caught the culprits but then saw their fear. "Because he is good natured . . . ," myth recounts, "he pities and forgives them." Such compassion was the source of Gluskap's power. The strict requirement that the Abenaki be generous originates in Gluskap's example. Hallowell noted that the Algonkian emphasized hospitality because "other-than-human persons share their power with human beings." Morality and mutuality were thus synonymous.[53]

Gluskap's lessons of social cooperation suffused Abenaki culture. The tribes derived both their concept of land "ownership" and their social organization directly from him. Among the Penobscot and Maliseet a myth relates that once a giant frog held all the world's water in its belly. When the frog refused to consider the people's plight, Gluskap slew him, creating streams and rivers. Unable to control their thirst, many people rushed to drink and were transformed into water animals—lobsters, crabs, eels, whales, frogs, yellow perch, and sturgeon. The survivors took the names of their relatives' animal forms and selected hunting territories adjacent to the new watercourses. The extended Abenaki family—human and animal alike—remained bonded despite persistent differences in outward appearance. The Penobscot used a special word to describe intimacy between human and animal kin. As Frank G. Speck noted, "the term *ntu'tem* 'my spouse's parents,' or in another sense 'my partner of a strange race,' " referred to animal relatives, just as it indicated relationships between hunting bands.[54]

*Ntu'tem* relations expressed with everyday immediacy the interests humans and other-than-human persons shared. When Gluskap left the world, his power—*Kta'hando*—continued as the "source of dynamics" of Abenaki life. Once Gluskap had fully transformed the world for Indian habitation, it became less fluid. Humans and other-than-humans lost much of their power to change form and to speak with one another. Only *made'olino-uk*, the shamans, had power to bridge the void. Yet the myths embody a practical sense of the individual's enduring responsibility for the social welfare of human and animal relatives. Shamanistic relations with a *baohi.'gan*, or spirit helper, retained and funneled power from the mythic era. Shamans considered the *baohi.'gan* part of themselves, and such an interpersonal solidarity created their power as it had Gluskap's.[55]

Shamans remembered and reordered the Algonkian cosmos. They recounted the mythic past and through esoteric rituals repaired other-worldly relations for the community's good. Some integrated bonds between ordinary and other-than-human persons into the ritualistic structure by interpreting dreams in which such persons appeared. The shamans' medicinal powers stemmed from the same concern for social relations. The Algonkian believed that social disorder caused disease. Shamans therefore, contended with malevolent persons or indicated to the sick how to ease some affront.[56]

Algonkian institutions emerged from this human/nonhuman symbiosis binding people and other persons to mutual responsibility and obligation. Myth, folklore, and practical experience reinforced the mutuality of humans in nature. Dire consequences resulted from failure to respect the integrity of other-than-human persons. Complicated prohibitions and a positive sense of intimate relations gave meaning to the Algonkian food cycle. Rituals surrounded hunting, fishing, and agricultural activities. In honor of the life they would take, the Algonkian carefully prepared themselves to hunt. The Micmac, Abenaki, and Montagnais all believed that "to keep animal's spirits favorable to men, and also to increase their numbers in the forest by inducing their spirits to submit to reincarnation, the bones must be treated with respect by those who kill the bodies." Algonkian subsistence activities were sacramental: the people's welfare depended on individual social responsibility.[57]

The Abenaki myth cycle and the operation of Kta'hando (power) defined a civilized-savage continuum that was less ambiguous than European social categories. For Europeans civilization and culture were synonymous. Civilized persons could be recognized because their behavior conformed to institutional hierarchies of status and social role. Algonkian definitions deemphasized organizational manifestations of civilization and focused instead on the social behavior that gave institutions personal meaning. The Algonkians did not believe that formalized social position accorded moral rectitude. People who belonged—who were "civilized"—received status for concrete social accomplishments. Europeans confused status and social ideals. The "godly" nature of institutionalized authority partially removed political and religious officials beyond the need for social recognition. Europeans formalized consensual processes. To achieve law and order beyond the folk community, Europeans depersonalized the exercise of authority.

Algonkian social and political behavior were synonymous. People constantly held the sachem accountable for his actions. "In fact," LeClercq marveled, "all his power and authority are based only upon the good will of those of his nation, who execute his order just in so far as it pleases them." Algonkian sachems led through persuasion and force of example, maintaining status only so long as they demonstrated concern for the people's welfare. Among the Abenaki and Micmac, sachems led family bands and defined their social purposes. They trained young, unmarried men to hunt and trap and claimed the animals for the benefit of all band members. Algonkian society had its fullest expression in the sachems' extended households. Individuals without relatives—especially orphans, the old, and the weak—sought their protection. Le-Clercq described how the sachem's authority derived from selflessness: "It is as if he had wished to say that his treasures and riches were in the hearts and in the affections of his people." The most influential sachems were also shamans of undisputed stature and their religious power suggests the social and religious ethic that permeated tribal politics.[58]

Algonkian social psychology indicates that solidarity had its psychic costs. Like Euramericans, the Algonkian experienced tension in making practical choices between communal ideal and personal impulse. They did not, however, use institutionalized power to strike a balance. Strict self-restraint minimized confrontations and ensured cooperation within and between family bands. Individuals rarely expressed anger openly because self-control was a central virtue. "It is considered shameful," LeClercq said of the Micmac, "to show anger or impatience for the insults that are offered, or the misfortunes which come." This emotional reserve tempered every facet of Algonkian life. An individual not only controlled "his *own* anger" but suppressed "open criticism of his fellows in face-to-face relations . . . to avoid arousing *their* anger."[59]

For the same reason the Algonkian were reluctant to discipline their children. Youngsters learned to avoid peer ridicule and to recognize the preeminence of kinship responsibility. They avoided anxiety by controlling their selfish impulses and complying with the demands of others. "They walk with dignity as if they had always some great affair to think upon, and to decide, in their minds," LeClercq noted of the Micmac. Algonkian personalities were cautious, restrained, and other-directed.[60]

Social concern sometimes operated in a negative way. While hospitality was an ideal, it could not always be practiced. On one occasion Pierre Biard and a company of Frenchmen shared some fish with five or six Micmac women who were "heavily burdened and weary." Just as the fish began to cook, however, other Micmac arrived. The women "fled quickly into the woods, with their kettle only half boiled, for they were very hungry." Biard commented: "The reason for their flight was that, if they had been seen, they would have been obliged by the rule of politeness to share with the newcomers their food, which was not too abundant." Under less trying circumstances the communal ethic prevailed. "All things (so long as they will last) are used in common amongst them," Thomas Morton noted of New England Algonkian. "A bisket cake given to one; that one breakes it equally into so many parts,

as there be persons in his company, and distributes it. Platoes Common-
wealth is so much practiced by these people."[61]

Individualism defined both mental illness and moral degeneracy.
Mythic cannibal giants variously called *Chenoo, Ki·wa'kwe*, and *Windigo*
personified the Algonkian struggle for social harmony. The Penobscot
name *ki·wa'kwe* means "going about in the woods." Such antisocial
beings were wholly noncultural, essentially nonpersons. The cannibal
giants existed outside the cosmos transformed by Gluskap and maintained by human domestic activities. While Gluskap provided a model
of proper behavior, the giants stood as the antithesis of social consideration. Individuals might become cannibals if they rejected kin values.[62]

Occasional encounters with cannibals reminded the Algonkian of the
fragile social values that kept their small bands from disintegrating.
Chretien LeClercq recorded an account of one Micmac family caught
deep in the woods during severe weather with no food. Pressed by "the
hunger which was devouring him alive," the man resolved to kill and
eat his wife so that he and his two children might survive. Perceiving his
intention, his wife frantically pleaded that it would be wiser to eat the
children: "Is it not much better that we put to death some of our
children, and that we eat them together, in order that I may be able to
rear and to support the smaller ones who can no longer live if once they
come to lose their mother?" The parents survived, but at terrible cost.
When they arrived at the summer village, the "leading men were as
much exasperated as surprised at the news of a deed so black and
barbarous." The Micmac ostracized the couple: ". . . they traveled the
woods day and night without ceasing, seeking everywhere in vain for a
rest which they could find in no place." Cannibalism, even committed
under such pressing circumstances, was the most heinous violation of
kinship values. The couple was ostracized not as punishment but
because cannibals were no longer human.[63]

The cannibal giants indicate the distinctions that comprised Algonkian analogues of European images of civilization and savagery.
Tales involving the giants reveal that communal relations were based on
the kinship hunting band for more than economic survival. These
stories indicate the social and psychological values that made life
possible in the Northeast's harsh winter environment. The Algonkian
knew that intimate relations between relatives were the most effective
method of ensuring solidarity. The small and seasonally mobile Algonkian societies scaled civilized behavior to the limits of kinfolk interaction. The Algonkian knew the civilized person by his concern for the

welfare of the people. Conversely, the savage was easily recognized by his self-concern and his utter contempt for humanity. By definition, then, the Algonkian were uneasy and reticent with outsiders.

Were Europeans human? The Algonkian were not sure. They certainly considered the violence that occurred at the time of contact as a symptom of savagery. Many Europeans acted in ways that evoked the ominous symbolism of cannibal giants. Here were powerful beings who posed as friends but who wreaked havoc. If Europeans were at first strangers, in time their incorrigible individualism struck the Algonkian as reprehensible. Clearly, Europeans could not be trusted. The Algonkian had their own brand of ethnocentrism, and their judgment of human character was rigidly behavioral: civilized persons acted as if they cared for people. Europeans rarely did so.

Most Europeans had no idea that they were being judged. Instead, Algonkian enthusiasm for metal trade goods led Europeans to premature self-congratulation. Explorers record Indian awe over the new material culture and Indian willingness to trade valuable furs for worthless trinkets. This eagerness for commerce induced traders to believe (naturally enough to their way of thinking) that Indians recognized European superiority in the utility of their products. The Algonkian did appreciate the practical advantages of trade but attached their own meanings to European goods.

Algonkian culture was so thoroughly socialized that even utilitarian objects played personalized roles in tribal life. Man-made objects, no less than persons of the natural world, demonstrated pervasive power independent from both their functions and the purposes of their makers. Everyday objects conveyed a living presence. Their creation dated from the mythic time when Woodchuck taught Gluskap to make tools needed to help his people. He showed the Algonkian how to construct canoes, snowshoes, and other useful objects in order to demonstrate his concrete concern. Tools were thus not the product of human ingenuity. Such objects were gifts and therefore had other-than-functional meanings. The Algonkian elaborately decorated their canoes and wigwams with family totems, and individuals adorned personal belongings in a similar fashion. A canoe, for example, retained the animate characteristics of the birch tree that had been used to make it.[64]

If the Algonkian rejected the rationale of European materialism (and they did), their response to alien social behavior was as decisive. At first the Algonkian thought that European trade goods were as socially purposeful as their own. The manner in which Europeans conveyed such products soon disabused them of the notion. The Algonkian quickly perceived the scale of commercial value that Europeans attached to their goods. In response, they demanded and received better prices for their furs. The Algonkian also went beyond commercial astuteness. They soon assessed the asocial motives of trade. "For they have learned from us," Pierre Biard stated, "that . . . nothing is readily given away." Indeed, the need for profits dictated otherwise. The Micmac told the priest: "We are not thieves like you."[65]

Algonkian estimations of European character were thorough. Traders had only to recommend individualistic ways of doing things to provoke the response: "You can have your way and we will have ours; every one values his own wares." Biard reacted incredulously to the intransigence of Algonkian self-esteem: "You will see these poor barbarians," he declared, "notwithstanding their great lack of government, power, letters, art and riches, yet holding their heads so high that they greatly underrate us, regarding themselves as our superiors." The Micmac frankly told Biard why they held the French in contempt: "They esteem themselves better, because they say, you never cease fighting and quarreling amongst yourselves; as for ourselves, we live in peace; you are envious of each other, and usually disparage each other; you are thieves and liars; you are covetous, without generosity and mercy; as for us, if we have a piece of bread, we divide it amongst ourselves." The Algonkian knew that Europeans held Indian nonurban cultures in contempt and judged their customs uncouth. The Algonkians, however, did not care, for they rejected urban materialism and urban manners equally. The Micmac told Lescarbot that "they do not come to seek after us."[66]

This disparity in social styles was only partially visible to Indians and Europeans but nonetheless established their historical struggle. Each people understood the natural and cultural dimensions of human activity in different terms and thus assigned divergent meanings to the same events. Two distinct systems of causality seem to have operated in Algonkian-European relations. Each system derived from the respective value orientations to the world. Each described different codes of social behavior. Europeans acted within the functional premises of their urbanized social, economic, political, and religious systems. Such behavioral assumptions affected the development of French and English communities in America as well as the course of Indian relations.

The Algonkian system is less easily grasped. The prime mode of causality that the Algonkian perceived emphasized kinship-oriented behavior as the norm. In relations with Europeans the Algonkian were concerned with two aspects of the same issue. First, their intensely socialized behavioral assumptions meant that they hoped to create relations of personal status to humanize the strangers. Second, they faced the challenge of recognizing and dealing with the impersonal character of European sociology. Contact threatened and undermined both Algonkian and European values.

Diversity in social organization resulted in different value orientations within European and American Indian cultures. Both cultures responded to human needs for order, stability, meaning, love, and sustenance. Similar in social purposefulness, the two cultures thereafter diverged. Europeans addressed abstract levels of social concern. Because of population size and its geographical dispersal, French and English colonials had to address social issues with large-scale organization. The inevitably imperfect result left a variety of social activities—especially ethnic, religious, and economic interests—beyond control. The ideal of European Christianity made the growth of institutional authority the hallmark of colonial social life. Algonkian cultures operated in the opposite direction. Their independent kinship units repudiated authoritarian integration and required individual responsibility to fill the vacuum. As a result, the Algonkian could not deal with Europeans until they had first united among themselves.

Extremes in social scale thus defined the great divide between the Algonkian and the Europeans. Indian peoples rejected government, but European colonial stability required punitive law and strict order. Given these opposed social styles, only personal relations between the northeastern peoples could bridge the differences. If any one of them held aloof and disdained communication, trust would be impossible. While it may seem that Europeans and the Algonkian were starkly opposed, this is only partly true. They shared common ground in economic, military, and religious interests. These situations created limited arenas for dialogue but also posed problems that impeded constructive alliance.

All northeastern peoples needed to recognize, address, and resolve underlying disagreements if they were to create lasting trust. Colonials carried old animosities to the New World. On the face of it, the conflict expressed itself in diplomatic efforts to ensure national security. Just below the surface, however, English and French were engaged in a mortal religious struggle. While both shared the same ideological belief in Christian progress, they differed in a basic way. Catholics were more tolerant of folk traditions and they reacted to the Abenaki favorably. In contrast, the English feared the profanity of everyday life and, since they also disagreed among themselves, found it difficult to communicate with Indians. At the most general level, then, any agreement among the three peoples would come to rest on the way that their religious beliefs intersected.

There were signs to suggest that alliances could be established. At least intellectually Europeans and Indians recognized a shared humanity. French and English declared that they had beneficent motives for colonization. The Algonkian offered membership in their kinship alliances. In this mutually expressed hope for positive association, both Indian and European ideologies of civilization and savagery oversimplified the complex social postures that each people assumed to facilitate communication. Arguments over status and sociality continued for as long as relations endured. Most important, the elusive ideal of alliance produced a troubled history of interaction.

# 3

# SOCIAL DEMONS AND RELIGIOUS
# DREAMS

*The Creation of the Abenaki-French Alliance*

Before they could deal with Europeans the Abenaki had to resolve conflicts among themselves. In fact, for two-thirds of the seventeenth century the tribes labored against internal disaster. An epidemic struck the tribes in 1616 and revealed their vulnerability, threatening the Abenaki's social identity and shaking their self-confidence. The Indians did suspect that colonials were responsible for the recurring sickness, but, as might be expected, they fell back on mythological explanations about the positive and negative effects of religious power, implying that they had only themselves to blame for the tragedy. Alternating epidemics of smallpox, measles, and plague came to symbolize the Abenaki's apparent inability to deal responsibly with one another.

Since religious values are at the heart of any social order, devastating illness and ethical deterioration among the Indians came to express tribal disharmony. The Abenaki would have agreed with French and English beliefs that the continuing epidemics were punishment for erring ways. They recognized that the fur trade created domestic conflict. Commerce pitted the bands against one another, and the liquor traffic disrupted family relations. The Abenaki quickly learned that their disunity worked to the traders' advantage, but that was their least important lesson. Post contact disease, drunkenness, and discord soon called them to religious and social reform.[1]

Catastrophe challenged the Abenaki's religious sense of history. Since their mythology encapsulated a practical sense of each person's responsibility for social welfare, sickness and excessive drinking urged ethical renewal. Gluskap had taught the people that they were to share moral strength and he showed them how to do it. Benevolent as he was, Gluskap had not established a world in which struggle was no longer necessary. Rather, "he wanted to show the man that he must not always wait for spiritual help, but do the things with his own labor, only appealing to spiritual power when necessity required it."[2]

The culture hero did not abandon his people. His gift of religious power—Kta'hando—continued to guide them. Even before Europeans arrived, the tribes received moral advice about confronting inevitable cultural change. With the aid of No-chi-gar-neh, the spirit of the air, they learned to use medicinal plants, to heed the spirits of dream and trance, and to use shamanistic powers for collective welfare. "You shall be great among your people," No-chi-gar-neh told the first shamans, "because your works shall bring great comfort to yourselves [and] also to all your people, for you shall be useful to them." No-chi-gar-neh also added an ominous admonition that defined the moral principles of Abenaki existence: "Being great, great must be your care in keeping yourselves in this greatness. You must never allow yourselves to become so small as to use your power upon or against your brother on any contention. Do not abuse one another with this power. . . because whoever abuses this power shall lose it." One tradition relates that until European contact Abenaki shamans adhered to No-chi-gar-neh's advice and "never showed any other kind of feeling only that was kind and brotherly."[3]

The Abenaki also recognized the divisive impact of early interactions. Europeans sparked disagreements among the religious leaders of the tribes. In their initial effort to assess the intruders, the Abenaki chose a few noted shamans "to watch the strange people's movements." Unfortunately, the overlooked shamans felt slighted, became jealous, and "began to agitate the minds of their friends to discord, each of them having a large influence among the people, [and] the whole country was thrown into different bands." Elders, who cited No-chi-gar-neh's warning that abused religious power would be lost, "advised peace and harmony." They were ignored.[4]

Thereafter, shamanistic rivalries rent the moral unity of the tribes and, according to the Abenaki way of thinking, unleashed epidemic sickness and disorder. At one level oral tradition about shamanistic violence seems to explain the intertribal war that Europeans observed during the early contact period. At another, the tradition corroborates documentation that shamans abused their power and may have contributed to that conflict. Among the Kennebec, Abenaki shamans not only used their powers to kill the settlers of the ill-fated Popham colony but also threatened to inflict sickness on any of their people who collaborated with the English. The settlement era thus began with the Abenaki divided, with intense shamanistic rivalries, and with Gluskap's gift of power violated.[5]

This religious and social crisis molded the way in which the Abenaki responded to Europeans and structured their rehabilitation. Mythology taught that "every stranger was a potential magical antagonist." The Abenaki thus understood that associations with French and English had to proceed with care. They were all the more cautious because they felt the effects of treachery even among themselves. Still, they sensed that alliance was not altogether impossible. They could see that some settlers, and especially the French missionaries, responded in selfless ways. Thus, if they feared that European strangers would use power against them, they also recognized that some colonials acted benevolently. This recognition of mutual humanity in time encouraged the tribes to think that they could adapt, preserving tradition while making sense of the moral challenge of contact.[6]

The French pioneered good relations because Jesuit priests and the Abenaki came to share powerful bonds. Although it took fifty years, the two peoples did learn to communicate. Their dialogue stands in vivid contrast to the distrust that characterized Abenaki-English relations. New Englanders dominated their closest Algonkian neighbors prior to 1640. In the Northeast both Massachusetts and Plymouth officially ignored the Abenaki with whom they traded. In the absence of effective local government, English settlers violently abused the Indians. Rejected, the tribes understandably concluded that the French were better friends.

It took all of thirty years for the French and the Abenaki to discover the common ground on which to take a stand. The developing alliance defied official French policies because Canadians worried that the Abenaki might pose an economic threat. In fact, the Abenaki were excluded from the Canadian fur market until the 1660s. Living between New

England and New France, the Abenaki could easily funnel furs south at French expense. Since the French and their Canadian Indian allies guarded against that possibility, the eventual association with the Abenaki was not based on mutual economic advantage.

Nor did the relationship grow out of Jesuit efforts to Christianize the Abenaki. In the main the Society of Jesus was occupied elsewhere. Abenaki knowledge of the French priests grew only by word of mouth, and the tribes interpreted as they wished the moral doctrines taught in distant mission villages. The priests considered the tribes unlikely candidates for conversion because the missionaries assumed that the English traders had corrupted them. As a result, the Jesuits gave the Abenaki only nominal attention throughout the first three-quarters of the seventeenth century.

The French-Abenaki alliance matured almost without attention, the relationship exemplifying the French and Indians at their most flexible with new people and new ideas. By 1675, when relations entered their first stage of sustained growth, both Jesuits and Abenaki knew how to deal with the problems of culture contact and moved toward each other deliberately. Since the tribes had concluded that the English were poor neighbors, they scrutinized the Jesuits for similar failings. The Jesuit missionaries for their part had seen their most carefully developed plans shattered in the clash of Indian and French cultures. Disillusioned by the rejection of Catholicism by most Indians, the priests could at least admire the Abenaki's religious devotion.

The Abenaki and individual Jesuit missionaries came slowly to share the same everyday world of conflict and the same hoped-for world of religious harmony. The Abenaki recognized that the demons of culture contact—European diseases, alcoholic beverages, and social conflict— wreaked havoc among them. Throughout the seventeenth century the tribes lived in a nightmarish landscape and turned to the Jesuits for help. If the priests were to win acceptance, they had to speak directly to the Abenaki's flagging optimism. The endurance of the relationship suggests that the Jesuits fundamentally communicated reassurance.

ALLIANCE EXPLORED

Although the plague of 1616 was devastating, the Abenaki weathered the storm. Other events shook the survivors in subtler ways. Beginning in 1625 Plymouth Colony began to trade among the Kennebec Abenaki, bartering corn for beaver pelts. By the end of the decade

Plymouth had implemented what Neal Salisbury has aptly called the "wampum revolution," buying shell beads in southern New England and exchanging them for Abenaki furs. As a result, the tribes found themselves drawn into the commercial orbit of the English who were slowly settling the coast of Maine.[7]

This regularization of trade created several related challenges that occupied the tribes until the mid-1650s. The first result was a deterioration of Abenaki relations with the English. Trade in southern Maine was conducted at arm's length and apparently with considerable resentment. In 1631 the Kennebec Abenaki killed Walter Bagnall, an English trader who had been cheating them. This response was no more drastic than English reaction to Abenaki misdeeds. In 1636 settlers on the Saco River appointed an officer "to excut any Indians that are proved to have killed any swyne of the English." The Abenaki reacted fearfully, rightly suspecting that they might be seized without warning. And "so I would," the trader John Winter observed, "if I Cann mett with them that did it."[8]

Tensions increased when the English made hard liquor readily available. By the mid-1640s drunkenness afflicted entire tribes. In the 1650s Plymouth Colony openly admitted that "there hath been great abuses in trading wine and other strong liquors with the Indians. . . [who] in their drunkenness, commit much horrid wickedness, as murdering their nearest relatives &c." Plymouth resolved to correct this "sad and woful" state of affairs. Unfortunately, while the English strictly banned traffic in liquor, the prohibition existed only on paper. The law stated that violators would lose their right to trade with Indians, but only after a third conviction.[9]

Between 1629 and 1650 the Kennebec Abenaki were the only tribe to balance relations with both the English and the Canadian French. Samuel de Champlain records that the Abenaki expressed a desire "to make a close friendship with us, begging us to help them against the Iroquois." The governor welcomed their overture because his fledgling colony at Quebec was desperately short of food and he hoped that "this nation might greatly relieve us, both by their supplies of grain and by taking part of my companions to winter among them." In July 1629 Champlain's brother-in-law, Eustache Boulle, returned from the Kennebec with a promise that the tribe would exchange agricultural produce for military aid against the Iroquois. Within days, however, New France surrendered to the English Kirke brothers and the fledgling Abenaki-French agreement died abruptly.[10]

When the French returned to Canada in 1632, conditions no longer favored economic and military alliance. The Kennebec did make the attempt. In the 1630s they tested the popularity of southern New England wampum in Canada's intertribal trade. They found a ready market but soon met opposition in developing it. The Montagnais and the French, at a competitive disadvantage without the shell beads, feared that the high demand for wampum would permit the Abenaki to become middlemen and funnel furs toward New England.[11]

The Montagnais persuaded the French to bar the Abenaki from the Canadian trade. When several Kennebec arrived at Quebec in the summer of 1637, a Montagnais sachem complained immediately to Governor Charles Huault de Montmagny. The sachem declared that the Abenaki had ignored him when "he had forbidden them to go up to the three Rivers." They also defied Montmagny's orders to leave Canada. "They went straight to the three Rivers, to exchange their porcelain [wampum] for the Beavers of the Algonquins." At Trois Rivières, M. de Chasteaufort, Montmagny's lieutenant confiscated their guns, forcing the Abenaki to return to Maine.[12]

Though the Montagnais feared trading competition, some of them saw a strategic advantage in extending friendship to the Kennebec. And despite the animosities that economic rivalry produced, the Abenaki continued to seek a military partnership against the Iroquois. It is significant that the Kennebec and some Montagnais realized that they had first to resolve differences among themselves. Quick settlement of intertribal disputes suggests the importance they attached to their developing relationship. In 1640, for example, a few Abenaki killed an Algonkin man in a drunken disagreement. The Kennebec "strongly disapproved" of such conduct and hurried two ambassadors with gifts to stop the Algonkin from taking revenge. These spokesmen received "a rather unfriendly reception," and only the intervention of two Christian Montagnais terminated the affair peacefully.[13]

Until this incident, the Kennebec Abenaki had not fully perceived the alliance that had emerged between the Montagnais, other Algonkian tribes, and the French. The Montagnais were the first of the St. Lawrence Algonkian to experience all the disorientations of culture contact. Displaced, pummelled by Mohawk raids, devastated by liquor and disease, and starving because of competition for limited game, the desperate Montagnais drew closer to the French. In their moves toward an alliance they first encountered Jesuit priests, who enjoyed the warm confidence of the devout Governor Montmagny.

With little appreciation of the vast forces disrupting the Montagnais world and with Montmagny's active support, the Jesuits unwittingly aggravated the Indians' crisis. The Montagnais had approached the French to ask for economic and military aid. Help was forthcoming, but so was an interference that threatened Montagnais identity. Since the French insisted that political and religious alliance went together, the Montagnais found more than they had bargained for. In return for assistance the Jesuits demanded conversion. This attack on traditional Indian beliefs came at a time when the Montagnais themselves feared the diminution of their religious power. Just as the Abenaki had sought the causes of crisis in their own traditions, the Montagnais deemed themselves responsible for their cultural disarray. Relentless Jesuit ridicule of their beliefs, shamans, and medicinal practices further undermined Montagnais confidence. It was plain that their once potent rituals had failed to bring relief. In 1639 the first Montagnais kin groups capitulated to the Jesuits and settled in a mission at Sillery.[14]

These Christian Montagnais forged relations between the Abenaki and French. In 1640 they intervened in the Kennebec conflict with the suspicious Algonkin in the hope of creating an alliance among all the tribes. Noel Negabamat, a Sillery headman, informed the Abenaki of the new order among Canadian Indians: "'If,' said he, 'thou wishest to bind our two Tribes by a perfect friendship, it is necessary that we should all believe the same. Have thyself baptised, and cause thy people to do likewise, and that bond will be stronger than any gifts. We pray to God, and know no other friends or brothers than those who pray like us.'"[15]

The growing influence of Sillery Christians on the distant Kennebec suggests the Jesuits' overall impact throughout the Algonkian Northeast. One of the Abenaki ambassadors who had negotiated with the Algonkin in 1640 returned to Sillery a year later leading eight canoes of curious friends and relatives. He joined a Montagnais war party against the Iroquois and on returning to Sillery "began to press urgently for his Baptism." The Abenaki sachem patiently accepted the Jesuits' demand that he prepare himself in the Christian faith. He memorized Catholic prayers, spent hours in the mission chapel, and unceasingly requested baptism.[16]

Such ardor pleased the priests, but they coolly tested his perseverance. "Father DeQuen refused him several times, in order to try him, — saying that he had to attend to others, who were more eager and better prepared than he; that he was a stranger, and that his word was not relied on." The Abenaki protested that he knew his prayers and catechism as well as the Montagnais Christians and that his soul was as much endangered as theirs. He observed that he had abandoned his kin and renounced leadership of his tribe in order to return to Sillery for instruction. Finally, he insisted that "he should not be refused on account of his being a Stranger, because Paradise is as much for those of his Nation as for the others." The Jesuits acknowledged these protests and at his baptism Governor Montmagny gave him the name of Jean Baptiste. True to his namesake, Jean Baptiste became a prophet calling his relatives to renewal.[17]

In the early 1640s other Abenaki individuals like Jean Baptiste examined the Montagnais and French alliance and were impressed. The experience of another Kennebec, who was given the name Claude, illustrates how the Christian alliance was able to overcome the Algonkian's characteristic reluctance to deal with nonrelatives. While at Sillery, Claude fell sick and the Jesuits sent him to the hospital nuns at Quebec. He observed how the nuns' "whole occupation was only to assist and succor the poor and sick." The nuns nursed many visiting Algonkian and won much goodwill. Such personal care firmly rooted French status and influence among the tribes: "These are so many precursors of the Gospel that God sends to his peoples," the Jesuits commented.[18]

Warm encounters with the French, along with Christian Montagnais visits to the Kennebec River, engaged the Abenaki's attention. Still, Montagnais overtures remained fruitless for several years. One Montagnais spent the winter of 1642−43 preaching among the Kennebec, but his words seem to have carried little weight. The *Jesuit Relation* explained: ". . . as those people have no acquaintance or commerce with any one else except some English who are wont to go there; and are much given to drunkenness by means of the liquor that they get in trade with the heretics, and with the vessels of the coasts—the discourses of our good Christian had not so much effect." The Jesuits concluded that the Kennebec were "an utterly infidel Nation" and consigned them to oblivion along with the Puritans who were blamed for corrupting them.[19]

Faced with Jesuit indifference, missionary activity among the Abenaki came first from within. By 1646 several of the Kennebec, some of them prominent, had been baptized and were residing at Sillery. These Abenaki decided to travel to their homes "to publish the Faith there, and to ascertain from the principal persons of their nation whether they

would consent to lend ear to the Preachers of the Gospel." The Kennebec Christians, led by Claude and Jean Baptiste, returned to Sillery in
August 1646 and reported that thirty men and ten women "would
embrace our belief." The Abenaki speaker declared, "All the others
exhorted me to come and seek a Father,—and said that they would be
very glad to listen to him before pledging their word."[20]

These quiet beginnings encouraged the Jesuits and they altered their
harsh opinion of the Abenaki. The priests remarked of one Kennebec
man: ". . . we see clearly that one Savage well tried, well converted, and
constant in his resolution does much more to extend the faith and attract
a whole nation, than a weak and inconstant multitude." Although the
Jesuits sought only a few earnest Christians, they responded favorably to
the Kennebec's request for a priest. The missionaries felt that the
Abenaki's wait-and-see attitude reflected their potential religious fervor. Governor Montmagny had more practical aims. He did not approve
of sending a priest until the Abenaki assured him that if one was sent
"they would no longer come here, and would give no offense to
Monsieur the governor regarding the trade."[21]

In August 1646 the Society of Jesus dispatched Father Gabriel
Druillettes to the Kennebec. He found the Abenaki beset by an epidemic against which their shamans were powerless. Druillettes responded to the crisis without hesitation, spending his days caring for
the sick and discrediting the shamans whenever possible. When the
priest returned to Quebec in June 1647, thirty Kennebec escorted him
and expressed regret at his departure: "We will say. . . that Father
Gabriel does not love us and does not care that we die, since he abandons
us."[22]

Missionary politics prevented the Jesuits from sending Druillettes
back to Maine as the Kennebec requested. The Jesuits drew back in
response to a request from another missionary group. Capuchin priests
had worked in the Acadian colony since the 1630s. While the number of
Capuchin missionaries among the Abenaki is unknown, the order had
twelve priests and five brothers in their Acadian missions in 1647. They
also had a permanent post at the mouth of Penobscot River which
Druillettes visited in 1646. It is not surprising therefore that the
Capuchins wished to include the Kennebec within their own mission
territory. Unwittingly, some of the Kennebec had carried a Capuchin
letter to the Jesuit Superior which asked that Druillettes be assigned
elsewhere. Despite Capuchin disapproval, the Jesuits resolved to send
Druillettes again, if the Kennebec asked for him. But when the tribe did

petition for a priest, the Jesuits had apparently changed their minds. The *Jesuit Relation* of 1651—52 reported the order "believed that other Missionaries nearer to their colony would be able to give them religious instructions."[23]

Gabriel Druillettes did not return to the Kennebec until the fall of 1650. Capuchin opposition partially explains the delay, but economic competition remained the major stumbling block. To protect their fur empire from the English, French traders continuously rebuffed the Abenaki. In July 1649 the Abenaki were told never to return to Quebec. Then events intervened. The Five Nations Confederacy dispersed the Huron peoples, destroyed the Jesuits' most ambitious mission, terminated the Canadian fur trade, and threatened the survival of New France directly. Suddenly, the Christian Montagnais and all of their allies, including the ignored Kennebec, became Canada's only defense. Always inclined to see the Iroquois as heathens viciously opposed to Christianity, the French drew closer to the Algonkian and prepared for a holy war.[24]

When Druillettes returned to Maine in 1650, he aimed to protect Christian Indians from Iroquoian savagery. This time he sought the Kennebec's military assistance as well as their souls. Strangled as much by the loss of Huron furs as by impending war with the Five Nations, the Quebec government also empowered Druillettes to negotiate a trading agreement with New England in exchange for an alliance against the Iroquois. Among the English Druillettes stressed the sacred character of the undertaking, arguing that the Five Nations perversely reviled Christian belief. The priest expressed both official and Jesuit opinion when he wrote to John Winthrop, Jr., that the Iroquois "not only have long harassed the Christian Cannadians near Kebec, and most cruelly torture them by slow fire, out of hatred of the Christian Faith, but they even intend by a general massacre to destroy my akenebek Catechumens dwelling on the banks of the Kenebec River, because they have been for many years to the Cannadian Christians."[25] Druillettes moved cautiously because the nominally Christian Kennebec were ostensibly within territory claimed by Plymouth Colony. While the tribe recognized no government beyond its own, it favored the anti-Iroquoian alliance. In 1650 only English support was wanting. Protestant New England received the Jesuit with polite tolerance but expressed no interest in fighting New France's war.[26]

Unable to win English support, the French again lost interest in the marginal Abenaki. Throughout the 1650s, as in the previous decade,

French indifference prevented an alliance. Druillettes believed that Kennebec interest in Christianity was genuine. He was all the more impressed because they could expect neither economic nor military aid from the dilatory French. Since the Abenaki were excluded from the fur trade, "they had no hope, either as individuals or as a people, of reaping any temporal advantage from the coming of our Father to their country," the Jesuits commented. In fact, the French did not admit the Kennebec to the Canadian fur trade until 1665.[27]

### RELIGIOUS SYNCRETISM

At mid-century the Kennebec were far more concerned with their deteriorating social life than with external relations. The early years of their alliance with the French and the St. Lawrence Algonkian coincided with a period of intense internal crisis. During the 1640s the tribe's interest in the mission at Sillery reflected a major aspect of their self-assessment. When they requested a priest in 1646, the Kennebec admitted their desperation. As it turned out, Gabriel Druillettes proved critically important to their religious regeneration. The Jesuit perceived the Abenaki's purposes and catalyzed an experiment in adaptation while the Kennebec themselves deliberately controlled the direction of religious change.[28]

Something more than compromise and something less than conversion emerged. While missionaries offered all Indians survival through cultural and religious adaptation, they often functioned as agents of destructive change. As a result, they sometimes triggered an angry nativistic backlash. Among the Abenaki, however, social disruption had occurred long before Druillettes appeared on the scene. The Kennebec already sought religious and social reform. They scrutinized Catholicism in the person of the priest only in an effort to revitalize their mythically grounded identity. Since the Kennebec clearly understood the causes of their crisis, the priest could not have manipulated them. In any case, Druillettes met them on their own territory and spoke to them in their own terms. In short, although the priest intended something more radical, the Kennebec took from his teachings only what would restore their own self-esteem.

The tribe needed to rejuvenate the religious integrity they knew to be the source of community health. Therefore, they urgently investigated Druillettes's power as a ritual specialist. When they requested a priest in 1646, the Kennebec were prepared to listen. Through their Christian kinsmen, Claude and Jean Baptiste, they offered concrete evidence of their openness. Instead of dispersing as usual to their family hunting territories, they promised to remain at their village throughout the winter to assess what a Jesuit might say and do. This offer to alter their residential pattern was unprecedented, for the tribe could not easily support so many people concentrated in one place. Hunting was difficult in February snows and starvation commonly stalked even dispersed family groups. But the Kennebec felt that extreme measures were warranted. In the spring of 1646 "a malady which caused vomiting of blood had destroyed a good part of their nation." The appeal for a priest came from people pushed to the brink.[29]

It was more than coincidental that Gabriel Druillettes's purposes intersected with those of the Kennebec. Appreciating the moral crisis that mass sickness created, Druillettes communicated his intentions by ministering to their ills, "winning their souls, the *Jesuit Relations* later said, "through the care he gave their bodies." He rendered whatever medical assistance was possible and taught Christianity to the extent that he could communicate it; only when death seemed inevitable did he baptize stricken Abenaki. These actions established the priest's credentials: in all that he did, his selflessness was manifest. Druillettes's benevolent behavior defused suspicion. Unlike many Canadian Indians who had explored the uses of Christianity only to conclude that it was dangerous, the Kennebec did not fear that baptism was actually a cause of death. Among them some baptized persons defied Druillettes's medical judgment and survived. That even a few survived impressed the Kennebec. Their families "published everywhere that prayer was good, and that it had cured their children."[30]

Druillettes's ministry was a matter of deliberate design. The Jesuits realized that allegiance could be won by behavior that expressed their supportive intent. Druillettes acted confidently as a "master" whenever moral issues of "Christian truths" were involved. He posed as a discerning "scholar" while learning the Abenaki's language and general values. The Kennebec thought it remarkable that the priest acquired their language with less difficulty than visiting Indians. They were even more impressed that on every occasion he communicated quiet assurance and tolerant humanity.[31]

Although Druillettes never understood the mythological criteria that the Kennebec used to judge his character, he nonetheless acted as the man of power they expected him to be. Even before his verbal ministry began, they had compared him favorably with their shamans. Medicine men, the Jesuit knew, were his only organized opposition. Druillettes shrewdly evaluated the shamans' traditional social roles and reversed them to his own advantage. Understanding that the shamans required payment for their attentions and did not nurse the sick, the priest eschewed gifts and lavished care. "This man is different from our Jugglers," the Kennebec marveled. "The latter are always asking, and the former never asks anything; the latter are almost entirely absent from our sick, but the former spends days and nights with them." They approved of Druillettes's humility; whenever he was given some choice bit of food, "he straightway carries it to our sick."[32]

In this way Druillettes undermined the prestige of Kennebec shamans. The Kennebec were inclined to blame the shamans for their troubles and the priest added convincing evidence. Because the Abenaki understood that beneficent power rested in manifest social concern, Druillettes's behavior proved that he was more humane than the medicine men. The shamans were apparently powerless, while the priest cured sickness. The Jesuit's success provoked the shamans' opposition, but even they eventually succumbed to his power. One shaman fell sick and sent for the Jesuit, "assuring him that he wished to believe and to pray in earnest." Druillettes spent time with the man and, believing him to be on the verge of death, baptized him. Sometime later it occurred to Druillettes to demand the shaman's "drum and his charms." The man recovered as soon as they were destroyed. His cure spelled doom for shamanistic power.[33]

The significance of the shaman's recovery rests on the destruction of his drum, which was the heart of his ritual power. The anthropologist Frank G. Speck described the essential role drums played in medical practice, observing that the Abenaki word for *shaman* means "the sound of drumming." Dr. Peter Paul, a respected Maliseet linguist, amplifies Speck's observation. He explains that the word *drum* refers to the act of begging or beseeching the religious powers for help. Thus, in witnessing the shaman's cure when Druillettes destroyed his drum, the Kennebec freshly appreciated the Jesuit's tremendous power.

Druillettes's shamanistic pose was successful because he spoke to the tribe's sense of crisis and offered solutions that accorded with the Abenaki's tenaciously held opinions of good and evil. The Kennebec later said of Druillettes: " 'He is not a man; he is a Nioueskou', that is a Spirit, or an extraordinary Genie." This testimony is again given weight in Dr. Paul's observation that the term *Nioueskou* means a person who is blessed or holy and came to be applied especially to Jesuit missionaries.[34]

The priest expressed a spiritual message the Kennebec could understand. He did not seek to immerse them in the intricacies of Catholic dogma. Rather, he declared that he could offer religious knowledge they lacked. In exchange he asked only that they acknowledge the importance of "he who created them" in their daily affairs. Moving from theology to practical action, Druillettes made specific proposals for the Kennebec's regeneration. On behalf of "he who created them" and "in token of their goodwill," the priest demanded three things. First, he asked that the Kennebec give up drinking liquor. They promised to do so and Druillettes observed that they "fairly well kept their word." Second, he required them to live peacefully with one another. Within their family bands the Kennebec got on well enough, but the priest noted that "as one sees in France, between two cities or hamlets. . . there may be seen also in this part of our America small envies between the various districts [bands] of the Savages." Again, the Kennebec quickly agreed to work toward unity. Finally, Druillettes demanded "that they should throw away their Manitou,—or, rather, their Demons, or fantastic charms." And "those who had some of these charms, or Manitous, drew them from their pouches; some cast them away, others brought them to the Father."[35]

These requirements addressed the causes of the Kennebec's crisis in the 1640s. The concept of one God—"he who made all"—confirmed their belief in pervasive personal power and seemingly promised to rejuvenate Gluskap's traditional ethic of social altruism. In this way Druillettes helped to identify the Kennebec's sense of responsibility for their own social problems. The priest explicitly equated sickness with sin, which he identified with the social disruptions of alcohol.[36]

It is a practical measure of the Kennebec's desperation and a gauge of their appreciation for Jesuit authority that they accepted their inability to deal with illness through traditional means. Druillettes taught them that the evil forces that opposed "he who made all" suffused shamanistic medicine. The Christian Montagnais had warned the Abenaki that postcontact sickness was an earthly reflection of the hellfire they drew on themselves forever. Druillettes went beyond such criticism. He stressed that a life of prayer could win sure redemption from the death of sin. He taught them that prayer transformed even death itself into triumph. Prayer, abstinence from drinking, and the practice of social decorum were, Druillettes promised, eloquent affirmations of a reestablished religious solidarity.[37]

The priest remained on his first visit among the Kennebec only for the winter of 1646–47. Yet when Druillettes returned in 1650 he found abundant evidence that his teachings had taken root. Many Abenaki assured him that prayer was powerful. Even in his absence the Kennebec had continued to recite the prayers he had taught them. When they showed Druillettes the methods that they had devised to remember Catholic rituals, he became convinced that they were genuinely devoted to Christ.[38]

What the priest saw as the Kennebec's conversion in fact hid far more complex processes. It is clear that the Jesuit had engendered a religious revival, but the tribe's devotion to prayer actually illustrates the way in which Druillettes reinforced traditional beliefs. The missionary did not inquire too deeply about Kennebec belief in orthodox Catholic dogma. It may even be that he consciously blended Christian and traditional rituals. On his 1650 journey, for example, his companions lost their way and found themselves without provisions. Just as the Abenaki would have done, Druillettes begged for help, offering a mass to save them: "The Father, seeing his people in this extreme destitution, had recourse to the God of men and animals,—offering him the sacrifice of his Son in those great forests; and conjuring him by the Blood shed by him for those people, to succor them in their necessity."[39]

As the imagery used in this statement powerfully declares, priest and shaman barely differed. Just as Druillettes finished the mass, an Abenaki hunter returned with news that he had killed three moose. The Abenaki drew the obvious conclusion. They told their people: "When we were on the point of dying from hunger, he prayed for us; and he who is the master of all the animals gave us meat, more than we needed for the rest of the journey." This was not an isolated example of overlap between Jesuit and Abenaki religiosity. Among the Kennebec, Christian prayers effectively supported traditional hunting values. One old man told the Jesuit: "This winter I have killed four Moose which I hunted down; I have slain two Bears, and put to death a good many small Deer. I think unceasingly of him who made all things; I often speak to Jesus, and he strengthens and comforts me."[40]

If hunting remained a sacred activity, the same was true of medicine. Druillettes's teachings did undermine the shamans, but the Jesuit's successes also fostered a syncretic intensification of medical ritual. Several people testified that they had rejected shamans who tried to cure them. More to the point, Druillettes learned that one man had received old shamanistic power over sickness in new Christian form. "His people told me," the Jesuit said, "that God often answered the prayers that he offered in behalf of sick persons, or for other purposes." Even Druillettes's condemnation of shamanism only appears to have caused a more radical change for the Abenaki than it actually did. When the priest ridiculed shamanistic medicine, he merely confirmed conclusions that the Kennebec had already reached on their own. They sought a priest in 1646 because it was woefully apparent that their shamans could no longer protect the community.[41]

The traditional nature of the Abenaki response to Catholicism deserves emphasis. Their blending of religious imagery illustrates the pragmatism that came to govern all levels of Abenaki relations with the French. The religious alliance developed because their ethical sensibilities were compatible. What the priest identified as demonic forces, the Kennebec had long recognized as malevolent other-than-human persons working through antisocial shamans. When one Abenaki avowed that Druillettes had driven "away by his orisons the Demon that wished to deprive me of my life," he admitted that prayer was a more powerful weapon than traditional medicine—even while implying that they were substantially similar.[42]

Neither the Kennebec sense of crisis nor Druillettes's religious solution forced the tribe toward radical social change. In fact, both responses were intellectually conservative: "The Demon has laid waste our country, because we did not know how we ought to have recourse to Jesus, who is his master." Even the pattern of religious revelation remained the same. Dreams and visions remained as commonplace after Druillettes's preaching as they had been before his arrival. Dream symbols did become superficially Christian: "Many of these good people," the priest related, "have assured me that their children, dying immediately after Baptism, had appeared to them from Heaven to encourage them to embrace the truths of Christianity."[43]

Such testimony confirmed Druillettes's expectations. He taught that Christ wished only for their obedience in return for protection against manifold demons. "Thou dost bid us combat and resist the Demons that attack us," the Abenaki told the priest. "They are many in number, but their strength is diminishing from day to day, and our courage is increasing." A complex demonology came to characterize Abenaki Catholicism; prayer gave them power to resist demons of sickness, social enmity, drunkenness, perverse shamanism, and polygamy. A single example exemplifies how the Kennebec combined the two religious traditions. They told Druillettes: "How many times have we seen persons in the last extremity, whom we thought bewitched, restored to health upon praying to him who is the master of all the Demons!"[44]

Two factors determined the Kennebec's positive assessment of Druillettes's power and thereby influenced the Abenaki-Jesuit accommodation. First, the tribe's mythology defined the personal character of socially constructive shamans. From this perspective Gabriel Druillettes conformed closely to Kennebec expectations. Second, their mythological traditions clearly described the purposes and pitfalls of religious power. In this light the devastating events of the early seventeenth century did not prompt them to repudiate their religious beliefs. To the contrary, they concluded that their difficulties derived from the widespread abuse of power, and through discussions with Druillettes they realized that revitalization was possible and in order. In sum, Kennebec traditions predisposed them to assess pragmatically the religious adaptation that Druillettes proposed.

THE ALLIANCE ESTABLISHED

While the Kennebec and Druillettes discovered common religious interests, the tribe did not immediately embrace Catholicism. For the next twenty-five years the tribes and the priests went their separate ways. The Abenaki remained oriented toward Acadia and New England; the Jesuits remained preoccupied among the Montagnais, the refugee Huron, and the Five Nations. But two factors slowly converged and drew them together. In dealing with Indian indifference to their teachings, the Jesuits learned that missionary activity had practical limits. Simultaneously, the Abenaki's communal crisis intensified. As a result, when dialogue resumed in the 1670s, the Jesuits were ready to acknowledge the legitimacy of Abenaki religious convictions. After repeated failures among other tribes, they were prepared to practice Druillettes's tolerance for Indian culture. They recognized that the Abenaki were eager to begin social and religious reform. And the priests understood that negative relations with English settlers had so disrupted the Kennebec's social values that internal conflict had become a way of life. As in the 1640s, the tribe responded positively. By the third quarter of the seventeenth century they increasingly sought Jesuit advice.

The Kennebec's second exploration of Catholicism came as an accidental side effect of war. In 1675 the Kennebec were drawn into a conflict raging between the English and the southern New England Algonkians. None of the Abenaki wanted any part of King Philip's War, as the conflict in southern New England is known, but extreme demands from local English settlers forced the Androscoggin and Saco to take sides. The English would hear no protest. Pressed by hostile frontiersmen and by English expectations that they submit, the Abenaki found themselves fighting a defensive war. The Kennebec and the Penobscot attempted to remain neutral, but when they failed to convince the English that they meant well, many chose exile over military involvement. The fortunes of war thus made these fugitives the nucleus of a new Jesuit mission and eventually a central link in an expanded Abenaki-French alliance.[45]

This extension of King Philip's War spelled an ecological disaster for the Abenaki. In the first place, it undercut the tribes' postcontact hunting economy, which by 1675 required European arms and ammunition. In fact, the outbreak on the northeastern frontier began when colonists demanded that the Abenaki surrender their guns to prove their peaceful intentions. The English applied economic sanctions. Faced with English refusal to sell them ammunition, the Abenaki experienced a severe shortage of major food sources. To make matters worse, the war also threatened Abenaki horticulture. In the fall of 1675 the English settlers so frightened the Kennebec that they fled to the Penobscot River, leaving their fields unharvested. Finally, the war barred the Abenaki from access to the animal and marine resources of their coastal lands. The Wawenock, who could not withdraw because of the short rivers of their territory, found themselves hard pressed by English hostiles who controlled the shore near Pemaquid peninsula.[46]

Although the Wawenock were likely the first to leave Maine, the precise tribal origin of the Abenaki in Canada remains obscure. It is known that a group of thirty Indians faced certain starvation in the spring of 1676 and fled to the French for assistance. These may have been the Wawenock, but the Saco or Kennebec are also likely candidates for the initial party. Whoever they were, the exiles sought only material aid—most important, food. As it turned out, the French could not give the refugees much help and the summer of 1676 was a hungry time. Yet these refugee Abenaki and the Jesuits formed an acquaintance that endured throughout the colonial period. Religious ties ultimately bonded the Abenaki and the French.[47]

The first Abenaki felt ambivalent about the mission. Having fled English violence only to confront Jesuit demands that they repudiate their religion and embrace the uncertain comforts of Catholicism, the exiles must have been perplexed. Most were elderly and chose to abandon their homes as the conservative, least disruptive response to a disastrous war. The refugees ran from change and sought security. They had not expected to be proselytized. The Jesuits noted that at first the Abenaki were "impassive," even "averse" to their teachings. The priests soon marveled, however, that there were "few of them who did not come Most Regularly to the Church, night and morning."[48]

It might be assumed that the aged Abenaki responded as politely as they could, since they were unable to support themselves and grateful for help. The record shows otherwise. The Jesuits provided little aid, yet the Abenaki freely participated in religious activities. The priests insisted that there was a marked change "in the morals of the majority of them," and despite the fact that many fell ill in the summer of 1676, the priests observed that the Abenaki had repudiated shamanistic healing rites. The missionaries also noted an uncharacteristic sobriety among the newcomers. Although drunkenness was "their greatest failing, almost all of them usually abstained from it."[49]

Promising as these beginnings were, the Jesuits hesitated to baptize the Abenaki at Sillery. They carefully tested the refugees' resolve and whenever possible inculcated "a veritable Dread" of profaning their baptism and "of losing its graces." Only young children and a few older persons were baptized. Among them was the Abenaki sachem Pirou-akki, whose gentleness, judicious management of his people, and eloquence struck the priests as excellent moral qualities.[50]

The thirty refugees left for their winter hunting territories in November 1676, but some Abenaki returned the following spring and the permanent mission began. While the continuing war between the Abenaki and the English encouraged this new migration, favorable reports from the first visitors surely contributed to the Abenaki's esteem of the Jesuits. With a determination that amazed the priests, the Sillery Abenaki traveled between Maine and Quebec, teaching their relatives what they had learned of Christianity.[51]

Because Sillery invited a fundamental social revitalization, the Abenaki usually settled at the mission in extended family bands. The immigrants fell under the supervision of Father Jacques Bigot, who occupied them with a thorough regimen of work and prayer. The apprentice Christians aided Bigot in his regular duties: teaching one another, chiding backsliders, and providing for the community's material needs. Relatives and friends of newcomers taught the daily routine, important rituals, and prepared them for baptism. One man coached the young boys in the Catholic catechism, prayers, and church music while a woman taught the girls. These responsibilities were onerous because the Jesuits carefully examined each neophyte over an extended period. With cautious optimism the priests praised Abenaki docility. "We have never seen savages say their prayers with more sedateness and devotion, or whose Singing has been more touching or more harmonious." Bigot added: "There have been none who have prayed as devoutly as these."[52]

The Abenaki reacted more profoundly to Catholicism in the 1670s than they had thirty years earlier. Nevertheless, they had the same motives in both periods. They continued to interpret the Jesuits in traditional religious terms, so missionary warnings against demonic activities again struck a responsive chord. Furthermore, Catholicism ensured the success of the Abenaki's hunting economy. The tribes would not have embraced any religion that failed to validate their reciprocal relations with animal persons.[53]

It appears that Catholicism again addressed the pressing anxieties of Abenaki life. Indian peoples knew that something was wrong and so feared Jesuit threats that they faced eternal damnation. It may be that they had too little hope, or that Jesuit portrayals of hellfire were frighteningly similar to the fate that befell captives in enemy hands. In any case, Catholic symbols of damnation could not be ignored. For the Abenaki, as for other Indian peoples, hell became a reality vividly conveyed by Jesuit pictures. Verbal and graphic depictions of unrelenting torment were a central element of missionary work. The Abenaki themselves hastened to show new arrivals visual evidence of the hellish fate that awaited the sinful.[54]

Fears about life after death and about right or wrong conduct that might win relief or everlasting pain characterized the Abenaki experience at Sillery. That fear manifested itself in every aspect of their lives. The experience of one Abenaki family, which the Jesuits considered exemplary, illustrates the emotionally charged atmosphere. Two young men fell fatally ill and Jacques Bigot told them they "must accept everything from the hand of God." This family had a difficult time adjusting to the deaths because they feared that the young men were not animated by an appropriate Christian resignation. "Alas," they said of one of the sick men, "we fear for him because after his baptism He manifested some Chagrin at His illness." Such scrupulous anxiety also typified the Abenaki's struggle with personal grief. After one young man died, his grandmother and mother "Regarded As a great sin the Cries that Their Sorrow caused them to utter from time to time."[55]

The Jesuits aggravated these emotions because they regarded self-inflicted physical mortifications as proof of Christian virtue. The women forcibly attempted to suppress their feelings. When given permission, Bigot observed, "they treat Their Bodies so harshly that I have been surprised at it, and have often been alarmed at the Blows of the discipline that I have heard when they had withdrawn secretly to some Spot remote from their Cabins." The mission Abenaki evidently felt that they needed to atone for past offenses. Much of their energy went into placating the spiritual forces of vengeance that attacked them. The widespread practice of self-mortification suggests how deeply they had internalized their own responsibility for postcontact crisis. As in the 1640s this reaction derived from that aspect of their mythology which related illness to social strife. And like Druillettes, Bigot deliberately affirmed this overweening sense of guilt to ensure that the Abenaki submit to Christian order. He taught them a prayer to express the uncertainties with which they grappled: "Jesus, may I see you in Heaven; may I never be damned. Keep me from anger, from evil speaking, and from drunkenness. Save me from the evil spirit."[56]

The Abenaki prayed because shamanism had failed to protect them. They embraced Catholicism as a group because they fervently believed that community health stemmed from the moral integrity of its individual members. Their devotion is all the more remarkable because epidemic diseases were common at the mission villages. In 1684 Jacques Bigot told sick Abenaki that God chastized them for their sins and to save them from hellfire. He promised them paradise as payment for acts of patience. It is not surprising that conservative Abenaki elders told the younger people that they died because they prayed.[57]

Christian Abenaki refused to be swayed by such arguments. Furthermore, because both conservatives and Christians valued communal solidarity, Sillery survived horrible mortality rates. One hundred and thirty people died from measles at Sillery during the summer of 1687. There continued to be grumblers, but the Jesuits isolated them among their fellows. In dealing with drinking, for example, Bigot declared: "I was not detaining here any one in order to make of Him a Christian in spite of Himself; that Those who did not Desire to be Christians, or who would not give up drunkenness, would give me pleasure by going away; that I was not anxious to have a large number of savages, but to have savages who would choose to be Christians." Bigot added, "Not one person went away."[58]

By entering the Canadian missions the Abenaki took an individual and a collective stand against social chaos. On one level Jesuit Catholicism diagnosed the severe problems besetting Indian communities. As in the 1640s, Jesuit teachings were compatible with mythological traditions about the causes of social discord. On another level the Abenaki war with the English in 1675−77 disrupted their trapping and agricultural economy and the Jesuits offered the refugees a community base far removed from the hostilities. Finally, Catholicism made it possible for the Abenaki to improve their ethical condition, especially in identifying the deterioration of social life that insidious alcoholism produced.[59]

## TOLERANCE AND ADJUSTMENT

Abenaki and French reactions to alcohol-related issues expose the barriers to intercultural alliance. For Indians alcohol had become a desirable way to attain psychic well-being. But the effects of alcohol ultimately eroded self-confidence. On one hand, drinking expressed the Indians' interest in exciting leisure activity; on the other, it unleashed deeply repressed resentments that even family members held against one other. Liquor provided the Abenaki direct access to the world of nonordinary reality which had always fascinated them. It also revealed the hidden problems in their communal life. They understood their predicament and were embarrassed. The missionaries also found alcohol a source of embarrassment, for the destructive liquor traffic belied French moral superiority and thus made the priests aware that French culture itself obstructed the conversion of the Abenaki. In opposing the liquor trade, the Jesuits eventually learned that they had to deal with the political implications of religious alliance.[60]

It took the Jesuits the better part of the century, but, by the 1670s they had become segregationists. Experience had taught them that civilized Europeans were not immune to moral savagery. Nor did they believe that the Abenaki were inferior to the French. In witnessing the terribly debilitating effects of intercultural relations, they frankly admitted that the French themselves were the problem. The Montagnais who first lived at Sillery taught the priests a painful lesson. Despite an ecclesiastical hard line—in 1660 the Canadian bishop François de Laval excommunicated liquor traders from the church—the priests met bitter failure. With the avid connivance of the French, alcohol destroyed the Montagnais mission.

Determined not to make the mistake again, the Jesuits lost no opportunity to forbid drinking when the Abenaki replaced the Montagnais at Sillery. They taught that the first line of defense against the evil rested in self-control. Such repression required community vigilance and the Abenaki's new moral leaders demanded total abstinence. Some of them policed the mission, accompanying known drinkers "to the Places where It is Most to be feared."[61]

Confronting the moral challenge that French society posed, the Abenaki and the Jesuits defied the assimilationist goals that had always formed Canadian Indian policy. From the start the French had optimistically assumed that they could integrate Indian peoples into colonial society: Indians would freely become ardent Catholics and obedient subjects of the king. The French thought that cultural accommodation would require not only missionary diligence but also a community of godly settlers who could lead by example when exhortation failed. In the 1630s Samuel de Champlain recorded an Indian response to this enduring French ideal:

> You say things that pass our understanding and that we cannot comprehend by words, as something beyond our intelligence; but if you would do well [by us] you should dwell in our country and bring women and when they come to these regions we shall see how you serve this God whom you worship, and your mode of life with your wives and children, your way of tilling the ground and sowing, and how you obey your laws and your manner of feeding animals, and how you manufacture all that we see proceeding from your invention. Seeing this we shall learn more in one year than hearing your discourses in twenty, and if we cannot understand, you shall take our children who will be like your own: and thus judging our life wretched by comparison with yours, it is easy to believe that we shall adopt yours and abandon our own.[62]

As the Indian reaction to Champlain indicates, the French resembled the English in the main tenets of their ethnocentrism. Agriculture, husbandry, government, and religion together defined the Frenchman's sense of the "good life" that would draw Indians to demand their own improvement. Because of the policy of integration, the trading company created in 1627 under the auspices of Cardinal Richelieu accorded Indian converts equal status with native-born Frenchmen. In the years following, the Jesuits joined Recollet priests and pious laypeople in attempting to make apostolic fervor the moral foundation of New France.[63]

The missionaries soon met opposition. Assimilation remained the official goal, but actual practice deviated from the ideal. Initially, the missionaries could not convince Indians that the French were morally superior. By the 1640s the Society of Jesus and the Ursuline nuns understood that Indians could not be educated for assimilation. Indian people not only preferred their own way of life but they revolted against imposed discipline. The Jesuits learned the hard way, but in time they came to understand Indian attitudes: "One must be very careful before condemning a thousand things among their customs, which greatly offend minds brought up and nourished in another world," Father LeJeune wrote. For the Ursulines, whose cloistered retirement made adaptation to Indian custom largely impossible, religious rapture shattered on the reef of reality. Indians sometimes admired the Ursulines' mystical fervor, but they remained attached to their life in the woods. Marie de l'Incarnation, the Ursuline superior who learned several Indian languages, expressed the unresolvable strains of religious passion, disappointment, and resignation:

> It will happen that a Savage, either Christian or pagan, wishes to carry off a girl of his nation and keep her contrary to God's law; she is given to us, and we instruct her and watch over her till the Reverend Fathers come to take her away. Others are here only as birds of passage and remain with us only until they are sad, a thing the Savage nature cannot suffer; the moment they become sad, their parents take them away lest they die. We leave them free on this point, for we are more likely to win them over in this way than by keeping them by force or entreaties. There are still others that go off by some whim or caprice; like squirrels, they climb our palisade, which is high as a wall and go to run in the woods. [64]

Indians often castigated the French for moral corruption and the Jesuits could hardly deny the accusation. French settlers adapted to Indian social mores so eagerly that they themselves became the object of frantically implemented programs designed to return them to order. Many French *coureurs de bois*—runners of the woods—voted with their feet. They chose the freedom of living and trading among Indians over docile submission to church and state. As a result, the French began to worry about their own civility. To further confound French ethnocentricism, the Jesuits also had to acknowledge that Indian peoples displayed admirable moral qualities. When dismal failure taught the missionaries that education could not achieve Indian assimilation, they joined the average settler in making a pragmatic adjustment. They accepted Indian notions of etiquette and ceremony, depended on Indian material culture—notably canoes, toboggans, snowshoes, and techniques of warfare—learned Indian languages, and conformed to Indian notions of status.[65]

The establishment of direct royal control of Canada in 1664 prompted severe criticism of this cultural accommodation. State policy clung to Champlain's hope that intimate contact and intermarriage would amalgamate colonists and Indians into a unique Canadian people. Of course, officials at Versailles thought that the new Canadians would remain more French than Indian. In line with this expectation Louis XIV and his minister, Jean-Baptiste Colbert, ordained that Canadian development required a thorough program of Indian "francisation," which the Jesuits had long since abandoned.[66]

Colbert misunderstood the missionaries' inclination to segregate Indian converts from the worst effects of contact. The minister thought that the Jesuits wished only "to maintain their own influence over them." Intendant Jean Talon reaffirmed such judgments in 1666 when he said that Indians "ought to have been taught our language long ago, and not oblige the King's subjects to study theirs, in order to be able to communicate with them." Colbert responded with a policy that Canadian officials were forced to accept. They did so with quiet acquiescence to Indian resistance as well as to the tenacious defiance of *coureurs de bois*. The minister hoped that "through the course of time, having only but one law and one master, they might likewise constitute only one people and one race."[67]

Church and state became polarized over this policy in the 1670s. Governor Louis de Buade, the comte de Frontenac, fueled Colbert's suspicions of the Jesuits. His first report on Canadian affairs expressed astonishment that none of the Christian Indians spoke French. Frontenac said that he had advised the Jesuits "that they ought, in their missions, bethink themselves, when rendering the savages subjects of Jesus Christ, of making them subjects of the King also." Not only did the governor of New France claim that Jesuit missions were "pure mockeries," he slandered their motives. He maintained that the priests thought "as much about the conversion of the Beaver as of souls." Colbert believed such fabrications and in 1674 nullified Jesuit plans to construct missions within the territories of the individual tribes. The king wanted Indians to be concentrated close to the French settlements, and he directed the missionaries to "lead them to civilized society, and to abandon their way of living, in which they can never become good Christians."[68]

Far-off metropolitan officials reassured themselves that their policy would augment New France's tiny population. They hoped that if Indians submitted, the *coureurs de bois* would soon return to the fold. Canadian conditions intervened. During the 1680s the governors of New France paid lip service to official dictates, but they did everything they could to protect Indians from undue interference. They annually reported the growing population of the Algonkian and Iroquoian missions, recorded difficulties in funding the villages, and described the problems of extending French law over them. They remained silent about their actual failure to fulfill the expectations of Versailles.[69]

The voluntary nature of Abenaki migrations to Sillery and Saint François de Sales is testimony to the Jesuit flexibility Canadian officials admired. The priests had to balance French and Indian presumptions about the nature of mission life. Along with Canadian officials with whom they cooperated, the missionaries did not openly criticize royal policy. Instead, they suggested that they attempted to comply. They complained about their limited resources and decried the destructive impact of unscrupulous French settlers on mission Indians. They hinted at the need for additional government funds and insisted that the liquor trade had to be controlled. In 1685 Jacques Bigot recorded Abenaki frustration with the role that liquor played in trade:

> Now we people are weak with regard to liquor, and a sharp warning was needed to stop us. Courage, our Father; watch the french well, so that they may not intoxicate any of our people. We are going away from the English solely because they tormented us too much, and would give us nothing but liquor for all our peltries; and we see here many frenchmen who wish to do the same.

The Jesuits asserted that the prohibition of alcohol within the missions encouraged the Abenaki to remain in Canada.[70]

The Jesuits constantly emphasized that if the Abenaki were to become culturally French, New France would be the loser. In 1679, for example, the priests noted that Abenaki hunters provided the colony with large supplies of furs. Even more important, Governor Denonville later agreed with the priests that the mission Abenaki were enemies of the threatening Iroquois Confederacy. Intendant Duchesneau admitted the wisdom of Jesuit tolerance: "The youth are all brought up *à la Française*, except in the matter of their food and dress, which it is necessary to make them retain in order that they be not effeminate, and that they be more at liberty and less impeded whilst hunting, which constitutes their wealth and ours."[71]

The Jesuits knew that assimilation was impractical and thus made a virture of adjustment. Recognizing that Catholic ritual embraced much of the Abenaki's traditional symbolism, they were content to translate their liturgy into the Abenaki language. And this religious program came to supplement the aboriginal song and dance cycle. The priests also appreciated the subtle cultural patterns that influenced Abenaki adaptation to mission life. They understood, for instance, that traditional agriculture was women's responsibility, so they did not expect men to work in the fields.[72]

While the priests encouraged the Abenaki to settle permanently in mission villages, they accepted the need to maintain the Indians' hunting and trapping economy. They understood that Abenaki social life could not be modeled on that of the Quebec settlers. Agriculture may have provided some staples, but hunting allowed the Abenaki to survive within the French trading economy. As a result, mission villages in Canada became what Abenaki summer villages had been long before contact—the agricultural and seasonal center of communal life. In effect, the Jesuits had no choice. Neither Sillery nor Saint François de Sales could provide the Indians with economic independence. Jacques Bigot explained that "the country in which They lived is much better than This one with regard to food, to hunting, and to fishing." The Jesuits' alliance with the Abenaki thus reaffirmed the principal elements of the tribes' aboriginal culture and attempted to minimize the worst effects of contact.[73]

The Abenaki missions reflected the hesitant compromise of French Indian policy in the 1680s. Church and state began to moderate their differences in order to achieve even limited alliance with the tribes. The Jesuits felt that the Indians had genuinely accepted Catholicism and the priests had little interest in assimilating them into corrupt Canadian society. French governors and intendants agreed. In Canada's need for warriors against the Iroquois and in the Jesuits' desire for converts, church and state had at last found common ground. It was enough that government cooperation with the priests attracted the Abenaki to live in Quebec villages. By 1689 over six hundred Abenaki lived in Canada and the Jesuits and governors optimistically planned to attract even more.[74]

The Abenaki who moved to Canada established a firm foundation for their alliance with the French. Shared values, civil fellowship in legal and economic relations, religious affirmations of a common identity, and joint political and military activity were the principal components of the association. Emotional reciprocity between the Abenaki and the Jesuits channeled relations. When the Indians compared the Jesuits to the English, or even to the French as a whole, the priests seemed exceptionally humane. Economic cooperation permitted the new missions to finance themselves, and Canada's conflict with the Iroquois drew many Abenaki warriors from Maine. Nonetheless, these were secondary factors in the creation of an alliance. It was religious dialogue that grounded trust.[75]

## MYTH AND RELIGIOUS REORIENTATION

The Jesuits became a pivotal force in Abenaki history because they helped the tribes bridge the precontact and postcontact worlds. Abenaki oral traditions record the long-range significance of the relationship. All too often historians describe Indian-white relations in terms that suggest that Europeans imposed problems to which the tribes reacted. The Abenaki, however, emphasized the moral challenge of contact, a challenge they understood and to which they responded in their own terms. In the old times Gluskap established ethical imperatives that would allow the Abenaki to adapt and maintain their social order. After contact the culture hero acquired even greater importance. Everything in Jesuit teaching affirmed the formative character of Abenaki mythology.

As a number of syncretic myths illustrate, Jesuit missionaries entered Algonkian tradition sometime in the seventeenth century. The tribes' critical response to the priests and to Catholicism is reflected in a wide variety of stories about Gluskap and the antiheroic cannibal giants. The new religion did not displace traditional beliefs. Rather, the Algonkian reinterpreted their religious position in light of missionary teachings.[76]

A number of cannibal giant stories indicate the symbolic adjustments that the Algonkian made to the new order. In aboriginal tradition the cannibal giants symbolized the antisocial forces that threatened communal life. The postcontact stories indicate that Indians regarded the Jesuits as benevolent shamans capable of resisting even the most dangerous of the fierce cannibals. One story reveals that the Micmac began to carve crosses on trees surrounding their villages to ward off the giants. The tale reflects the strength of the new belief because it was the older, more conservative Indians who advised the use of the cross as a protective device.[77]

Another story, this one from the Montagnais-Naskapi, suggests that while traditionalists were no longer able to thwart cannibal malevolence, Christian Indians could. A tale from the same group explicitly states that Indian spiritual power had degenerated. When a hunting party failed to kill a giant, one of its members despaired that "we cannot do it [because] our magic power is too weak." With the aid of his guardian spirit the shaman among them perceived both the giant and a priest coming toward the camp. Rushing to greet the priest, the shaman declared: "We are all going to die here because the *witigo* has come among us and we cannot kill him." The missionary replied with confidence: "Oh, no, my child, he is not dangerous. We will kill him." Walking out onto the frozen lake, the priest confronted the cannibal giant, "raised his crucifix, whereupon the *witigo* fell dead on the ice." These stories suggest that once the Jesuits came to appreciate Algonkian communal values, they began to behave in ways that the Algonkian could recognize. Only the good man, the individual who had successfully integrated his own personal needs with Algonkian kin-defined ethical norms could victoriously confound the giant.[78]

In fact, all of the Algonkian seemed to have assessed the priests positively. Certainly, their traditions record a conviction that traditional belief and Catholicism were compatible systems of religious power. While it is uncertain whether the aboriginal Algonkian believed in a supreme deity, twentieth-century Abenaki acknowledge a Great Being who combines the traditional attributes of power with that of the Christian Holy Spirit. Similarly, they recognize an evil spirit and their concept of the underworld, which was originally peopled with several classes of hostile beings, is now associated with hell. There is some evidence that shamanism and Catholicism continue to be seen as antithetical systems of power. Although shamans operated in the nineteenth century (and to some extent in the present), their powers seem to have gradually separated from a religious attempt to ensure community well-being.[79]

Perhaps the most dramatic evidence of the Algonkian's response to Catholicism and of their overall reaction to Euramerican contact is found in Abenaki and Micmac accounts of Gluskap. Taken together, these syncretic treatments indicate the basic flexibility of mythic traditions and emphasize a fundamental conviction that Gluskap remains at the center of Algonkian history. One Penobscot creation myth observes that the Great Spirit "made Adam out of earth but he did not make Gluskabe." Instead, "Gluskabe made himself out of dust that was kicked up in the creation of Adam," although he could not speak until the Great Spirit "opened his lips." While the Great Spirit may have been responsible for the creation of the world, he heeded Gluskap's advice about its ultimate arrangement.[80]

Several other accounts assert the basic equality between Gluskap and Christ. In a contest of power the two matched each other's magical feats. A Micmac and a Penobscot source ascribe Gluskap's creation to Christ, but their assessment of the culture hero's character is in harmony with mythological tradition. The Micmac story presents Gluskap as Christ's first-created being who then fabricated human moral order—as he had done in the precontact myths. The same story describes Adam, who is second-man, as the father both of European peoples and of evil in the world. In the Penobscot tale Gluskap derived his strength from the Great Being who made him responsible for instructing the people: "I will be thy teacher," the Great Being said, "and you will be their teacher." The linguist Dr. Peter Paul explains the harmony between traditional beliefs and Catholicism when he observes that Gluskap was just like Jesus: both were sent to improve the people's understanding of right and wrong and both had similar missions for human welfare.[81]

These mythological and folkloric accounts are crucially important to understand the Algonkian's sense of postcontact history. They expose both the moral problems Euramericans posed and the tribes' religious and social adaptation. A Penobscot tradition records Gluskap's prophecy that French and English would compete for Abenaki lands. The same tale observes that the Abenaki themselves would face many temptations but that with Gluskap's blessing they would adjust to Christianity. He told them that Euramericans "will show you the things that caused the death of the Great Spirit, and . . . will teach you to bow down to these things; and bow you may; but never forget that the Great Spirit is in the air, in the sun, moon, and in all things which your eyes can see.—Here the teachngs of Klose-kur-beh ended." In departing this world Gluskap apparently admitted the primacy of the Christian God. Nevertheless, there is a widespread belief among the Abenaki and the Micmac that Gluskap continues to exist. They still remember his promise to return at some future time of need.[82]

# 4

# POLITICS OF LAW AND PERSUASION

## English and French Contrasted

The Abenaki embraced Catholicism because the Jesuits had won their trust. This religious alliance demonstrates the crucial role face-to-face relations had to play in constructive associations between Indians and Euramericans. The anthropologist Robert Conkling has shown that the Abenaki scrutinized the character of the missionaries and as a result granted the priests a charismatic authority. At Sillery, at Saint François de Sales, and later in Maine the Jesuits acted as sachems. But even then they were constrained by Abenaki politics. Like the sachems, the missionaries might advise, exhort, and persuade, but they could not force compliance.[1]

English relations with the Abenaki were far less flexible. Settlers in Maine always viewed Indians with suspicion and their hostility reaped bitter harvests throughout the colonial period. Since they had little firsthand experience and virtually no intimate contact with the Abenaki, distrust defined the English outlook. The settlers wanted Abenaki furs and land. Little else concerned them. Unlike the French, who could rely on missionaries and Acadian traders to smooth relations with the tribes, few English won Abenaki trust. Indeed, the Abenaki and English misunderstood each other to the point that the slightest rumor of hostility was capable of triggering violent disagreement.

The lawlessness that prevailed in colonial Maine contributed heavily to the poor relations between the Abenaki and the English colonists. For much of the seventeenth century various English governments struggled for control of the Northeast. Sir Ferdinando Gorges, the Mason family, Plymouth Colony, Massachusetts Bay, and the Duke of York, among others, claimed jurisdiction over Maine. The territory passed from one government to another throughout the century. These rivalries made insecurity a way of life on the frontier. The settlers, frequently left to govern themselves, acted on their own. To ensure their own interests they often repudiated external control and competed intensely with one another. Political turbulence prevailed and relations with the Abenaki went unregulated. Individuals purchased the tribes' prime lands without governmental surveillance. Traders cheated Indians and illegally sold them liquor. In most situations the Abenaki were treated contemptuously. They responded in defensive anger.[2]

Complex internal problems profoundly affected New England's Indian policy. Puritan Massachusetts aggressively subdued rival settlements in New Hampshire and Maine during the 1640s and 1650s. But the contemporary ethic of expansion exacted high costs. Territorial growth outstripped English ability to govern far-flung settlements and to regulate relations with Indians. Nonetheless, the Puritans sought to impose their will everywhere. Their conquest of the southern Algonkian tribes confirmed the English belief that all Indians ought to submit. A clash of Indian and English interests was one result, as was an intensification of intertribal rivalries.[3]

The pattern had been established in the 1630s. The Pequot War of 1637 derived from intense competition among the English colonies, between those colonies and Dutch rivals, and between Euramericans and Indians who desperately jockeyed for economic and political independence. Indians struggled in vain. The war shattered the Pequot tribe, hedged in the Narragansett, and assured English hegemony. The conflict also hardened English antipathy to Indians in general, convincing the mass of the population that they faced an ongoing threat. As historian Neal E. Salisbury has put it, the English saw in these events " 'a world turned upside down' with barbarians triumphing over civilization, Satan over Christ, anarchy over order."[4]

Convinced that their newly founded city of God faced enemies outside and traitors within, the English perceived satanic conspiracies wherever they looked. This belief did not directly provoke violence in Abenaki-English relations, but it did make communication extremely difficult. The Puritans expected hostility from all Indians and the Abenaki's close relationship with the French fueled English fears. The Puritan colonials viewed with alarm what they considered the insidious influence of French "papists" among American Indian "heathens." Adding their contempt for Indians to a long-standing Francophobia, the Puritans saw a Catholic threat in the guise of pagan savagery. The Abenaki thus emerged as French puppets. Discounting ample evidence that the tribes remained politically autonomous, the English repeatedly ignored Indian efforts to communicate and recklessly provoked their anger.

The Pequot War had a much deeper impact on Massachusetts's sense of historical purpose. In reflecting on the theological significance of the conflict, the Puritans conceived of the Indians in symbolic terms and perceived both external and internal threats to Massachusetts's inward-looking communalism. The Puritans were so deeply committed to the creation of godly communities that something like tribalism came to characterize their social order. Their ideal centered on the congregational church—an experiment in bringing Christian order to the individual town, to the Puritan colony, and to the world at large. But the English soon discovered that congregationalism and colonialism worked at cross-purposes. Religious communalism gave the town greater significance than colonial government. While the towns accepted allegiance to the General Court at Boston, the Puritans distrusted all forms of government. Thus, at the very time when Massachusetts was subordinating local Indian tribes to its rule, the towns were largely going their own way.[5]

Such local independence made the application of law elusive. When the English compared themselves to the Indians, they deemed their own religious and political order superior. But even while they condemned Indians for godlessness and lawlessness, the Puritans were ambivalent about the way in which law functioned. The communal ideal in New England towns stigmatized legal proceedings as antisocial. The Puritans looked first to Christian love as the means of enforcing social compliance. Townsmen carefully scrutinized one another, used neighborly chiding to regulate interpersonal behavior, and ultimately relied on friendly arbitration to resolve disputes. Given this emphasis on active community involvement, the Puritans felt that people who resorted to legal suits were expressing an unreasonable and ungodly desire to be "revenged" on their neighbors. Civilized people respected the law but did not need it.[6]

In theory, law existed to legitimize the resolution of conflict. In practice, however, Puritans realized that increased reliance on the courts exposed the failure of their religious ideals. Many people assumed that those who called on the law did so for selfish reasons. Such individuals were considered uncivilized. As a result, the communal ideal provoked a symbolic inversion. Some Puritans feared that anyone who took disputes to court was a social degenerate who had become Indianized. At the same time, those who refused to submit to authority were condemned as Indian heathens. The Puritans were caught in a double bind: those who used the law and those who acted outside the law were equally savage. If Christian neighborliness failed to regulate behavior within the New England towns, government was also unsuccessful.

Even while they distrusted and often subverted government among themselves, the English condemned Indians as lawless. Unlike the Abenaki, who placed no political or legal limits on personal liberty, the English clung to a belief that only hierarchical legal authority could create civil order. That faith blinded them to the tensions that disrupted their own communities and aggravated their relations with the Abenaki. On the frontier, where English and Indians met in the flesh, formal legal agreements, and the officials who were supposed to enforce them, were unknown or disregarded. In these face-to-face interactions, where individuals did or did not comply with laws regulating contact, the proclaimed superiority of authoritarian English politics faltered. The unhappy results emerged in annual cycles of tribal grievance and Abenaki retaliations against English offenders.[7]

### LEGAL IMPASSE AND WAR

Recent historical studies emphasize the legal irritations that drove Indians to defend their independence. The tribes closest to English settlements suffered continuous erosion of their sovereignty as colonial governments gradually asserted control over Indian-white relations, commerce, land ownership, and ultimately intratribal affairs. In seventeenth-century New England Indians had access to the courts, but the proceedings were seldom fair. Historians indict the English not only for first imposing law on the tribes but then condemn colonials for denying Indians justice.[8]

This interpretation concentrates on issues of legal equality but generally ignores the differing cultural assumptions the English and the tribes made about social and legal order. If law was to be at all effective,

it had to control everyday relations with Indians. At this level law
simply did not work. New England governments could not regulate the
frontier. Throughout the colonial period the English thought that
Indians were God's instruments to chastize New England for its failure
to achieve religious solidarity. It followed that the English had first to
govern themselves. Reflecting on the first Abenaki war of 1675—77,
the minister William Hubbard admitted that lawlessness was as much
an internal as an external problem. He condemned those "scattering
Plantations in our Borders . . . [where] many were contented to live
without, yea desirous to shake off all Yoake of Government, both sacred
and civil, and so transforming themselves as much as they could into the
Manners of the Indians they lived amongst."[9]

Along with Hubbard, most Englishmen justified their contempt for
the Abenaki on the grounds that small-scale tribal life was little more
than anarchy. As an immediate result, the English were blind to the
Abenaki's actual attempts to prevent frontier violence. English failure
to appreciate the existence of legal order among the tribes—let alone its
nature or the manner of its execution—typified New England's continuing struggle with Indians. Certain that the inherent superiority of their
own institutions would fill the assumed political vacuum in Indian
cultures, the settlers demanded tribal adherence to English law. Yet the
colonials were always the first to flout authority. As contemptuous of
Boston officials as of the Abenaki, the settlers of coastal Maine made
Indian war inevitable.[10]

The Abenaki reaction to the English in the last quarter of the
seventeenth century constitutes a critique of colonial law. Abenaki
politics and law were strictly consensual, in contrast to the English
system which gradually made authoritarian law the cornerstone of social
order. The tribes had already achieved New England's communal ideal
and they endeavored to preserve it. While tribal law was adamant in its
insistence on personal freedom, the Abenaki usually followed the pres-
sures of public opinion. Legitimate authority derived only from the
active and free agreement of every person. The tribes had spokesmen to
express their considered views, but such leaders were not comparable to
English political officials. Abenaki sachems persuaded, cajoled, and
molded public opinion. They could not and did not govern.[11]

The sachems could agree to peace because their peoples earnestly
desired it. But they could not prevent violent reprisals against English
offenses. Frontier violence thus derived as much from the Abenaki legal
system as from the English. Hard pressed by frontier aggressions,
individual Abenaki were legally free to defend and revenge themselves

as they saw fit. While this state of affairs would suggest that feuding became a way of life, in fact it did not. During the war of 1675 — 77 and during King William's War as well, individual Abenaki men did not strike back as tribal law permitted. Rather, they chastized the English only after lengthy consultations among themselves.

The settlement of coastal Maine created an even broader field for conflict. It raised for the Abenaki, as for the English, ominous threats to their consensual solidarity. When Abenaki sachems declared that they could not restrain their young men, they frankly admitted the limits of tribal law, politics, and diplomacy. The English responded with similar arguments about the nature of frontier violence, but there was a telling difference in their reasoning. Faced with local incidents beyond governmental scrutiny and control, officials advised the Abenaki that the criminals were bad men outside the reach of law. This admission confirmed the Abenaki critique of colonial government. The Abenaki could not restrain their warriors because of legal principle; the English could not temper frontier aggression because their laws did not function.

The Abenaki and English finally began struggling with these legal misunderstandings in the 1670s. The causes of conflict were not apparent to contemporary historians whose religious views confused sin and lawlessness. Puritan divines like William Hubbard and Cotton Mather condemned the settlers' moral degeneracy in one breath and in the next excused their lawlessness, claiming that it was only English disregard of Christian duty that caused conflict with the tribes. Sin was judged more dangerous than criminality. As a result, Hubbard and Mather ignored the direct provocations against the Abenaki. They knew that the settlers maltreated their Indian neighbors and yet they dismissed the Abenaki's many defensive attempts to placate the English.[12]

In the 1660s the Abenaki and the English tentatively agreed that criminals in both societies had to be restrained. Since the tribes controlled the frontier, the English were forced to recognize Abenaki sovereignty. In a remarkably evenhanded agreement the two peoples decided that Abenaki sachems would deal with Indian criminals while the Indians would appeal to English courts when they were wronged. The agreement was soon forgotten. The settlers were little inclined to negotiate with the Abenaki, and the tribes themselves were unfamiliar with written laws and the English court system.[13]

This failure to reach diplomatic agreement on legal issues directly contributed to the eventual outbreak of war. The settlers held Indians in such contempt that their violent behavior undercut all official attempts to communicate. Late in the summer of 1675, for example, several sailors tested the then popular belief that Indian children knew instinctively how to swim by upsetting an Indian woman's canoe and dumping her child into the Saco River. The woman rescued her baby but it died soon after. The incident provoked open war because the child's father, Squando, was the Saco sachem and because Abenaki law required that he take revenge.[14]

The English excused themselves for causing the war. While William Hubbard had no love of lawbreakers, he considered the incident "some little Colour or Pretense of Injury" and observed that Squando's child might have died in any case. "Surely," Hubbard added, "if their Hearts had not been secretly filled with Malice and Revenge before, they might have obtained Satisfaction for the Wrong done." The minister apparently could not understand why the Saco and their Androscoggin allies declared war against the English. He insisted that the child's death "was only an Occasion to vent the Mischief they formerly had conceived in their Hearts."[15]

By obscuring the actual causes of the ensuing three-year conflict, Hubbard's published justification misled English readers. He made the Abenaki seem hot-blooded when they actually were defending themselves in the only way possible. Similarly, by implying that the Indians were lawless, he glossed over repeated English provocations. Convinced that all Indians "naturally delight in bloody and deceitful actions," the settlers demanded that the Abenaki surrender their arms and ammunition as the only acceptable assurance of neutrality. It was irrelevent to the settlers that the Abenaki would starve without guns. Thus, the Abenaki arena of King Philip's War had all the markings of a self-fulfilling prophecy. The English feared their Abenaki neighbors, thought that the French conspired with the tribes against New England, and suffered the rejection of their arbitrary demands.[16]

At first the Kennebec and Penobscot Abenaki attempted to stay out of the conflict, despite flagrant abuse from local settlers. As illustrated in the extraordinary efforts of one frontier official, Thomas Gardiner of Sagadahoc, the English could not distinguish between hostile and friendly tribes. Gardiner did not believe that the Kennebec or Penobscot endangered English security. He placed responsibility for the conflict on the colonist's extreme demands for the surrender of Abenaki guns. "I do not find by Any thing I Can discerne," he wrote, "that the Indianes East of us ar[e] in the least our Ennimies, [they] only fly for fear from Any boats or English thay se & good Reason for thay well Know it may Cost them their Lives if the wild fishermen meet with them."

Gardiner's neighbors felt less sympathetic, however, and accused him of trading ammunition with the Abenaki. Arrested and sent to Boston, Gardiner managed to prove his innocence. As he had predicted, the Kennebec and Penobscot remained at peace during the winter of 1675 – 76.[17]

A 1676 conference between English representatives and the still neutral eastern tribes further exposes the tensions that dominated relations. Quick to perceive the delegates' anxiety, the Penobscot sachem Madockawando assured the English of their personal safety. Nevertheless, when Silvanus Davis replied that "therein they *dealt like men*" (implying that they usually did not), he provoked Madockawando's anger: "You did *otherwise by our men*, when fourteen came to *treat* with you; and set a *Gaurd over them*, and took away *their Guns*: And not only so, but a second Time you *required our Guns*, and demanded us to *come down* unto you, or else you would kill us, which was the Cause of our leving both *our* Fort, and *our Corn* to our great Loss." The Penobscot sachem identified the provocations that pushed the Kennebec and Penobscot toward war. As Madockawando observed, the English imperiously expected compliance with their extravagant demands. Simultaneously, they refused to take responsibility for the anger they provoked.[18]

The English delegates recognized the truth in Madockawando's accusations, and their reply underlined the lack of trust that made accommodation impossible. The English stated that the settlers of whom Madockawando complained "were not within the Limits of their Government." The representatives nevertheless insisted that the Abenaki comply with all English demands and refused to appease Madockawando. The sachem made it clear that without diplomatic compromise war was inevitable. To reestablish a sense of mutual trust, he insisted that the English recognize the tribes' neutrality by again selling them powder and shot. Madockawando asked "whether they would have them dye, or leave their Country, and go all over to the French." The English replied that good faith was simply impossible. "If we sell you Powder," they inquired in turn, "and you give it to the Western Men [Saco and Androscoggin Abenaki], What do we do but cut our own Throats." Under these circumstances necessity as much as outrage forced the Kennebec and the Penobscot to join the Saco and Androscoggin against the English.[19]

Striking out against English inflexibility, the Abenaki terrified settlers from the Pemaquid peninsula to Piscataqua River during the summer and fall of 1676. But some Kennebec again sought an accommodation. At the end of October, a Kennebec sachem, Mogg, offered to return all captives and to reestablish peace. The settlers at once sent Mogg to Boston to negotiate an agreement. It turned out that the distant government was no more astute than the settlers in appreciating the Abenaki view of the war. The government failed to understand that peace required a mutual agreement that could defuse future disagreements. Instead, the English thought that Abenaki sachems could be forced to subdue their headstrong warriors. The treaty Mogg concluded was drafted "in the name of Madockawando," whom the English erroneously believed to be head sachem over all the tribes. In actuality, Madockawando had taken no part in the preliminary discussions and wielded little influence beyond the Penobscot River.[20]

To complicate matters further, the English contended that the tribes alone were at fault, and the treaty naively required the Abenaki to indemnify the settlers for wartime damages. It even enjoined them to attack any other tribes, such as the Saco and Androscoggin, who might remain hostile. While it is true that the Abenaki disagreed among themselves on how to deal with the English, the one-sided terms of Mogg's treaty ensured its repudiation. When the English brutally murdered several Abenaki during another peace conference in February 1677, the action returned the Kennebec and Penobscot to active participation in the war.[21]

Incapable of realistically discussing peace terms, Massachusetts lost the initiative to officials of the duke of York. The New York government took possession of Pemaquid in 1677, claiming jurisdiction over Sagadahoc, the territory between the Kennebec and St. Croix Rivers. While the Abenaki readily agreed on terms with Pemaquid authorities, they reluctantly made another overture to Massachusetts because they desperately needed ammunition and trading goods. A letter signed by the Kennebec sachems Diogenes and Madoasquarbet detailed the Abenaki sense that the English were inherently deceitful. The sachems began:

> To the governor of Boston
> this is to let you understand, how we have been abused. we love yo but when we are dronk you will take away our cot & throw us out of dore if the wolf kill any of your cattell you take away our gons for it & arrows and if you see an engon dog you will shoot him if we should do so to you cut down your houses kill your dogs take away your things we must pay a 100 skins if we brek a tobarko pip they will prisson us becaus there was war at

naragans you com here when we were quiet & took away our gons & mad
prisners of our chief sagamore & that winter for want of our gons there
was severall starved . . . now we hear that you say you will not leave war
as long as on engon is in the country we are owners of the country & it is
wide and full of engons & we can drive you out but our desire is to be
quiet . . . we would fain know whither you did give such order to kill us
for bringing you prisners is that your fashing to come & mke pese & then
kill us we are afraid you will do so agen . . . you may see how honest we
have bin we have kiled non of your English prisners if you have any of ours
prisners you wold a knocked them on the hed do you think all this is
nothing.[22]

When Massachusetts replied, the colony again refused to recognize
the thorny issues preventing peace. Since the southern Algonkian tribes
had been decisively defeated, the English felt no need to placate Indians.
Neither the government nor the settlers believed the Kennebec accusation that the war derived only from English abuses. Instead, Massachusetts interpreted the conflict in a narrowly legalistic manner, informing the Abenaki that the offending settlers "were disorderly
persons that lived out of our Jurisdiction." The English expressed a hope
that future incidents "may be prevented, by a more orderly & full
setlement of Government in those parts." The sentiment masked
Massachusetts's determination to curtail the Abenaki's independence.[23]

Only the timely mediation of Sagadahoc officials permitted Massachusetts and the Abenaki to reach an agreement. Despite what it felt
were Massachusetts's "difficult Termes," Sagadahoc persuaded the
Abenaki to accept a general cessation of hostilities in August 1677. To
allay English fears, the tribes promised to avoid traveling near the
settlements and released approximately sixty captives in return for six
Indians. These terms were formalized in April 1678 when the Abenaki
recognized English property rights. Massachusetts, however, admitted
Indian sovereignty over Maine: the colony agreed to pay the tribes an
annual quitrent "of a peck of corn for every English family."[24]

The treaty of 1678 was unsatisfactory from every point of view.
While the text defined both Abenaki and English property rights, it
neither addressed the emotional polarization that divided the two
peoples nor established mechanisms to negotiate the dangerous conflicts
that continually erupted. In the years following the treaty's ratification
the English did attempt to minimize irritations, especially those that
took place in trading situations. In 1680 the Province of Maine banned
all liquor sales to the Abenaki (every pint sold in violation of the law was

assessed a twenty shilling fine) and created a licensing system for traders. Court records indicate that violations were common and the tribes must have been irritated. But most important, fear of the Abenaki remained uppermost in the settlers' minds and therefore constituted the most imposing barrier to peace. The Province of Maine expended considerable funds on fortifications and thereby communicated distrust.[25]

Relations with the Abenaki remained volatile, fueled by rumors that disturbed both Indian and English communities. Early in 1684 reports flew up and down the coast to the effect that a French trader, the baron de Saint Castin, would lead the Abenaki to war. One settler testified that an Indian sachem declared "that his hart would never Be well till he had killed some of the Einglish againe and threatening that he would Burne English houses and made the English slaves to them as they ware Before." Expecting the worst, the Province of Maine ordered the militia into garrison and directed settlers to arm themselves against the impending attack. In February the authorities reported to Boston— wrongly, as it turned out—that the Abenaki had gone to Canada "to fetch guns and ammunition" and that Moxus, the Kennebec sachem, had supposedly said "that all his men have left him, and that he has no control over them." This news so alarmed the inhabitants of Casco and Cape Porpoise that in March they "laid aside all business to strengthen their defense."[26]

These events were only symptoms of the settlers' anxious reactions to the Abenaki. In April 1684 Governor Thomas Dongan of New York and Sagadahoc assured the Council of New Hampshire that there was nothing to fear from the Indians. In fact, his officers at Pemaquid had recently confirmed peace with them. Governor Edward Cranfield of New Hampshire, however, felt far less confident. In May he wrote to the Lords of Trade that the Abenaki "have been very disorderly, and have threatened to kill the English." Rather than discussing the issue directly with the tribes, the governor aggravated tensions. While Cranfield and the governor of Massachusetts both promised to satisfy any Abenaki grievance, they wrote to Dongan asking for Mohawk aid in subduing the tribes. This ill-considered request again inflamed the frontier. A story that "two hundred Mohawks were coming to exterminate the eastern Indians" spread quickly among the Abenaki, animating them in turn. John Hagkins, the Pennacook sachem, was so upset that he wrote to Cranfield: *"if you never let 'Mohogs' kill us, we'll be submissive to your worship forever."*[27]

These alarms alerted the English to the utter inadequacy of the 1678 treaty. New Hampshire and the Province of Maine jointly concluded a more comprehensive agreement with the Pennacook, Saco, Androscoggin, and Kennebec Abenaki in 1685. In affirming that there should be a lasting friendship between them, this later treaty established mechanisms for resolving difficulties. English criminals were to be tried by their magistrate and Abenaki offenders by their sachem. In return for protection against the Mohawk (or for the implied assurance that the English would not enlist their services), the Abenaki agreed to inform the English of any hostile Indians and to assist in the colonies' defense. Finally, to relieve English fears of sudden attack, the Abenaki promised to give "timely notice" should they decide to change their usual place of residence. If any Abenaki failed to comply with this last provision, the treaty authorized the English to arrest or attack the offenders.[28]

The treaty of 1685 proved no more successful in easing tensions than had the 1678 agreement. Within three years relations between the settlers and their Saco and Androscoggin neighbors had deteriorated seriously. The Abenaki resented the settlers' refusal to pay the quitrent the 1678 treaty had guaranteed, but other grievances also irritated them. Already suspicious of the growing number of English in southern Maine, the Abenaki were particularly angered by settlers who persistently placed nets across the Saco River, blocking migrating fish, a major food resource in the spring. A related issue caused even greater resentment. English cattle continually damaged the Saco's unfenced corn fields. Despite repeated complaints to local authorities, tribal rights were ignored. Since the settlers refused to discuss the issue, the Abenaki spoke "verey threatning words to the English of Shooting" the animals, Colonel Edward Tyng reported. He added that "the English ware much to blame in not keeping out their Creatures." Finally, in utter exasperation, the Saco killed four or five wandering cows.[29]

The settlers' failure to address these complaints violated the 1685 treaty. As the Sacos took action in their own defense, the English needlessly escalated the confrontation. Soon after the Sacos began to kill invading cattle, news arrived from Boston that there had been some trouble with Indians in southern New England. In Governor Edmund Andros's absence, the lieutenant-governor of Massachusetts ordered the Province of Maine to seize all Indians suspected of hostilities. Incapable of distinguishing frustration from uncontrolled fury and perhaps eager to serve local economic interests, the English seized twenty men, women, and children, "some of whom were so old and feeble that they were forced to be carried when ashore on others backs." The Abenaki were sent to Boston not because they threatened the settlers but rather, as Colonel Tyng expressed it, "that they might be hostages of our pease."[30]

The tribes tried to avoid open conflict, but English provocation finally drove them toward war in 1688. The Abenaki first retaliated in kind, seizing several English and inquiring of one, Captain Walter Gendall, why the Saco had been treacherously apprehended. Despite Gendall's lame reply that some English had been killed on the far-distant Connecticut River, the Abenaki decided to negotiate. Released to convey that message, Gendall reported to Tyng that the tribes would return the English captives if their people were also freed. Tyng rushed two men to soothe the Abenaki, even though he doubted that the conflict could be resolved. He reported that the Indians seemed "very imperious." Yet the Abenaki remained quiet and even released more captives to Tyng's agents. Paradoxically, Tyng ignored these overtures and informed Boston that the Abenaki "Intend a warr with us." He even feared that the Indians and French had already formed a "Strong Combination."[31]

This confrontation repeated the classic pattern. As usual, the settlers viewed the Abenaki suspiciously, ignored their own provocations, refused discussion, and pushed the Abenaki toward violent defense. Members of the governor's council admitted as much, deploring "that so rash and Early a Seizure of Indian Women and Children should produce such a Hurry and Expense." Hoping to placate aroused tempers, the councillors hastily dispatched their Saco prisoners back to Maine. Unfortunately, local events aborted that belated conciliatory gesture.[32]

After long discussions with Henry Smith, one of their captives, and in spite of factional disagreement among themselves, the Abenaki agreed to negotiate. Most were willing not only to release their prisoners but also to pay for any destroyed property "in Beaver as the English should value itt." But their representatives, along with Smith, were fired upon in their canoes when they attempted to parley with Captain Gendall. Wounded but undaunted, Smith jumped ashore. Instead of seeking asylum, he angrily demanded that Gendall read the Abenaki's letter. When his demand was refused, Smith returned to the understandably outraged Abenaki. Violence continued, Gendall himself was killed, and his men remained silent about the actual cause of open hostilities.[33]

Because the English lacked "a perticuler order to Execute" the Sacos who had been returned tardily to Maine and because military officers feared an Abenaki onslaught, the captives were sent back to Boston. With them went English willingness to discuss the explosive situation. Government officials did not try to assign responsibility. Headstrong settlers thus created the second Abenaki-English war, just as they had the first. They left its prosecution, or resolution, to Boston officials who were too far away to govern. Since neither the English nor the Abenaki could resolve the confrontation, violent incidents confirmed mutual impressions of perfidy.[34]

Throughout the seventeenth century problems of political scale greatly strained social relations in the Northeast. Jurisdictional disputes over Maine made the region a microcosm of the larger power struggles of Europe. In the background loomed the rivalry between French and English for control of Acadia, especially the territory between the Kennebec and St. Croix rivers. But international power plays over Abenaki lands were minor in comparison to the disputes among the English themselves. Plymouth Colony asserted an uncertain claim over the region of the Kennebec. Massachusetts first imposed and then purchased authority over Maine west of Plymouth's territory. Within the bounds of Sagadahoc, officials of the duke of York opposed Massachusetts's expansion, developed a rival Indian policy, and thus came to symbolize the threat of arbitrary royal power.

The accession of the duke of York to the English throne increased colonial tensions. In fact, the frontier events that led to open war with the Abenaki in 1688 cannot be understood apart from the issues that pushed Massachusetts into revolt against royal authority. In 1684 James II abolished the charter that had justified Massachusett's political independence. At the end of 1686 Sir Edmund Andros, well known in New England for his eight years as governor of New York and Sagadahoc, assumed the government of the entire Northeast from New York to Maine. Andros was extremely unpopular and dissatisfaction with his administration focused in 1688 when he attempted to make peace with the Abenaki. Andros's arrogant manner only convinced New Englanders that they faced an internal conspiracy equal to the Abenaki threat.[35]

Refusing to confide even in members of his own council, Andros incited unrest among the people he governed. During the winter of 1688–89 disturbing rumors accused the governor of conspiring with the Abenaki and French to subdue New England to the will of foreign powers. Andros blithely disregarded such reports and visited frontier towns, self-righteously demanding to know on whose authority the settlers had acted against the Indians.[36]

Returning from New York only to discover Massachusetts at war with the Abenaki and the Saco imprisoned, Andros was furious. Few New Englanders were acquainted with the actual conditions of the outbreak, and it seemed to them that Andros lashed out with "an unaccountable displeasure." Since the governor denounced his councillors and militia officers as "high offenders," his private conferences with the captive Saco appeared to agitated observers all the more ominous. Confident that the Saco were innocent, Andros ordered them released. "It's affirmed those very men [the captive Saco] have done great part of the mischief sustained by us," the ill-informed but growing opposition commented. Suspicions mounted when Andros sent a delegation to Quebec "upon some Errands and Business as were not communicated and laid open to the Council." Boston grieved: "We are again Briar'd in the Perplexities of another Indian war, how or why, is a mystery too deep for us to unfold."[37]

These rumors against Andros were intricately bound to general fears of the Abenaki. Although most English did not realize it, the governor had strengthened New England's defenses at the same time he attempted negotiations with the tribes. That Andros's cautious steps served only to increase antipathy toward him measures the settlers' fear of conspiracy. People in Maine believed that the governor had replaced loyal Protestants with pro-French Catholic officers. Rumor again intervened, inflating a quiet meeting between Andros and two Indian women at Pemaquid into a full-fledged plot.[38]

While still at Pemaquid seeking peace, Andros learned that James II had fled to France and that William of Orange had entered England to accept the throne. The governor realized at once that Protestant New England would welcome the removal of Catholic King James, and he hurried back to Boston. Discovering on his return that the council had enlisted soldiers to defend the frontier, Andros nullified their orders. Historian Thomas Hutchinson later described colonial response to the governor's seemingly conspirational actions: "He had a more favorable opinion of the Indians than the Inhabitants who had suffered so much by them and imagined he should be able to preserve peace with them." Thoroughly exasperated, for these and many other reasons, the people of Boston rose in armed rebellion and Andros surrendered on April 18, 1689. A makeshift committee assumed the powers of government and imprisoned Andros in Boston harbor—as much for his safety as for his reputed crimes against New England.[39]

The Glorious Revolution had both an immediate and long-range impact on Massachusetts's relations with the Abenaki. The settlers, convinced that they faced an internal conspiracy, at once rid themselves of suspected "papist" military commanders, producing further uproar on the already distraught frontier. What is more serious, the revolution terminated Andros's complex efforts to reach an agreement with the Abenaki. Andros had combined force with persuasion to bring the tribes to terms, and his policy was on the verge of success in the spring of 1689. Denied all advantages of trade, the Abenaki had suffered so severely during the preceding winter that "they scarcely did subsist." Even so, a vital parley with Madockawando failed when the sachem realized that Andros had been deposed and that "the land [was] in confusion." After capturing the fort at Pemaquid in August 1689, the Abenaki left the retreating garrison a bitter parting message: "Sir Edmund Andros was a great rogue and had nearly starved them last winter, but he was now a prisoner, and they no care for New England people; they [will] have all their country by and by."[40]

Over the long run, then, the Glorious Revolution increased civil disorder and thereby undercut all efforts to end conflict. An attempt to confer with the Saco and Androscoggin in the winter and spring of 1690–91 began and ended in violence. By 1692, when Massachusetts was made a royal province and Sir William Phips was named its first governor, the English cared nothing about the origins of the conflict. They knew only that the Abenaki and French had been too long successful in terrorizing the frontier.

## FROM RELIGIOUS TO MILITARY ALLIANCE

The first two Abenaki wars with the English derived from fundamental differences in legal order. Both peoples admitted the need for agreements that could resolve and defuse conflict. But satisfactory political arrangements could not be obtained. In expecting that the tribes submit to English law, government officials demanded too much of the Abenaki. Given the authoritarian character of colonial politics and the lawlessness of the frontier, the English could not sanction any compact that would leave the tribes independent. The Abenaki, for their part, had difficulty comprehending the legal ideology that made the English unreasonably rigid.

The tribes did attempt to reassure both their English neighbors and distant officials in Boston. Experience taught them, however, that even repeated assurances could not banish distrust. The historical record shows that the tribes continually sought redress and constantly failed to achieve even compromise. It also reveals a political irony. Massachusetts pretended the superiority of centralized government but failed to control its frontier. The Abenaki, who apparently had no government, managed to act with political unity. English officials could not force settlers to live by the legal terms the treaties of 1678 and 1685 imposed on the tribes. Administrative ineptitude was bad enough, but the Abenaki also suffered innumerable insults from English traders, fishermen, and farmers. Naturally, the tribes resisted.

The French displayed a fundamental respect for Indian rights which the English did not share. The Abenaki occupied a privileged position in the French empire. They had, in fact, dual citizenship, which gave them considerable political clout. New France accorded Christian Indians the same political rights as native-born French subjects. Many of the mission Indians were Abenaki whose relatives and allies in Maine shared this political status. There was much visiting back and forth and in Canada the Abenaki were treated as French subjects. Still, the French made no effort to subordinate the tribes to Canadian authority and managed to resolve two major difficulties that troubled English-Abenaki relations. They found the means to coordinate political relations between French and Abenaki subjects when they accepted the corporate existence of the mission communities within New France. They also recognized the existence of tribal law. As a practical result, they learned to work within the independent tribes, adding persuasive French voices to the continuing Abenaki search for political consensus.[41]

During the 1680s and throughout King William's War the French were far more successful than the English at communicating with the Abenaki. Unlike the English, who stayed close to their settlements, the French lived in or near Abenaki villages. Since the French were little interested in agriculture, they did not threaten to dispossess the tribes. But more to the point, the Acadian French used trade with the Abenaki to build constructive relations. Temporary and permanent liaisons between Frenchmen and Abenaki women were common, and such relationships were only one indication that the French had come to respect their commercial allies. When disagreements arose, Indian custom prevailed. While the English held themselves aloof, some of the French met the Abenaki directly.

The Penobscot, Passamaquoddy, and Maliseet knew the French as traders, occasionally as compatriots living and marrying among them, and sometimes as members of the same church. These eastern Abenaki were early acquainted with Recollet missionaries, but none of them had the Kennebec's opportunity for religious dialogue. Still, in discovering a system of reciprocal status, Acadian French and Abenaki learned that they could test and therefore come to trust each other's mettle.[42]

Acadian relations with the tribes shared the difficulties that troubled the alliance between the Kennebec and the Jesuits because Indians and colonists did not conform to expectations in Versailles. Metropolitan officials were too far away to perceive the interpersonal character of the relationship. They had little power to impose their will over so great a geographical and psychological distance. Indeed, for much of the seventeenth century Acadia lacked an effective local government. By the 1680s Acadia had gone its own way even more than had Canada. Since its localized Franco-American culture was protected by royal indifference, the tiny colony had already developed a mixed French and Indian heritage.[43]

But Acadia was not the social amalgam that royal officials had planned for Canada. The settlers remembered their national origins in religious practice, language, music, and folklore, but their sense of civil identity was tied to everyday relations with English and Abenaki neighbors. Acadians accommodated themselves to the demands of a far-away government when necessary but responded more often to Boston than to Versailles. Sometimes they resisted, especially against threats to their tiny, fiercely independent communities. The Northeast itself molded their development. Acadians quickly became *coureurs de bois*, trading, fishing, and hunting with the Micmac and Abenaki. They also farmed and raised cattle enough to produce a small surplus for trade. The colony was in fact an economic satellite of fishermen and traders from Massachusetts. Unlike Canadians who feared and guarded against their Iroquoian and English neighbors, Acadians associated comfortably with Boston merchants. In turn, the English left much of the Indian hinterland to Acadia's sphere of influence.[44]

Seventeenth-century Acadia was nonetheless a battleground for competing French and English interests. New England merchants particularly envied the profits Acadians gained from the fur trade. As a result, the territory east of the Kennebec River passed repeatedly from one colonial power to another. Furthermore, conflict among the French traders contributed greatly to Acadia's uncertain grasp on the region.

These rivalries were only terminated when an English squadron seized the colony in 1654. Distracted by events on the Continent, France made only feeble efforts to recover Acadia and the colony remained under English control until the Treaty of Breda in 1667. In the summer of 1670 Hector d'Andigne de Grandfontaine received the Penobscot River from the English and his deputies accepted the St. John River in New Brunswick and Port Royal on the Nova Scotian peninsula. Nevertheless, Acadia continued to languish after the repossession. Ostensibly subordinate to New France, the Atlantic colony was often ignored, incompetently governed, and threatened constantly by New England.[45]

A few individuals, Jean Vincent d'Abbadie de Saint Castin the most prominent among them, maintained French presence among the eastern Abenaki. The younger son of a noble house of Béarn, Saint Castin arrived in Canada in 1665 with the Carignan Salières regiment. In 1670, as an ensign under Grandfontaine, the eighteen-year-old Saint Castin participated in the reassertion of French sovereignty over the Penobscot River. He was there in 1674 when the Dutch attacked and with several Abenaki traveled overland to inform Governor Frontenac of the trouble. During this challenge to French authority his elder brother died and Jean Vincent became the third baron of Saint Castin.[46]

Despite his social standing, Saint Castin preferred a life bound by the intimate circle of the Abenaki world. More adaptable *coureur de bois* than haughty aristocrat, Saint Castin disturbed Acadian priests and political authorities. Early in the seventeenth century Captain John Smith had noted that French and Indians lived together as a single nation. Saint Castin (along with a number of his now invisible Acadian countrymen) wholeheartedly embraced that tradition. Until the 1680s he lived as he pleased among the Penobscot, trading mostly with Boston merchants and making annual visits to Port Royal to fulfill his religious obligations. His confessor on those occasions undoubtedly chided him for spiritual indiscretions—and possibly for his tenuous allegiance to France—but the baron persisted in his errant ways. Generous alms to the church marked his temporary contrition. Once absolved, Saint Castin returned quickly to the freedom of the woods.[47]

Except for a few individuals like the baron of Saint Castin, the French had only a vague idea of the international politics that began to affect Acadia during the 1680s. For his part, Saint Castin joined his Penobscot allies in seeking neutrality. Along with them he would have remained a quiet, unassuming neighbor of the English except that metropolitan authorities in France and the colonies of Massachusetts and New York began to contest control of the fur trade, the fisheries, and the tribes. The fragile détente between English and Acadians began to fracture in 1682 when Louis XIV commissioned a new fishing corporation and denied Massachusetts's right to dry fish on French shores. During the next year Thomas Dongan, governor of New York and Sagadahoc, ordered the French either to submit or depart his province between the Kennebec and St. Croix rivers. This demand took both Acadian and Canadian officials by surprise, as did Dongan's 1686 seizure of wine and trade goods recently received by Saint Castin from New Hampshire. Dongan contended that neither French nor other English colonials could trade with the Sagadahoc region.[48]

New France remained preoccupied elsewhere, looking first to the hinterlands of the Saint Lawrence River, then to Dongan's dangerous alliance with the Iroquois, and finally to English encroachments in Hudson's Bay. Dongan's threats against the Acadian French received only nominal attention, not just because of Canadian diffidence, real as it was, but also because Versailles thought that all of these problems could be resolved through diplomatic channels. Officials in France were wrong. The 1686 Treaty of Neutrality between England and France did not ease northeastern conflict.[49]

Saint Castin played a central role in Acadia's defensive reactions during the 1680s. Since France failed to strengthen the Acadian government, the settlers competed viciously among themselves for most of the decade. Acadian governor François Marie Perrot, for example, vied openly with Saint Castin for control of the fur trade. Perrot's removal from office in 1687, along with increasing pressure from Sagadahoc, pushed Saint Castin to ally himself unequivocally with French interests. The king expressed personal interest that the baron reform his manners to comport with his status. After a second attack from Sagadahoc in the summer of 1687, Saint Castin took action. He requested thirty soldiers and funds to enlist the Abenaki in order to protect his fort on the Penobscot River. The baron promised that he could attract four hundred Indians, and the Acadian governor agreed that the project was urgent. A year later Governor Louis Alexandre des Friche de Meneval assured the king that the baron had embraced a more dignified way of life. Saint Castin had stopped trading with the English, ceased his debauched relations with the Abenaki, and had married Mathilde, the daughter of the Penobscot sachem Madockawando.[50]

Although Saint Castin lent the French credibility among the Abenaki, he had little or no impact on Canada's Indian policy. To assure his own interests, he kept government officials informed as the English asserted control over Penobscot and Passamaquoddy territory. Still, neither Saint Castin nor the eastern Abenaki were involved with the outbreak of war between the western Abenaki and the English. In fact, as late as October 1688 Canadian governor Jacques-René de Brisay de Denonville remained oblivious to the English and Abenaki conflict (even though Jesuit missionaries had witnessed the outbreak of war). In his annual report to metropolitan officials in Paris, Denonville said only that the English wished to live peacefully with the Abenaki and to that end sold trade goods to the Indians at low prices. Contrary to English suspicions, and in spite of his own nebulous fears of pressure from the English colonies, Denonville had no part in the Abenaki attack against New England.[51]

Events soon sharpened the governor's anxieties, but he did not focus them on the Abenaki. In the fall of 1688 Sir Edmund Andros of the Dominion of New England reported solicitously that he had directed the Iroquois Confederacy to cease its war against New France. It struck Denonville uneasily that such professed benevolence hid Andros's responsibility for a recent raid against Saint Castin's post on the Penobscot. Although Denonville could not prove it, he suspected that Governor Andros had also been behind attacks on Canso and Chedabucto in Acadia. While otherwise confused about Andros's intentions, the French governor knew that the English had reasserted hegemony over the Iroquois: Andros had gone so far as to halt a delegation from the Five Nations on its way to see the French governor. While determined to resist imperial gestures on the New York frontier, Denonville did not understand that a diplomatic collision had been set in motion over Abenaki territory.[52]

Only the Jesuits and a few traders living in Acadia had any interest in the Abenaki—and their concerns were religious or economic, not political. At Denonville's request, Father Bigot traveled to Maine in 1688. Both men wished to attract more Abenaki to the already flourishing Canadian missions. In fact, the trip raised French consciousness about issues disturbing the Abenaki. On his return Bigot asked the governor to prevent French traders from exchanging liquor for Abenaki furs. The priest argued that the trade sparked violence within the tribes and inevitably produced bad feelings toward the French and their religion. Prefiguring disagreements that would grow more vicious over time, outraged traders demanded in turn that the priests be barred from Abenaki villages.[53]

Governor Denonville himself sided with the priests, stressing the difficult task they faced. He claimed that they worked with men who had neither discipline, law, nor subordination. He thought, in short, that the Abenaki lived so brutishly that if Catholicism did not master their hearts, nothing could come from an association with them. Following Jesuit advice, Denonville limited himself in 1688 to a suggestion that Abenaki leaders be given presents to offset Governor Andros's calculated generosity.[54]

Later in the English-Abenaki war, even after Denonville officially noted English aggressions against the tribes, the French ministry failed to see the obvious military potential of their Abenaki allies. Louis XIV and his ministers urged Denonville to halt the English advance but offered no practical advice. The French court also made a tepid complaint to Great Britain regarding Massachusetts's behavior, but neither side discussed the Northeast until early in 1690. When French leaders finally realized the ominous character of Acadian developments, the Abenaki offensive seemed even more valiant for its independence.[55]

The bureaucratic scale of French colonial affairs, especially the enormous distance impeding administrative communication, made reports from visiting priests crucial to French strategy. Nevertheless, in 1688–89 the missionaries played only an observer's role. While the priests fostered spiritual alliance, they noted the Abenaki's successful war against New England. Their reports implied to metropolitan officials that Abenaki warriors might defend Acadia as well.[56]

Pierre Thury, a priest of the Foreign Missions Seminary of Quebec who had resided among the Penobscot since 1687, described the Abenaki's raids against the Maine frontier. He noted with satisfaction that the warriors confessed their sins before attacking. Thury witnessed one battle that proved Abenaki prowess. In August 1689 the Indians surprised the village and fort at Pemaquid. Thury admired the Penobscot's military tactics as well as their honorable conduct in accepting English surrender without further bloodshed. The Abenaki declared that there had been enough bad faith and advised the English not to return. Thury claimed that the Abenaki castigated the English for troubling them over the practice of their religion. In all that he wrote the priest stressed the religious fervor of the Abenaki. During their attack on Pemaquid the Penobscot women and children had kept a perpetual rosary for their warriors' safe return.[57]

Thury reported that the Abenaki were already united in faith and interested in a broader alliance. They told Thury they could strike as far

as Boston if they had 200 Frenchmen with them. Similar reports from
Jesuits on the Kennebec prompted a new appreciation of the Abenaki's
importance to Canada. Intendant Champigny noted their efficiency in
that they had captured Pemaquid with only the ammunition received in
1688. The French did not immediately see the Abenaki's full military
potential. But as the Jesuits continued to argue that the Indians should
be attracted to the Quebec missions, Canadian officials came to observe
that once resettled the Indians could defend the colony against the
Iroquois and the English.[58]

The campaign against Pemaquid demonstrated the Abenaki's effective military techniques. At the end of 1689 the minister of marine
concluded confidently from his desk at Versailles that with Indian aid
the French might defend Acadia. He therefore opposed the Jesuit policy
of inviting the Abenaki to Canada. Instead, the priests were encouraged
to live in Maine. After his recall to France, Denonville discussed the
situation with metropolitan officials and observed that the priests'
reputation among the Indians, added to their fluency in the Abenaki
language, made them essential to French policy. Missionaries alone,
said Denonville, could govern the "savage peoples," keep them faithful,
and "prevent their revolting against us every day."[59]

Denonville overestimated Jesuit influence, even though he should
have known better. For French and English alike the European outbreak
of King William's War obscured the Abenaki's purposes in striking
against the English colonials. Dramatic French and Abenaki military
forays opened the Euramerican conflict but were only one part of an
escalating war fever that engulfed the Northeast. After two years of
ineffectual actions, New England resolved in February 1690 to rebuke
the Abenaki enemy. A few days later the Mohawk demanded an assault
on Canada and castigated the English because "they ate, drank and slept
much but left the war to them." Thus, the French decision to use
Abenaki arms against New England came as much from a need to thwart
a dreaded alliance between the English and Iroquois as from a sincere
identification with the Abenaki cause.[60]

Reappointed to save New France from its many enemies, Governor
Frontenac at once demonstrated the formidable power of the French
allied with Indians. He aimed to teach the English a painful lesson
about joining the Iroquois. Three Canadian forces went out, and four
towns smoldered: Schenectady on February 13, Salmon Falls in March,
and Fort Casco and then Fort Loyal in Maine at the end of May. This last
party comprised sixty Canadian Abenaki under command of René

Robineau de Portneuf. Beyond terrorizing the frontier, as Frontenac had hoped, these attacks greatly encouraged the Abenaki, who continued the war after Portneuf returned to Quebec. During the summer of 1690 French officers joined the Abenaki and they were "always masters of the battlefield."[61]

Having demonstrated the military advantage of alliance, Canadian officials had to alleviate problems of supply that undermined Abenaki determination to wage war. Cut off from English trade, the Abenaki required arms and ammunition, and Canadian officials quickly noted that this need could be used to control the tribes. Although the Penobscot told Governor Frontenac in 1691 that they would fight with or without French supplies, they also requested six canoes of materiel: blankets, hoods, shirts, tobacco, knives, gunpowder, and lead for bullets. They argued persuasively that their families were starving, and it seemed obvious that strategic raids would cease if they ran out of powder and shot.[62]

Since the French ministry had already decided to vigorously protect Acadia—and the Abenaki were crucial to that design—Governor Frontenac had no difficulty lobbying for their cause. When Joseph Robineau de Villebon arrived in Acadia shortly after Port Royal fell to Sir William Phips in 1690, he too emphasized the Abenaki's importance. Villebon reported that the western Abenaki had recently signed a truce with the English because of French negligence. Hoping to strengthen the Abenaki's resolve, he demanded generous supplies and a chaplain for his garrison. To lead the warriors, Villebon recommended the Sieur de Portneuf, who was distinguished for his command of Abenaki language and customs.[63]

The king and minister of marine realized that Acadia could neither be reconquered nor retained without Abenaki assistance. To get that help, both men understood that Acadian officers would have to satisfy Indian expectations. It became official policy to do so. The ministry established a special fund of 3,200 livres to provide the tribes with arms, ammunition, provisions, and utensils. Unfortunately, this policy rested on a limited recognition of Abenaki motives. The king apparently thought that the warriors had so committed themselves to his service that they would subordinate their interests to his. Nonetheless, he did respond to Abenaki demands, directing his officers to tell the warriors:

> that on the advice that has been given his Majesty of their obedience to his
> services, and of the offers they made the previous year to wage a greater

war than in the past against the English, his Majesty is well pleased to give them the aid they have demanded, and assures them that they will always be given the same protection during the war and after the peace.[64]

The French gifts were timely because they paid for a successful fall and winter campaign. As Governor Frontenac advised the king: "It is impossible to describe the ravages these Indians commit for fifty leagues around Boston . . . capturing daily their forts and buildings; killing numbers of their people, and performing incredible deeds of bravery." Four hundred Abenaki joined Villebon's officers in several forays against the English, including an immensely successful attack on York in 1692. On that occasion the death of a distinguished clergyman, Shebael Dummer, convinced the English that religious prejudice had instigated the Abenaki war.[65]

For their part, the French worried that the alliance was too fragile and hoped that patronage might strengthen it. Villebon reported that Abenaki supplies had warded off disaster: "Had the English succeeded in gaining our Indian allies over to agree to a peace with them after the fall of Port Royal, there is no doubt but that Canada would have been entirely exposed and, I dare add, lost." Villebon may have overestimated New England's military power, but he noted correctly that "the Indian never feels so much encouraged as when he sees himself sustained." The ministry shared Villebon's optimism. Although the king had not yet learned of the 1691 and early 1692 campaigns, he renewed the Abenaki fund and improved it as well. He financed fifty more soldiers and sent another 406 livres for gifts to Abenaki sachems. He intended, the minister of marine reported, that the Abenaki might wage war without depending on hunting and trapping as usual.[66]

But local issues had a more immediate impact than presents from the French king. Successful English attacks against Penobscot and Kennebec villages destroyed vital supplies of corn and struck the Abenaki hard. French persuasion could not overcome the Indians' sudden sense of adverse momentum. When an illustrious alliance led by Madockawando, Moxus, Egeremet, Worumbos, and the Sieurs de Portneuf and de la Broquerie failed in its attack on Wells, the Abenaki foresaw more bad luck. "It has so far been impossible," Villebon wrote, "to overcome the superstition that, if they receive such a reverse when they set out on the warpath, they must stop at once, no matter how large a party, or how insignificant the action." Portneuf and Saint Castin vainly urged further attacks, but the Abenaki "retreated swiftly, each to his own district."[67]

The tribes were not inclined to take advice. They knew that the French, while quick to urge their allies to war, were tardy in their own defense. English raids slowed the Abenaki war, and French acts of cowardice and malfeasance exposed the inequality of the alliance. At Saint Castin's persuasion, the Abenaki gathered at Mt. Desert Island in the fall of 1692 to meet two French supply ships, the *Joli* and *Envieux*. Although Saint Castin promised action against the fort Sir William Phips had reestablished at Pemaquid, French naval officers refused to attack because of threatening bad weather. Not even their annual supplies soothed Abenaki disappointment, and the tribes left for their fall hunting "disgusted at the refusal to attack."[68]

Louis XIV shared their anger and attempted to make amends with increased subsidies. The 1693 grant included support of an additional forty soldiers and the usual gifts for Abenaki warriors. But the minister of marine identified two disturbing issues. First, he observed that local officials had not effectively used the king's supplies during 1692. To rectify colonial indirection, the minister relied on exhortation: the Abenaki must be led to war. Second, the king had learned that the Penobscot and Kennebec felt that they had not received a fair share of the war supplies. This complaint prompted a redefinition of alliance. Since the Kennebec and Penobscot were closest to the English, and thus most susceptible to attack and the most zealous in war, the minister accorded them more presents than their sheltered Maliseet and Micmac allies. The front-line Abenaki were to be given roughly half the supplies: 1,000 pounds of gunpowder, 3,000 pounds of lead, 15 rifles, 30 shirts, besides cloth and food. In addition, their sachems were to receive guns, ammunition, shirts, fancy hats, and blankets. The remaining materiel was to be distributed among other allies so that they too might continue the war.[69]

Welcome as these subsidies were, they did not win the Abenaki's allegiance. Since 1675 alliance with the French had produced mixed reactions among the tribes. Although the association remained grounded in warm, personal relations, the French found it difficult to appreciate the Abenaki's situation. In 1693 metropolitan officials had just begun to realize that their policies troubled the tribes. Aware that the Indians were disgruntled with French passivity, the king and minister nonetheless failed to review the terms of the alliance. Acadian officials realized that wartime conditions were intolerable and that French supplies could not replace the Abenaki's need for traditional resources. Villebon reported that the Indians continued to grow crops and their trapping economy remained vitally important. French supplies of munitions could not ease these pressing needs. Abenaki faith-fulness and Anglophobia, real as such sentiments were, misled French officials at Versailles. Although the tribes were quite willing to accept military assistance, they did not think of themselves as fighting a French war. Moreover, the Abenaki considered the French ineffectual allies.[70]

POLITICS OF PERSUASION

Since the French could not provide the Abenaki with enough goods to continue the war, the Indians began to consider the possibility of peace with Massachusetts. Many remained exasperated with the English, but the Abenaki could not bear the cost of fighting. As a result, in August 1693 some of them concluded a peace treaty with Governor William Phips. As it turned out, the agreement only formalized misunder-standings.

In stating that the tribes promised to "forbear all acts of hostility" and to "abandon and forsake the French Interest," the text fostered two misconceptions. It made the Abenaki the sole aggressors and attributed the war to French instigation. The treaty further declared that the Abenaki would cease all acts of "private Revenge" and stipulated that the tribes must apply to the Massachusetts governor for redress of any "wrong or injury done on one side or the other." These terms were unilateral, for Phips required that the Abenaki submit themselves as subjects to the English Crown "to be Ruled and Governed by their Majties Laws."[71]

The treaty wholly conformed to English pretensions of innocence. Furthermore, its terms legalized erroneous assumptions about the character of Abenaki politics. The English naively thought that the treaty itself would effect the political transformation of the tribes, but the Indian signers were certainly unaware of such implications. The Abenaki continued to assert their sovereign status. Nevertheless, the treaty of 1693 formed the foundation of every later treaty between the tribes and Massachusetts. Thereafter, the English claimed that the tribes were subjects, although numerous Abenaki "rebellions" effec-tively exposed the lie.

There is compelling evidence that the Abenaki asserted political independence even in 1693. In signing the Phips treaty the Abenaki deliberately shunned French control. Since the tribes' newly established neutrality exposed the vulnerability of Canadian frontiers, the agree-ment pushed Villebon to urgent measures. The French took heart in knowing that the tribes resented the treaty's one-sided terms. Julien Bineteau, a Jesuit on the Kennebec, informed Villebon that the Abenaki still despised the English but that more effective French support was mandatory. Villebon agreed: "There is every reason to be apprehensive of these negotiations unless the Indians receive considerable presents from us."[72]

If the Abenaki felt no reason to wage war, the French were determined to persuade them. Pierre Thury, for one, needed no prodding and hurried back to the Penobscot to criticize Madockawando for signing the Phips treaty. On this and other occasions the French swayed all Abenaki by exploiting the influential opinions of a partisan few. Commander Villebon intervened among the Penobscot, pleading with Madockawando's son, who had just returned from France: "I made known to him his father's behavior, and said that, having been made so welcome in France, it was his duty to induce his father to change his mind." Although the young man promised aid, he later found that he could not help, "fearing to endanger two of his kinsmen whom his father had given as hostages to the English at Pemaquid." Villebon clung to a slim hope that the Abenaki might be convinced to abjure the treaty because the sachem Taxous had not signed it.[73]

Villebon requested that a Maliseet sachem, Manidoubtik, "see Taxous on my behalf, and to urge him to raise a faction which would put an end to these negotiations." Taxous replied vigorously "that he was making preparations to assemble a war-party of considerable size in the spring." Reassured, Villebon asked that Canadian soldiers be dispatched to hearten Kennebec warriors. He spent the winter of 1693–94 exhorting the Maliseet and Micmac and they promised "to be at hand by the end of April."[74]

Persuasion, then, became the basis of French diplomacy and the Abenaki responded. Even the lukewarm alliance symbolized in each French gift seemed preferable to notorious English treachery. Reminding the Abenaki of English transgressions, however, could move them as presents could not. The French of course downplayed their own failings. The Penobscot wanted peace, doubted promises that Louis XIV could protect them, but listened when Thury warned "of the danger in which they placed themselves by negotiating with the English, who, under the guise of friendship and extensive trade, would not fail to betray them as they had in the past."[75]

Such arguments were not immediately successful. Even with three Kennebec leaders and Father Bigot arguing the French cause, the

Penobscot would not repudiate the Phips treaty. Nevertheless, representatives visited Villebon on the St. John River "to obtain the gifts sent to them by the King the year before." Especially honored was Taxous, if honor exists in flattery aimed at manipulating a man's resolve. "I adopted him as my brother, and gave him the best suit of clothes I had," Villebon wrote. Taxous replied warmly that he would "induce Madokawando to join him, or render him contemptible to all the young men." Increasingly, French maneuvers played on the emotions of the youngest Abenaki warriors, who were more inured to the hardships of war.

Despite glowing promises, the Penobscot remained suspicious of French support. When they divided their presents they discovered "that they had received only a portion [of] . . . what had been sent to them by the King." Sebastien de Villieu, an officer at the scene, noted that this fresh evidence of French ineptitude almost destroyed what remained of Indian goodwill. "To complete our undoing," he wrote, Madockawando insisted that Phips return the Abenaki hostages given as sureties for the treaty on July 5. Hoping that Phips would keep his word, the Penobscot bided their time—which worked to Madockawando's advantage, if not to his credibility, because a major objective of the war had been to regain captive kinsmen. Once the Penobscot had decided to wait, the French argued uselessly. Pierre Thury was no less urgent than Villieu "and was no less troubled than he, on learning that a minister had come to the fort of Pemaquid to teach the Indian children how to read and write."

Countered by Madockawando, Villieu hurriedly formulated arguments to estrange the Abenaki from the English. He urged the Penobscot to take a few English captives and thereby secure their kin held in Boston. If that stratagem failed, Villieu maintained, they could still assemble those English already taken captive and exchange them for their relatives. He offered to write to Phips "that he must treat the Indians in his power well if he wished the English prisoners to be kindly treated." Had it not been for Madockawando's steadfast opposition, Villieu believed that his strategies would have been accepted.

The ensuing discussions clearly show the manner of French influence. Villieu realized that Abenaki politics rested on vagaries of social consensus. Seeking a compelling argument, Villieu finally divided the Penobscot on an issue even more fundamental than the safe return of Abenaki hostages. One disgruntled Penobscot told Villieu that Madockawando "had sold the lands and river of their nation to the English." He had in fact conveyed to Governor Phips title to lands on

St. Georges River without consulting his people. Egeremet, the Kennebec sachem, witnessed the transaction, and they both threw their hatchets into the sea "to make it impossible for them or their descendants to recover them again."[76]

Villieu informed Pierre Thury of this startling development and the priest "was quite prepared to believe it." When a letter from Father Bigot confirmed the sale, Thury and Villieu conferred with Taxous. "This had a wonderful effect," Villieu exulted. "Taxous, as chief, declared loudly that Madokawando had made peace, but as for himself he wished to make war and was preparing to set out." Waiting only for the arrival of Maliseet allies, Villieu gave a feast at which the warriors jeered Madockawando's relatives. In short, community contempt persuaded where French arguments had failed. Villieu was relieved. He had feared that without Madockawando's active support the Penobscot might have wavered even at the last moment.

The sachem's capitulation to community opinion unleashed quiescent Abenaki anger, but other problems surfaced. Repudiation of the 1693 Phips treaty could not resolve the intertribal tensions that wearied the war-torn peoples. Arriving at Durham, New Hampshire, exhausted and without food, Kennebec scouts sent Penobscot and Maliseet warriors to attack three small houses with "very little plunder." The allies were displeased to discover that the Kennebec had reserved for themselves a richer, more densely settled site where they killed 104 persons and took 27 captive. Piqued by this ill treatment, Taxous grew even more exasperated when young Kennebec warriors declined to share their captives—a request, Villebon remarked, not normally "refused between chiefs." Despite the affront, the Penobscot "set out to crack a few heads in a surprise raid north of Boston."[77]

Far from simply inciting the Abenaki to war, the French based wavering policies on careful analyses of existing intratribal factions and negotiated earnestly between rival interests. In contrast to English enmity, the Abenaki found, even in feeble French support, some substance for alliance. Then, too, Sir William Phips's greed left them little choice. Their decision to make war came at great cost, and some Abenaki soon regretted renewed hostilities. Starvation threatened them throughout the war, and the desire to free their countrymen held in Boston grew more intense. All of this led to heated arguments.

War produced a political crisis among the Abenaki because it damaged traditional tribal methods of reaching consensus. When Madockawando secretly conveyed lands to Phips, he undermined the prestige of all sachems. His self-interest made suspicion common in Abenaki politics, and French eagerness to use such emotions aggravated divisions within the tribes. Rival factions particularly troubled the Penobscot, but more fundamental problems ensued. When their sachems acquiesced to headstrong Kennebec warriors in 1693, the leaders' authority collapsed. It is significant that the French, rather than the English, appreciated these social problems—even while they contributed to them. It remained for the Jesuits to attempt to mitigate tensions.

# 5

# SEEKING NEUTRALITY

*Abenaki Diplomacy in Intercolonial Relations*

Because the English did not recognize their own responsibility for the first two Abenaki wars, they could not reach any agreement with the Abenaki. To compound this miscommunication the English saw the Abenaki-French alliance only as a religious threat. New Englanders claimed that Canadian officials incited the tribes to war. They believed that the French bought allegiance with arms, ammunition, trade goods, and provisions. New Englanders concluded that "political priests" were playing on the Indians' ignorance of "true" religion and seducing them for the "perfidious" French Catholic cause. Such erroneous seventeenth-century beliefs have often misled historical investigators.

Historians who emphasize French conspiracies among the Abenaki are unaware that growing tensions between New France and New England did not cause King William's War. Rather, the Abenaki conflict alerted Quebec and metropolitan officials to New England's aggressions against its Indian neighbors. In witnessing the tribes' military prowess, the French were alerted to the extent of English vulnerability. Massachusetts remained convinced that it dealt with a religious conspiracy, and the French believed as earnestly that the Abenaki distrusted English character. In identifying with Indian complaints against the English, the French achieved common cause with the Abenaki.[1]

The French did threaten English interests in the Northeast, but New Englanders consistently exaggerated the role of French priests in the colonial wars. It followed that the English ignored Abenaki motives. The Jesuits did try to lead the tribes but were only partially successful. If Catholic and Calvinist zeal gave war a religious tinge, there is little evidence that these polarized passions affected the Abenaki. The Indians did not need theological proof of English duplicity when their own experience more than sufficed. Nor did French goods, lavish as they were, purchase loyalty. Even in the most generous years, there was never merchandise enough to meet Abenaki demand. Furthermore, although the French king wished to support the tribes during the war years, he failed to act accordingly. French largesse supplemented the Abenaki's trapping income, but traditional foods from agriculture, hunting, and gathering remained crucial. In short, the Abenaki-French alliance was based on something more than mutual economic or military advantage.

Still another reason accounts for English misunderstanding of French diplomacy among the tribes. While the Abenaki and the Acadian French opposed the English for related reasons during the 1680s, the outbreak of European war superseded local tensions. The English dismissed the causes of Indian anger and grew more convinced that the French were at fault. As a result, Massachusetts was unwilling to compromise with the tribes, forcing the Indians to make unpalatable choices throughout the colonial wars. The Abenaki might submit to a kind of martial law—virtual captivity under direct English control—or accept a newly vital but inadequate commercial and military association with the French. Caught in the middle, the Abenaki nevertheless held firm, refusing to submit to the English yet often resisting French leadership.

Only the missionaries recognized that military alliance directly threatened tribal autonomy. Working to ease resentments, the priests played a special, ongoing mediatory role that had no parallel in the haphazard vagaries of English diplomacy. Men like Jacques and Vincent Bigot and Sebastien Racle among the Androscoggin and the Kennebec and Louis-Pierre Thury among the Penobscot and Passamaquoddy were far more than the pernicious political agents the English believed them to be. Speaking for the tribes to war-harried officials in Quebec, the priests were largely responsible for whatever success French policy enjoyed. They sometimes appealed the Abenaki's case directly to metropolitan officials in France. On other occasions they neutralized conflicts arising from official diffidence and disagreements over trade.[2]

The Jesuits became political middlemen because Canadian officials appreciated the trust the priests had won among the tribes. Since the government relied heavily on the Jesuits for vital information about Abenaki morale, French officials quickly heeded the missionaries' demands. They realized that the priests listened to the Indians attentively and reported faithfully. In fact, the missionaries' overwhelming influence, accompanied by their commitment to eradicate French abuse, accounts for the remarkable response of an otherwise cumbersome French bureaucracy. Ineffective as French policy remained, it had no counterpart in English diplomacy. Because the English held the Abenaki at arms length, the Abenaki of course embraced the French.[3]

After 1693 Abenaki, French, and English responded only to the events of the moment and were largely incapable of resolving fundamental tensions. The English relied so extensively on written treaty agreements that even their awareness of English frontier aggressions did not clarify the tribes' position. Phips's treaty marked the Abenaki's submission, so the English thought, and subjects they would be. The French, conversely, posed an even more serious threat to the tribes because they endangered tribal solidarity in ways that the English did not. Priests, traders, and officers had but to warn of English treachery to engender angry, partisan disagreements within and between the tribes. And the French missed no opportunity to recall past English transgressions.

Caught up as the English and French were in their own strategic interests, none of the English and few of the French comprehended the Abenaki's diplomatic purposes. Historians have made the same mistake. The intercolonial wars have obscured the tribes' attempts to find some middle ground between the Euramerican colonies. If historians have erroneously placed blame for the outbreak of King William's War on French instigation, they have also failed to examine the role that the Abenaki played in the conflict. The tribes were neither complacent nor passive. They relentlessly pursued several limited objectives—attempting to make peace, to establish commercial relations, to protect their missionaries, and to placate Euramerican suspicions. But the ideal of alliance molded the tribes' every response. Even war, impelled as it was by anger, frustration, and the Abenaki desire for revenge, reflected that larger ideal.

Many of the Abenaki goals disturbed the French. During and after King William's War, Abenaki negotiations with the English directly threatened the defense of Canada and Acadia. After the 1697 Peace of

Ryswick the French began to quarrel among themselves about the implications of tribal diplomacy. As a result, French interference in tribal politics continued to provoke resentment. The priests, traders, and military officials might warn about English duplicity, but their own activities effectively alerted the tribes to another lie. The Abenaki realized that the French were as self-serving as the English. So the Indians pursued détente at every turn. They desired English trade yet clung to the syncretic Catholicism they shared with Jesuit missionaries. Ultimately, these purposes proved unacceptable to both the French and the English, and the Abenaki found themselves in the midst of another Euramerican war that began in 1702.

The period 1675—1713 thus established divisiveness as the fundamental issue at contest in the Northeast. Although Abenaki and French shared compelling religious beliefs, the advent of the intercolonial wars undercut even that common bond. It was one thing for the Abenaki to experience solidarity with particular Frenchmen who deserved trust. It was quite another to grapple with the strategic implications of an alliance with distant French governments in Quebec, Acadia, and Versailles. Alliance with the French became as troublesome for the tribes as relations with the English. The Abenaki did the best they could under the circumstances, meeting pragmatic politics with practical compromise.

## WAR AND TRIBAL DIPLOMACY

When the tribes returned to war in 1693 they repudiated the treaty signed with Sir William Phips, permanently embittering relations with the English. Since Governor Phips did not comprehend the nature of Abenaki politics, he had taken Madockawando's and Egeremet's word that they would bind their tribes to peace. The sachems, of course, could not enforce their pledge, especially when they sealed their promise with a controversial surrender of prominent Abenaki hostages. Wrongly assuming that the sachems represented tribal willingness to capitulate, Phips himself imposed extreme expectations on the agreement. He confidently declared that "their Subjection now made will oblige them to be cautious of any new eruption."[4]

Given this unrealistic sense of tribal diplomacy, Phips became even more intransigent after the tribes' renewed outbreak. Since the Abenaki had submitted to English authority, he expected them to seize the warriors responsible for the attack "that they may be taken into safe custody, and proceeded against according to Law as False Traitors, Rebels and Murderers." In what had long since become an English tradition, Phips also ordered the militia "to surprise and seize what and so many of the Indians as you can, and bring them away with you, that we may oblige the return of our Captives and delivery of ye principal Murderers."[5]

Bluster and duplicity remained the major tools of Phips's diplomacy, although he might have used trade to bring the tribes to terms. A year after the return to war, the Abenaki again decided to negotiate for the return of their captives and to reestablish trade. (The French themselves observed that the Indians were "much afflicted" because they had not received the king's supplies in 1694.) Convinced that discussion was impossible, the English responded with violence. Four Abenaki were killed while visiting Fort Mary at Saco in early November 1694. A few weeks later, Bomazeen, a Kennebec sachem, and two companions inquired after Abenaki captives held at Boston. They too were taken captive. William Stoughton, the lieutenant-governor acting in Phips's absence, stated publicly his conviction that the dead and captured "were doubtless now sent for Spies."[6]

Completely disregarding the Abenaki's anger at this fresh evidence of English treachery, Stoughton indicated that he would negotiate, but only on his terms. The Abenaki were not impressed. They had no reason to fear Stoughton's threat to prosecute severely "the Chiefs and Savages" responsible for the repudiation of Phips's treaty. Nor did they accept his demand that they release all English prisoners along with the warriors who had "assisted and acted in this bloody tragedy." Instead, the Abenaki replied energetically:

> Writing with too much haughtiness, thou obligest me to reply to thee in the same style. Now, then, listen to the truths I am about to tell thee of thyself; of thee, who dost not speak the truth when thou sayest that I kill thee cruelly. . . . Thy heart must ever have been addicted to wickedness and deceit. . . . Thou hast covered [the flag of truce] with blood; As for me, I could never resolve even to act in that manner, for therein I have an extreme horror of thy unparalleled treachery.

Nonetheless, the Abenaki proposed to exchange prisoners within thirty days. They also admonished: "Take special care not to fail in what I tell thee. If thou dost not obey exactly, thou will draw down calamities on thyself, thy cattle, thy provisions and all thy substance."[7]

Apparently the English disregarded the threat. On the appointed day they failed to meet the tribes. Late in May 1695, however, the Abenaki made yet another attempt to communicate. They traveled to Pemaquid to exchange captives only to hear an English excuse that contrary winds had prevented the transportation of prisoners. Both sides spoke heatedly but temporarily averted a crisis. The English commander gave the Indians a stone "as an emblem of the durability this peace ought to have; and the Indians conforming to their mode of expression, placed another Stone beside that of the English." The Abenaki also exchanged eight prisoners for promises that a later conference nullified: Massachusetts's commissioners demanded that the tribes surrender all captives while they themselves refused to release any Abenaki until this condition was met. The tribal spokesmen "broke off the conference" in anger.[8]

While the English fumbled with these Abenaki overtures, after 1693 French officials embraced political realism to keep the tribes at war. If the alliance was to meet Canada's military needs, compromise with the tribes was essential. Basically, Commander Villebon in Acadia and Canadian officials at Quebec understood the delicacy of alliance in ways that both the English and administrators in France could not. Villebon argued that it was imperative that the French join Abenaki warriors against Fort William Henry at Pemaquid, an objective the tribes had long advocated. The alliance would then be secure, he claimed. While the Abenaki resented the fort, it also attracted them "with all sorts of merchandise." Villebon added a strategic consideration sure to capture the ministry's attention: with Fort William Henry demolished, the French could extend their border to the Kennebec River, where one officer and a few soldiers could deter English expansion. Writing from Quebec Intendant Champigny stuck a comparable note in advising French officials that the Abenaki, if pressed to exasperation, were quite capable of destroying settlements in Canada itself. In short, French colonial authorities were worried, about "the lovers of peace [among the tribes] who desire to draw breath after so many years of fatigue"[9] and who resented even their allies.

Pierre Thury wrote with even more sensitivity in the fall of 1694. He advised that war produced intolerable tensions that superseded the Abenaki's affection for the French. Thury noted that only the desire to free their tribesmen and a need for supplies had led them to negotiate with Massachusetts. "All these considerations puts our savages in great perplexity, because by themselves they are not capable of resisting the English and of leaving their country to establish elsewhere, they can do

neither without exposing themselves to die of hunger and misery."
Moreover, the priest declared, the Abenaki resented hollow French
promises of aid. They knew they were caught between the callous
English and the demanding French. Without prompt aid, he emphasized, the Abenaki would turn against the French within a year.[10]

The desperation of the tribes can be glimpsed in accounts of the
Acadian fur trade, the only source of goods on which the Abenaki could
rely. In expressing relief that peace with the English had been aborted,
Intendant Champigny observed that renewed war meant the Acadians
could continue to profit from the fur trade. Indeed, in the spring of
1695 the minister of marine strengthened the connection between the
military alliance and commerce. The king himself admitted that the
annual presents could not meet Abenaki requirements and ordered that
the trade be conducted to undersell the English.[11]

Louis XIV's decision came none too soon. In June 1695 the Abenaki
told Villebon that they had again parleyed with the English because
they needed goods. To make matters worse, metropolitan authorities
had already decided that the allocation of annual gifts had to be revised.
This decision placed the western Abenaki in jeopardy and pushed them
that much closer to the English. The Kennebec and Penobscot were to
receive only two-fifths of the supplies instead of the half to which they
had grown accustomed. Another two-fifths was to be divided between
the Maliseet and Micmac. Apparently unaware of the western Abenaki's
predicament, the French naively thought that gift-giving, as the
Abenaki practiced it, would effectively convey the king's warm support. Villebon was therefore to reserve the remaining goods as presents
for visiting Indians.[12]

French policy, then, did adjust to tribal demands, but compromise
left much to be desired. In 1695 M. Tibierge was sent to examine
Acadian affairs and describe the Indian allies' economy. He agreed with
Villebon that it was vital to destroy Fort William Henry, if only to
preserve the fur trade for Acadians. Tibierge discovered that the Penobscot produced most of the furs and observed that since Saint Castin
possessed a fortune of some 40,000 livres, the trade was considerable.
He estimated that the Penobscot trapped 30,000 livres of fur annually—a sum that made the king's presents nominal at best. The scope of
this trade can be further glimpsed in a 1695 complaint lodged by the
Acadian Company against the Sieur de Villebon. The military commander refused to sell the company some 15—16,000 livres of beaver
pelts.[13]

Since the French could not supply the Abenaki with the goods they needed, the tribes continued to negotiate with the English. Again, their overtures failed. In 1695 the tribes angrily terminated discussions when the English refused to release hostages. "It is not considered necessary to put fire beneath their bellies" any longer, the French declared, "in order to induce them to visit the enemy with the bloody effects of a just fury." More important, the ship *Envieux* finally arrived with provisions. "What a strange thing is prejudice," Champigny exclaimed. The Abenaki had been so convinced "that the English were masters of the sea . . . that, had it not been for the arrival of this ship, I know not what result would have been expected from such excessive terror which overpowered in their minds all the good disposition they seemingly entertained, to be revenged on their enemies."[14]

In actuality, Abenaki successes came at prohibitive cost. The English frontiers were largely depopulated by 1695; thus, by driving settlers to inaccessible and better-defended towns, victory brought defeat. The Indians remained hostile, but, Canadian officials explained, they could not wage war over great distances. Thus, Frontenac and Champigny did not openly contradict the king, who had ordered the Canadians to abandon their defensive posture. They did, however, frankly detail the limits of military alliance and joined Villebon in urging an attack on Fort William Henry.[15]

Only English hostility kept the tribes at war. Despite Pierre Thury's vehement warnings, in 1696 both the Kennebec and Penobscot responded to an English invitation to trade. Early in the spring, when their needs were greatest, a party spent several days at Fort William Henry. Suddenly, the English boldly killed two of the Kennebec: Egeremet, a leading advocate of peace, and his son. Three soldiers seized Taxous, but a Penobscot warrior saved him. The English carried only one Indian into the fort and he cost them the lives of six men. The Abenaki lost three. They renewed war, killing twenty-three men to revenge Egeremet's death.[16]

Once again, French resolution bolstered the tribes just when they felt most discouraged. After two years of dilatory action, the minister of marine finally approved direct involvement. Pierre Le Moyne d'Iberville arrived with ships in August 1696, and the Abenaki were more than ready to lay siege to Fort William Henry. In contrast to the extreme provocation the fort had created, it fell without much struggle. Fearing the inevitable, Commander Chubb accepted Saint Castin's offer of protection. Thomas Hutchinson, an early Massachusetts historian, commented: "The reason of the garrison's requiring an extraordinary caution against the rage of the Indians, was this, they were conscious of their own cruelty and barbarity, and feared revenge."[17]

For a time the demolition of Fort William Henry accomplished all that the French had hoped for. The Abenaki startled the frontier with new energy and gave the English no respite. Early in 1697 they killed or captured thirty families near Boston. In July they killed fifteen or sixteen settlers and in their anger even burned one man in the Iroquoian manner. They successfully attacked Lancaster early in the fall and killed or captured twenty-six.[18]

The Abenaki remained steadfast in their opposition to Massachusetts but nevertheless grew increasingly exasperated with their French allies. On August 20 Pierre Thury and Taxous explained the Abenaki's frustration: "The Indians were getting restless because the ships had not arrived" and their provisions were desperately low. In October Father Thury and Penobscot representatives traveled to Quebec where Champigny responded to their demands for food and ammunition. Their situation remained critical, however, because the English had burned Kennebec and Penobscot crops the previous fall. The Abenaki found the winter of 1697–98 the most difficult in recent memory.[19]

The European peace treaty signed at Ryswick in December 1697 failed to bring relief. The English simply saw no need to deal with the tribes directly. English attitudes had stiffened during the 1690s as war repeatedly demonstrated that the Abenaki were able enemies. Faced annually with ignominious defeat, the English had increasingly blamed the French. As the war drew to a close, officials in England and Massachusetts attributed the Abenaki outbreak of 1688 to the instigation of the baron de Saint Castin. The English concluded that the tribes were subservient to the French. Massachusetts wrongly assumed that the European peace would halt the Abenaki along with their French allies.[20]

Massachusetts again paid a heavy price for its miscalculation. The Abenaki had not fought for the French, and they honored no European peace that disregarded their interests. The Massachusetts General Court complained: "It was discovered soon after the publication of the peace of Ryswick that a treaty between European princes however exalted and powerful was not sufficient to restrain American savages, who, even if they had some notion of international compact, were not willing to acknowledge, as binding, promises in which they had no voice." Although the legislature accurately assessed Indian sentiment, Massachusetts continued to rebuff Abenaki demands. The tribes had fought alone before King William's War began, and they remained at war after the Treaty of Ryswick. When Massachusetts exchanged captives with the French, there was not a single Abenaki among them. Since 1698 marked the tenth year of Indian captivity, the tribes were unwilling to respect a one-sided peace.[21]

Abenaki determination confronted the inexperience of the newly appointed governor of Massachusetts, Richard Coote, the earl of Bellomont. The tribes' persistent harassment of the frontier appalled Bellomont, and he added his own aggressive signature to Massachusetts's long-standing and ineffectual Indian policy. At first he believed "it would be easy to engage the Five Nations to make war on them and extirpate them." Later, he appealed to the French, informing Governor Frontenac that he had ordered the Iroquois to free their French captives. "I doubt not, Sir," Bellomont added, "but you will, on your part, also issue orders, for the release of all the King's subjects, both Christians and Indians." Frontenac, however, realized that the Abenaki would wage war until they had recovered all of their captive relatives.[22]

Frontenac's reply perplexed the agents Bellomont sent to muzzle the Indian enemy. They reported that in spite of the French governor's orders and "on the pretext that their own people were still detained at Boston" the Abenaki would not release their English prisoners. The agents refused to meet the Abenaki because, they argued, Indians were subject either to the French or English crown. Diplomatic differences should therefore be discussed by the colonial governors rather than with the tribes themselves. Failing to comprehend obvious political realities, Bellomont's agents threatened the French governor when they learned of a recent Abenaki war party. They bluntly stated that "unless Count Frontenac disciplined his Indians better, obliging them to release their prisoners and preventing them from sending out hostile parties, Lord Bellomont would find the means to bring him to reason."[23]

Ignoring repeated warnings from French officials, Bellomont followed a needlessly complex plan to force Abenaki submission. In August 1698 he asked the Skachkook to persuade the Abenaki "to make a perpetual peace" and migrate west. The governor's thinking seems confused because he realized that the Skachkook were not close English allies. He observed that they had "been driven out of the eastern parts by the New Englanders, [and] are still acknowledged by the Eastern Indians [the Abenaki] as part of themselves." Nevertheless, while the Skachkook did not act as intermediaries, the overture itself was important. In January 1699, when the Abenaki finally renewed Phips's 1693 treaty, an uneasy peace settled over the frontier.[24]

## THE IDEOLOGY OF INDIAN WAR

The English found it difficult to reopen lines of communication with the Abenaki. Good faith was not entirely lacking, for the English earnestly wished for peace. But they did not expect it. The English truly did not understand why the tribes had resisted for the better part of twenty-five years. For both the settlers and the government the inter-colonial wars proved the conspiratorial collusion between the Indians and the French. The end of King William's War failed to change that conviction.

The colonial English and French knew that the Treaty of Ryswick created only a brief interlude in an ongoing European conflict. Under the circumstances, suspicions were natural, and the English fervently believed that the Abenaki were merely biding their time. They feared that the tribes waited for the inevitable outbreak. The Abenaki, for their part, had no love for the English, but peace was a welcome respite. While they genuinely attempted to reassure the English, the Abenaki's continued attachment to the French Jesuits undercut all their protests. In short, the painful Indian war had conditioned the English to expect the worst.

The war years were bitter for New England, and the survivors remembered painfully once prosperous towns and villages now reduced to ashes. Both King Philip's and King William's wars undermined New England's sense of confidence. Orthodox opinion—repeated weekly at meetinghouse, deplored annually in days of fasting, and trumpeted in election sermons—reminded faithful Protestants of the sorry spiritual digressions that had drawn disasters on them. Twenty-three dead and twenty-six captured at Quochecho; thirty slain at Salmon Falls, with another fifty led into *"the worst captivity in the world"*; fifty dead at York, and a hundred carried away; ninety-four lost at Oyster River, and a hundred other places fallen to Abenaki onslaught. Such dramatic sorrow quickened New England's sense of religious crisis. Neither outlying farms, garrison houses, nor forts hindered the feared Indian and French enemy.[25]

But not all New Englanders so internalized responsibility for the devastation. Settlers on the frontier felt only what seemed to be frenzied oppression. The English recalled the carnage—war whoops, flashing tomahawks, murdered children. These became the images of a fury they did not comprehend as the heritage of their own defensiveness. They could not understand the Indians' sense of legitimate war. Instead, symbols of annihilation merged with memories of religious conflict. Colonization had begun with the certainty that French Jesuits would wreck havoc on the new Israel. Seventy years later it was evidence enough that French and Abenaki had conspired together and struck like arbitrary lightning. Such an ideology of conflict was now firmly set in the English mind.[26]

English relations with the Indians contrast dramatically with the accommodation achieved between French and Abenaki. The royal charter of Massachusetts had asserted that the principal end of English settlement was "to win and invite the natives of the country to the knowledge of the only true God and Savior of Mankind." No such effort was made toward the Abenaki. As the seventeenth century closed, Reverend Cotton Mather decried English irresponsibility: ". . . had we done but half so much as the *French Papists* have done, to proselyte the *Indians* of our east unto the *christian faith*, instead of being *snares and traps* unto us, *and scourges in our sides, and thorns in our eyes*, they would have been *a wall unto us both by night and day.*"[27]

New England's symbolic reaction to the wilderness and to the Indians who inhabited it forms a haunting theme in the region's historical consciousness. Influential colonials believed that angry Indians reflected the disorder of English social and spiritual life. "God is not among us," Cotton Mather declared to the General Court in 1689. It seemed to the English that wilderness overwhelmed their communities. At least for Mather, Indians provided a bad example. They were infamous for three scandalous vices that the English imitated. Indians are "*liars* of the first magnitude; one cannot believe a word they speak." Moreover, complained Mather, they are sluggards, refusing to work. Finally, "they are abominably indulgent of their children; there is no *family government* among them." While the English embraced all these faults, Mather argued that they were especially foolish to indulge their children. Fathers refused to discipline their families despite widespread spiritual scandal. "But O how much do our people Indianize in every one of those abominable things!"[28]

Other New Englanders recognized the problem, but this theme of spiritual irresponsibility and the divine justice of Indian retribution found its fullest explication in Cotton Mather's writings. His awareness of God's anger intensified during King William's War. He realized that

English failure to regulate Abenaki relations created the conditions for Jesuit success. "God forbid that a *Popish Priest* should out do a *Protestant Minister* in his Industry," Mather exclaimed. He admitted that poor relations with the English had alienated the Indians. As one official on the frontier noted: "I Observ'd the Jesuits allwayes gain'd more on them by their blamless watchfull carrage to them then by any other of their artfull methods. Example is before preceipt wth them." Although Mather did not approve the methods by which Jesuits "Diaboliz'd" the Abenaki, he came to the same conclusion: English behavior invariably scandalized Indians.[29]

Mather believed that the frontier settlers provoked divine wrath. "*Let not People be any more so Foolish, as to think of taking Root, in Ungospellized Settlements; Lest I Once more do Suddenly Curse their Habitations,*" the Puritan God thundered. "Sirs," Mather avowed, "You cannot but look on Sin as your main *Troubles*, the main Author of all your *Troubles*." Mather enumerated a long list of frontier vices but particularly condemned the covetousness of English traders of rum—"That *Branch* of the *River of Death*." He promised that when the Abenaki found themselves suffering hellish torments, they would upbraid the settlers: " '*Tis you English men, that have brought us hither!*' "[30]

Mather reacted even more furiously because the Jesuits taught the Abenaki "to uphold a *Daily Worship of God* in their Families." The minister remonstrated: "It has even struck a cold Horror upon us, when we have been told, That some of our *English* People never heard a *Family-Prayer* in their Lives, till they came into the *Wigwams* of the Indians." The self-appointed prophet concluded that English-induced drunkenness was far worse than Jesuit idolatry. "Both of them are Damnable; but *your part* is far more inexcusable than *Theirs*," he decried. "They *think*, that they *Save* the Souls of the *Pagans*, you *know* that you *Damn* them." In such terms Mather expressed an ingrained English fear of wilderness: the frontier corroded the carefully constructed social regulations that ensured domestic and international order.[31]

This thinking had tragic implications for English relations with the Abenaki. For the English could not conceive that the Indians also regretted war and sought peace. Mather expressed a common denial: since the Abenaki had no community life, they could not be trusted. He claimed that the great God who creates war "had further intentions to chastize a *sinful people* by those who are *not a people*." In his history of Massachusetts, *Magnalia Christi Americana*, Mather denied English responsibility while simultaneously castigating the settlers for inciting hostility. He transformed Abenaki humanity into bestiality, calling Indians "ravening savages," "rapacious wolves," "serpents," and "monsters." He thus reminded the English of the greater war between the city of God and the devil's wilderness. Mather believed that the war itself derived from Indian witchcraft. Their "chief *Sagamores*," he claimed, "are well known unto some of our captives to have been horrid *sorcerers*, and hellish *conjurers*, and such as conversed with *daemons*." The French alliance with the Abenaki, added Mather, further perverted nature. The "half Indianized French, and half Frenchified Indians," combined Catholic and pagan corruption. French officers, Mather reported in inflammatory terms, armed themselves with relics and indulgences.[32]

Adding a final distortion of tribal sentiments, Mather said that the Abenaki deplored the way in which Catholicism had corrupted them. While captive in Boston, Bomazeen supposedly admitted that the Jesuits had misrepresented the true Christian religion. According to Mather, Bomazeen declared that

> the *French* taught 'em, that the Lord Jesus Christ was of the *French Nation*; that his mother, the virgin *Mary*, was a *French Lady*; that they were the English who had murdered him; and that whereas he rose from the dead, and went up to the Heavens, all that would recommend themselves unto his favour, must revenge his quarrel upon the *English* as far as they can.[33]

Because King William's War was otherwise inexplicable, the minister blamed the French and their satanic allies from the invisible world. He was especially graphic in reporting the strange experiences of the town of Gloucester. Although far from the frontier and heavily armed, Gloucester was infested by spectral Indian and French forces. Mather's published account of the month-long engagement quoted one minister's conclusion: ". . . the *devil* and his agents were the cause of all the molestation which at this time befel the town. . . . I would take upon me to entreat your earnest prayers to the Father of mercies, that those apparitions may not prove the sad *omens* of some future and more horrible molestations to them."[34]

As a result, when the English began to reexamine relations with the Abenaki, their fears of Jesuit intrigue guaranteed continued misunderstandings. The government thought that trade would control the tribes, but amicable commercial relations could not dissipate distrust. Since the English had no personal contact with the tribes, antipathy for the Jesuits soon convinced them that a "papist" conspiracy leavened all

Indian attempts to communicate. In November 1699, for example, Captain Silvanus Davis and John Nelson reported that Indians around Casco Bay were "uneasy and imperious." Two hundred Abenaki gathered and demanded to know whether the Earl of Bellomont intended "to dispose of their land without their consent." Unfortunately, Davis and Nelson interpreted this query in conventional terms. They advised that the tribes ought to be provided with inexpensive goods and argued that forts should be erected "to maintain our boundaries with the French." They also urged "strict measures" against private traders and "that all prudent means be taken for the removal of the French missionaries."[35]

The Massachusetts council agreed with this practical advice and provided £300 of goods to be sold to the Abenaki. But distrust remained. "Nobody doubts," reflected Governor Bellomont, "but that the French missionaries prompt 'em to this insolence, and how to help it I cannot tell." The governor did believe that the "most natural and proper way" to end the threat would be to settle Protestant missionaries among the Abenaki. But he confessed that he "could find none that will go and live among and teach the Indians Christianity."[36]

Lord Bellomont grew increasingly disturbed during the winter of 1699 — 1700. Rumors traveled the length of the frontier from Casco Bay to Albany, New York. Everyone feared that the Indians intended a mass uprising. Various alarms included the Mohawks, all of the Five Nations, the Canadian mission Indians, the Pennacook, and the Abenaki in the anticipated insurrection. Some hotheaded English advised Bellomont to disarm the Indians, but he was cautious enough to refuse. Rumors flew with winter snow, expressing English certainty that an outbreak was imminent. "We are satisfied a great war is intended," said Benjamin Sabin, "not as of old a paganish, but [now a] papist war."[37]

To calm these apprehensions, Bellomont issued a proclamation in March 1700 addressing Indians' corresponding fear of English treachery. He directed all English subjects "to endeavour by all opportunities and possible wayes . . . to undeceive the sd Indians, and to inform them of the utter falsehood and untruth of any such reports." But in also ordering the settlers "to repel and resist any hostile attack or Violence," he did little to calm the frontiers.[38]

Lord Bellomont was as misled as the settlers. He accepted as fact innumerable reports that Catholic missionaries incited the Indians' furor, declaring that "if some Indians inform us aright, the Governor of Canada is as deep in the design as his Jesuits." Colonel Romer, an engineer who inspected frontier forts at Bellomont's request, confirmed the governor's bias. Romer reported that four Jesuits lived on the Kennebec River, claiming that they "do great hurt to the King's interest, and that of the public, because they instil into those people hatred for his Majesty and his Subjects." He noted that two more Jesuits resided at the head of Saco River. Because of the "horrible cruelty of French papists and Indian Infidels," Romer recommended extensive fortifications along the eastern frontier.[39]

Exaggerated English fears underlay the rumors of conspiracy. Suckquans, one of the Skachkook sachems, reported that many Indians believed that "the English of New England were so jealous of their Indians that they would not suffer them to go out a hunting without some English went [with them], and gave them so little powder that they could not go far." In the same vein Robert Livingston, an Englishman who understood Indian affairs, wrote from Albany: "We are fearful here that the English to the eastward are too rigid and jealous of their Indians, and their keeping them so in awe does rather exasperate them [rather] than keep them under." The New Yorker decried the "unskilful management of Indian affairs [which] have formerly proven very fatal to that country."[40]

In effect, Bellomont had inherited an Indian problem that required him to assuage frontier fright. Given the circumstances, the governor could do little. Lieutenant Rayment wrote from York county that the Indians inquired why there "was so many souldiers posted there." When Rayment replied "because the Indians threatened to make war and burn the English houses," the Abenaki expressed surprise. One sachem, called Captain Tom, vowed that they intended no such outbreak "because the English and they were Brothers." While he did claim that the Pennacook felt disaffected, Captain Tom also emphasized that the Abenaki remained friendly. In any case, Rayment reported that the Indians could not afford to go to war. Unsuccessful at hunting, the Abenaki were "very poor and pinch't for want of provisions."[41]

Neither Bellomont nor the New England governments under him found the Abenaki's economic dependence reassuring. Under Bellomont's direction the General Assembly of New Hampshire sent an impassioned plea to King William in April 1700. The petition described the ordeals New Hampshire had suffered at the hands of a "barbarous and Treacherous Enemy" whose "bloody Nature and perfidy" was further excited by "Popish Emissaries from ffrance who have taught 'em that breaking faith with, and murdering us is the Sure way to gain paradise." Denouncing the vile deeds of French priests, the assembly accused the Jesuits of "poysoning" the Abenaki with their "Hellish Doctrines." This memorial was all the more remarkable for its unsubstantiated presumption that the Society of Jesus was subversive and for its blindness to English provocation of the tribes.[42]

A few Englishmen displayed a levelheaded sense of the issues, because they knew that the Jesuits had not instigated the Indians to a new war. Peter Schuyler, Robert Livingston, and H. Hansen, who had firsthand information, reported that the Onondagas were "wholly ignorant of any ill design the Eastern Indians [Abenaki] have upon the English." In Massachusetts Samuel Sewall saw clearly that the peace treaty was too general. "I should think it requisite," reflected Sewall, "that convenient Tracts of Land should be set out to them; and that by plain and natural Boundaries, as much as may be; as Lakes, Rivers, Mountains, Rocks, Upon which for any English man to encroach, should be accounted a Crime." Sewall also believed that without such regulations "the French Friers will persuade them, that the English, as they encrease . . . will never leave till they have crouded them quite off their Lands."[43]

Bellomont remained convinced, however, that the confrontation derived only from French schemes among the Abenaki. "As the French apply themselves to court them from us," he rather inaccurately declared, "our caresses must increase, any bare compliments will not do with them." The governor told the Massachusetts legislature and council that "the French Missionaries have debauched the Eastern Indians from their obedience to the King." He added: "I wish you would this session without further delay make a law for punishing such Popish missionaries." His reasoning stemmed from false assumptions about the way in which the Abenaki ought to behave. In accusing the Jesuits of "debauching" the Indians, Bellomont wrongly implied that the tribes had promised subjection to the king. He imagined that they would be more submissive if the priests were removed. On June 6, 1700 a joint committee began "to consider methods to obviate the industry of the French Missionaries in debauching the Five Nations, and to bring the Eastern Indians, under the obedience of His Majesty." Eleven days later the General Court banished Jesuits from all territories claimed by Massachusetts. Such were the methods of Bellomont's diplomacy.[44]

The governor clearly failed to perceive the basic issues that troubled English relations with the Abenaki. Consequently, he advocated policies that only served to increase tensions. In a candid moment Bellomont admitted to "our want of care, and indeed of justice and kindness" which drove the tribes to the French. But his policies passed over these problems. He saw no reason to trust Abenaki claims of friendship: "All the thinking people here believe the Eastern Indians will break out against the English in a little time."[45]

Under Bellomont's guidance, in an effort to guard against the outbreak the English feared, the General Court reenacted a law regulating trade with the Abenaki. Aware that itinerant traders abused the tribes, the government designated the fort at Casco the exclusive trading post. To attract Indians to that site, the governor stationed a gunsmith at the fort to repair firearms and sharpen hatchets. These concessions pleased the tribes, but the trading act met only some of their needs. Because the truckhouse was so far from the centers of Abenaki population, illegal traders continued to exploit the situation. Even the Council of Trade and Plantations in London learned of colonial dissatisfaction with Massachusetts's trading laws.[46]

Even as Bellomont initiated these limited commercial concessions, he attacked Jesuit influence among the Abenaki. The General Court funded salaries for "three able Learned Orthodox Ministers" to teach Indians the "true Christian Religion." In September 1700 the Reverend Jonathan Remington became chaplain at Fort Mary in Maine "to instruct the Indians." In December another missionary was attached to the new fort on Casco Bay. These developments heartened Lieutenant-Governor Stoughton, for he particularly despised Jesuits. He thanked Father Bigot for assisting English prisoners during the previous war but nonetheless denounced the Jesuits' "pernicious and damnable principles." Stoughton believed that "papist" intrigues meant that the Abenaki were "not to be trusted on their most solemn protestations of fidelity."

It mattered little that Father Bigot objected to English views of the Society of Jesus. Stoughton addressed the priest frankly: I can offer you no encouragement in teaching English subjects "your idolatries," Stoughton began. "It would be more pertinent & profitable for you to Repent of your Blasphemies belched out against the Most pure and holy Christian Religion which we profess." He concluded: "I strictly Comand & Require you to withdraw your self out of the King of England's Jurisdiction, where you now are, and that you cease from levening the Indians with your pernicious principles & practises."[47]

Bellomont had yet another plan to leash the Abenaki—this one was the least likely to succeed. At an August 1700 meeting with the Skachkook at Albany he suggested that they invite the Abenaki to settle in eastern New York. Because several Abenaki attended the meeting,

Bellomont was encouraged that they might accept his proposal, especially if it came from the Skachkooks. He himself made no effort to speak to them. To further this plan, Bellomont recommended that beaver and other furs be admitted custom-free into England because the Abenaki and other Indian allies of the French would be attracted to settle among the Iroquois.[48]

The Abenaki responded directly to Bellomont's policies when they met Massachusetts commissioners on June 3, 1701. Lieutenant-Governor Stoughton hoped that an agreement could be reached to prevent the tribes from "being debauched by the French" and that "presents and assurances of full supplies for Trade" would win them to English interests. Thus, when the commissioners offered the Abenaki protection "against any that shall invade or disturb you," they implied that they had the French in mind. The Indian spokesmen rejected this offer, preferring to look first to their own defense. The commissioners then accused Acadian traders of cheating the Abenaki and therefore asked that relations with the French be terminated. The tribes again demurred and observed that if they did reject the French, they would not be allowed to visit relatives living in Canada. "Besides," the delegates explained, there are "many amongst us [who] care not to be deprived of the liberty of going wither they please."[49]

The Abenaki carefully looked after their own interests, even when they confronted extreme English demands. But they shrewdly placated the commissioners in declaring that they saw little necessity of "going to the French since we may be so well supplied with what we want from the English." They did appreciate learning about "the likelyhood of a War." With the bitter experience of past conflicts in mind, the Abenaki declared: "We desire to keep ourselves free and not under command of any party." They also proposed a practical way to resolve disagreements, asking that the English consult them before they were blamed for any attack that might occur.

Curiously, the commissioners ignored this vital attempt to improve communications. Instead, they reminded the Abenaki of the practical benefits of trade "so that you may have no pretence or occasion of going to Canada or to the French in these parts for want of this or any supply whatsoever." In turn, Indian spokesmen ignored English concerns about the French and merely inquired if the Penobscot, who were not present, might be included in the new trade agreement.

While the tribes were willing to compromise on many issues, they responded heatedly when the commissioners maligned the religious core of the French alliance. The English invited them to join "the true

Christian Religion" that did not espouse "those foolish superstitions and plain idolatries" the Jesuits taught. These remarks aroused the Abenaki's truest sentiment. "It much surprizeth us that you should propose any thing of Religion to us," they declared, "for we did not think any thing of that nature would have been mentioned." The Abenaki reminded the English that they had never before offered to teach them anything about religion. "Being instructed by the French," they ended the discussion, "we have promised to be true to God in our Religion, and it is this we profess to stand by."

This meeting startled both the commissioners and the Abenaki. The English had assumed, as had Bellomont, that the Indians would reject the French as soon as their need for trade was met. Furthermore, they believed that the Abenaki would eagerly accept Protestant missionaries. The religious issue defined the basic division between tribal and English interests. While the Indians required commerce and favored neutrality in any intercolonial conflict, they would not repudiate their priests. Successful relations, as the English slowly discovered, required something more than inexpensive trade goods and perfunctory offers of true religion.

The Abenaki nevertheless favored attempts to maintain peace, as they informed the English in December 1701: "If there should happen to be War between England and France we would have all calm and quiet in this Land. . . . [and] not have it affect us." They also requested that two sloops loaded with blankets and provisions be sent to the major rivers to trade. The council's favorable response pleased the Abenaki delegates. "Now the Country will all see That the Peace is more strong," an Abenaki named Sampson Hegin affirmed. Hegin was overoptimistic. The English continued to distrust Indian sentiments. When the Penobscot later requested the construction of a trading post at Pemaquid, the English refused, retorting that it would probably be destroyed if a war broke out.[50]

The conference of 1701 exposes the fundamental contradictions of Massachusetts's Indian policy. At a basic level, the commissioners' proposals revealed the impact of twenty-five years of frontier war. In attempting to persuade the tribes to forsake the French, English officials implied that the Abenaki had few serious grievances. Settlers and government assumed that French Catholic agents had instigated bloodly conflict, following Cotton Mather's religious interpretation of King William's War. The English further supposed that the tribes would perceive that their own interests lay in plentiful and inexpensive trade goods. As a result, Massachusetts policy increasingly relied on commercial bribery to win the Abenaki's regard.

## THE UNEASY PEACE

In both their vigorous war against New England and cautious alliance with the French, the Abenaki maintained political independence. But years of contact with Euramericans had changed the material circumstances of their lives. By the end of King William's War, guns, iron hatchets, kettles, hooks, cloth, and metal implements had replaced many traditional tools. Commercial hunting and trapping flourished, although agriculture and gathering activities remained important. These changes benefited Abenaki bands because trade goods were used in ways that strengthened social values. Nevertheless, acceptance of European material culture threatened Indian liberty.

Two factors disrupted the economic adaptation of the tribes in the seventeenth century: hostile relations with Massachusetts undermined the Abenaki's trapping economy and a positive relationship with the French involved them in the ongoing competition between France and England. Before contact, relations outside the hunting bands had been of little importance. Neither war nor peaceful intertribal relations had called into question the economic, political, or social integrity of Abenaki life. This stability prevailed until 1675, when King Philip's War made economic conflict pivotal. Abenaki desire for trade goods required constructive affiliation with the English, but the closing years of the century frustrated this connection.

Association with the French throughout King William's War complicated fundamental disagreements with Massachusetts. The Abenaki did not understand the ideological polarizations or the strategic concerns that divided Euramericans. In their response to both the French and English the tribes strove only to preserve the status quo. Throughout the war numerous rebuffs from Massachusetts drove them again and again to the French, who at least attempted to provide trade goods and for their own reasons nurtured the tribes' anger against the English.

Peace did little to ease tensions. The Treaty of Ryswick required that Canadian political and religious officials redefine relations with the Abenaki, and the Acadian commander Villebon found himself in the ironic position of implementing peace. It fell to the French to halt Abenaki raids on New England, and the French ministry expected Villebon to provide trade goods that would ensure fidelity. To Villebon's dismay, the policy worked no better in peace than it had in war. When the Abenaki finally concluded a treaty with Massachusetts in 1699, they indicated a preference for English goods. Furthermore, the English deliberately undersold even subsidized French goods.[51]

The French soon began quarreling among themselves over the potential effects of a commercial alliance between the Abenaki and the English. Villebon hoped that the tribes would prevent Massachusetts from resettling the Kennebec River, at least until an international commission could award the territory to the French. The tribes, however, refused to buffer New France and ignored Father Deschambeault's efforts to dissuade them from trading with the English. Their obstinacy came from long experience with the French. They had learned well the limits of alliance. Peace only brought missionary interference and reinforced Abenaki determination to serve their own advantage.[52]

Father Thury returned to a long since abandoned Jesuit goal: settling the Abenaki into a single village. Such a congregation would permit intensified agriculture and, more important, would simplify religious instruction. Throughout the war Thury had enjoyed official support in fighting the reluctance of Penobscot men to grow crops—traditionally a woman's task. Thinking that the Indians would eventually abandon the hunting economy that grounded their social and political identity and support themselves solely by farming, Thury worked toward modifying the Penobscot's economy. To some extent he succeeded. His postwar plans began with a village chapel to symbolize the Abenaki's religious and civil transformation.[53]

The scheme proved premature, for Thury could not convince the tribes to repudiate the seasonal mobility of their hunting and trapping economy. Although long allied with the French in religious sentiment, personal affection, and military enterprise, the tribes retained a lively autonomy. Eventually Pierre Thury admitted that resistance made his goals unrealizable. Because the Abenaki would not limit themselves to an agricultural economy, he transferred his ambitions to the Micmac.[54]

While the Abenaki did not wish to abandon their way of life, they sought to preserve a religious alliance with the French. In the fall of 1702 they sent a party of forty, headed by the Jesuit Pierre LaChasse, to visit Governor Louis-Hector Callière of New France. Aware that the Canadians feared English influence among the Indians, the Abenaki declared that they were ready to obey the French governor. He welcomed such reassurance and to allay their frankly admitted need for English trade gave them guns, powder, and shot. Although Callière could not provide the gunsmith they required, he did offer to repair their arms and sharpen their hatchets free of charge at Quebec. Moreover, he promised to open a trading post that would serve them at reasonable cost.[55]

Trusting that Catholicism would bind the Abenaki firmly to the French, Callière took a tolerant but cautious view of their relations with the English. He spoke against the hidden treachery of the English but urged the tribes not to strike the first blow lest peace be jeopardized. Callière did compliment the Indians for rejecting Protestant ministers and assured them that Catholicism was "the only road to eternal happiness." Finally, the governor vowed that the Jesuits would continue to teach and advise the Abenaki.

To maintain positive relations between the Jesuits and Abenaki during the tense opening years of the eighteenth century, Callière had to give the priests his unqualified support. The missionaries not only met active opposition from Massachusetts but came under severe criticism from Acadian officials and traders. Convinced that the English could not be trusted with the Abenaki, many Acadians disagreed with Callière's caution. Arguing among themselves, the priests themselves reflected the larger debate over Abenaki relations with the English. As early as 1699 Sebastien Racle and Vincent Bigot differed over tribal negotiations with Massachusetts. To avoid scandal the Jesuit superior recalled Racle, probably because he opposed the English.[56]

Two years later Acadian Governor Jacques-François de Brouillan still feared that inexpensive English trade goods would turn the Abenaki against the French. Although in general he praised the Jesuits, Brouillan criticized one of the Bigot brothers for allowing the tribes to make peace, and later Brouillan lodged a similar complaint against Father Anthony Gaulin, who lived among the Penobscot. Metropolitan officials shared the governor's concerns: Bigot was withdrawn in the spring of 1702 and Racle returned to the Kennebec.[57]

The Sieur de Villieu, an officer working among the Abenaki, agreed with Brouillan's estimation and castigated the Jesuits repeatedly. He complained to the minister of marine that the priests went so far as to cultivate friendships among the English. Villieu boasted that he would harrass Gaulin from his Penobscot mission. The priest strongly resented being labeled a "seditious and turbulent spirit" and asserted that Villieu wished to sell the Penobscot liquor and to "cheat them right and left." Despite the priest's anger, Villieu continued to supply the Penobscot with brandy. Appalled that the French would undermine the religious alliance, village sachems, with Gaulin's earnest support, accosted Villieu. They pointed out that the French liquor trade had turned the Maliseet into drunkards just as the English had corrupted the Kennebec. They warned Villieu away from their village: "You can stay at the seashore with the other Frenchmen and we will come to trade there."[58]

Such incidents, coupled with Brouillan's vehement criticism of the Jesuits, deeply troubled Governor Callière, who complained to the minister of marine in November 1702. Asserting that Brouillan maintained a dangerous independence from Quebec, Callière feared that the Acadian governor would enforce contradictory policies among the Abenaki. The Canadian governor thus anticipated unnecessary confusion and asked the minister to eliminate the problem. Callière wanted Brouillan to comply with all orders sent to the governor-general of New France. Intendant François de Beauharnois joined Callière in urging that Abenaki affairs be administered from Quebec. Since the St. John post had been abandoned, he observed, the Indians would find it easier to collect supplies in Canada.[59]

While the French developed new administrative mechanisms to regulate Indian relations, the English began to seek a long-range accommodation with the tribes. The outbreak of war between England and France prompted the new governor of Massachusetts, Joseph Dudley, to placate the Abenaki. He went to the lower Kennebec River in July 1702 and, understanding that frontiersmen feared Indian attack, urged the tribes to remain east of the Saco River. He promised to send supplies directly to the Abenaki and asked that they inform him of any hostile parties, French or Indian. These proposals satisfied the Abenaki because they too realized that the settlers were paralyzed with anxiety. "The more we see the English stir about," they told Dudley, "the more we go amongst them, that they may not fear." The Abenaki knew the strength of their bargaining position, and when they asked for a trading house on the lower Kennebec, Dudley acquiesced. He also acknowledged their complaints about the cost of English trade goods. He told them that he would investigate the prices of goods at Boston and "let you have the goods as cheap as may be, and the merchants live."[60]

Some Englishmen distrusted Dudley's overtures and their sentiments illustrate the futility of any agreement that did not calm the frontier. John Wheelwright wrote from Maine to warn the governor that the Abenaki would be faithful only "So Long as it may stand with theire owne Interest." Wheelwright declared that the Indians would side with the French because the Jesuits taught them "that theire is no faith to be kept with Heriticks sutch as they account us to be." Although Dudley remained optimistic, he too feared the Jesuits. "Nothing but the French Priests amongst them will put them out of a temper towards us," he informed the Council of Trade. The governor continued to hear reports "that the French priests . . . are daily using means to draw [them] off from their obedience to H[is] M[ajesty]."[61]

Frontier alarms grew more intense throughout the winter of 1702– 03 but the tribes remained quiet, watching the English strengthen their defenses. Not even a violent incident between an Englishman and some French and Abenaki disturbed the peace. When a few Indians revenged the attack, Dudley and the sachems resolved the issue coolly. This is not to say that the tribes merely submitted to the governor's will. Many among them resented this fresh evidence of English treachery, and in June the Boston newspapers reported that the Abenaki were two-thirds "for peace and one Third for warr." In a meeting with the Indians Dudley chose to overawe the tribes with reports of English victories in Europe. He expected little difficulty from the Abenaki: "Indians are able like Wolves to disturb men," he bluffed, "but not to do them any damage; they are not able to hurt us in the least, and I value them not, no more than the paring of my nails." Such bravado masked Dudley's inability to muster Abenaki support. He asked them to apprehend war parties sent against the frontier and even offered the sachems commissions in the Massachusetts militia—all to no avail.[62]

The Abenaki politely declined involvement: "Their desire is to be as Neuters; not to medle nor make, nor to stir or act in any thing one way or other." The governor savored these sentiments and again offered the sachems military commissions in what he thought was an inoffensive manner: "And if I would honor them so far as to make them Captains and to send them a present now and then," Dudley said, "why it is honor: not that I desire they should be expos'd to fight upon any occasion." Still, the Abenaki remained aloof, remembering that events during King William's War had often misled them.[63]

Dudley interpreted the Abenaki's reticence as "Sullen Temper Demands" and failed to see that some of them did attempt to placate the English. Despite the professed neutrality of the tribes, one Kennebec sachem took a stand that threatened to compromise the Abenaki position. Fearing that the English would indiscriminately retaliate against the slightest sign of hostility, Moxus sent spokesmen to inform Dudley that a French ship had arrived at Mt. Desert Island. Grateful for this information, Dudley rewarded Kennebec delegates with new coats, shirts, neck-cloths, and hats.[64]

Even this bold maneuver could not alleviate growing tensions. The new French governor in Quebec, Phillippe de Rigaud de Vaudreuil, feared that Abenaki affections would be swayed by Massachusetts's commercial seductions. As Moxus understood all too well, Vaudreuil had abruptly terminated Callière's watch-and-wait policy and had sent officers to Maine to foment war. Moxus warned Dudley in vain. These Frenchmen, along with Micmac allies, found a few willing warriors among the Abenaki tribes. Their combined forces attacked Casco and Wells in August 1703.

As Vaudreuil had planned, Dudley's moderate diplomacy ended with this raid. That most Abenaki remained neutral was not apparent to the English, who failed to differentiate Indian friends from foes. Unlike Vaudreuil, Dudley could not manipulate Indian factionalism to serve his own advantage, not even to achieve peace. And much as the tribes wished to live in peace, they could not legally restrain their warriors. Massachusetts formally declared war on the Pennacook and Abenaki on August 18, 1703.[65]

The Abenaki's sudden involvement in Queen Anne's War exposes the problems the Jesuits faced in mediating between Quebec, Versailles, and the tribes. Although the English typically suspected that Jesuits incited the Abenaki to war, there is no evidence that they did so in this instance. In fact, if Brouillan's exasperation with the priests is any indication, some of them had actually supported the Abenaki's desire for neutrality. In 1702 Governor Brouillan of Acadia had accused Sebastien Racle of encouraging another tribal agreement with the English. The minister of marine reacted furiously and wrote to the Jesuit Superior in France ordering that the missionary be removed from the Kennebec. Racle realized his vulnerable position and attempted to mollify irate French officials. After the attack on Casco and Wells, with all chance of Abenaki neutrality aborted, he defused criticism by assuring Vaudreuil that "the Abenakis would take up the hatchet whenever he pleased."[66]

The Abenaki did not want military involvement in the war, and their missionaries helped them to avoid it. While Racle attempted to placate Vaudreuil, other Jesuits met at Norridgewock on the Kennebec River to discuss the desperate situation of the tribes. After weighing various alternatives, they urged the governor to harbor the Indians in new Canadian missions. In effect, the priests became mediators between

French officials and the tribes. Jesuit missionaries Anthony Gaulin and Joseph Aubéry argued convincingly that the Abenaki would starve without English trade. Furthermore, Vaudreuil believed that once relocated the Indians could form an effective barrier against the Iroquois. Both factors convinced the governor that an Abenaki move to Quebec was to their mutual advantage. By the outbreak of Queen Anne's War, then, the Jesuits had become strong advocates of Abenaki interests. Although forced to work around Vaudreuil's policies, the priests did their best to protect the tribes.[67]

Ironically, the minister of marine reversed French policy just when Vaudreuil pressed the unwilling tribes into the war. The minister did not accept the governor's assertion that Abenaki and English should be kept perpetual enemies. He preferred, in fact, that colonial officials work toward neutrality with New England. The minister feared that in recoiling from Indian aggressions, the English would persuade the Iroquois to abrogate the treaty they had signed with New France in 1701. Since the Abenaki had so "brilliantly" broken with the English, he understood that it would be difficult to restrain the warriors. Still, the minister believed that Vaudreuil should try to "dispose them to that Neutrality." Distance, however, confounded the minister's orders as it had during the previous war. By the time his dispatches reached Quebec, the migration of the tribes was already complete.[68]

The Abenaki themselves reacted to the proposed move with disturbed emotions, although most submitted in the end. In May 1704 the Androscoggin informed Intendant Beauharnois that they would move to Canada; his promises of new fields, fortifications, and a chapel helped to calm the more reluctant among them. Likewise, Vaudreuil assured the Indians that they would have the war materiel they needed. Despite official persuasions, however, the Saco flatly refused to leave their lands. While the Penobscot were also reluctant, they too eventually agreed to reside within French bounds. The governor reported that if the Abenaki "felt any difficulty in quitting their ancient abode, they acquiesced with a good faith when they understood our reasons."[69]

## QUEEN ANNE'S WAR AND THE HERITAGE OF EXILE

Queen Anne's War brought the Abenaki a new awareness of the negative effect of alliance with the French. Trusting French promises of aid, most moved to Canada to avoid active involvement. A few warriors participated in half-hearted raids against New England, but almost from the beginning the migration proved a mixed blessing. Governor Vaudreuil refused to accept Indian neutrality and only grudgingly provided them with necessary trade goods, food, and war materiel. And after 1700 the Canadian fur trade collapsed from oversupply, denying the Abenaki even a market. As the war passed, the tribes grew disillusioned and began acting for themselves.[70]

Nevertheless, the Abenaki had made a wise decision in abandoning their homes. Granted, Canadian conditions were difficult for the migrants, but the Jesuits had accurately anticipated Massachusetts's threat to the tribal villages in Maine. Under Dudley's leadership the English attacked directly. For the first time their forces marched during winter. "I hope," said Dudley, that "I shall keep the war at a good distance, but their waters and swamps Eastward are so unpassable that it is impossible to root them out." That this vigorous offense destroyed only deserted villages perplexed the English. They did not realize until 1706 that the Abenaki had abandoned their lands.[71]

Apart from a few desultory raids, the Abenaki soon became frustrated with the war. Vaudreuil heeded the minister's desire to limit the conflict but sent out small war parties to preserve the tribes' flagging friendship. Usually, mobile bands struck unexpectedly against the English frontier and then retired into the woods. Waged from Quebec, this extraordinarily arduous warfare achieved little. It is not surprising that the warriors began to lose interest and attacks diminished. This was the only war in which the Abenaki fought explicitly for the French and they were little motivated beyond their past resentment of the English. Most of them disliked life in the Canadian villages, and metropolitan indifference to their well-being made the war seem remote. Inadequate support discouraged them.[72]

Fear of losing Abenaki allegiance, lukewarm as it was, eventually prompted the minister of marine to provide more generous supplies. By 1707 he concluded that the tribes should be encouraged to attack New England. But it was not until 1708, when metropolitan officials learned that Massachusetts had serious military designs against Acadia, that the tempo of the war picked up. In a sudden turnaround the minister chastized Vaudreuil for his lax conduct: His Majesty, said the minister, "is not satisfied with the inactivity in which you remain with such numerous forces as you have." He ordered the governor to dispatch numerous parties against New England and even "to go yourself to attack them in their posts provided you be sure of success." He added that these bold campaigns were to be accomplished "at the least possible expense."[73]

The minister expected too much, too late. The Abenaki were no longer interested in fighting a French war. In response to the minister's order Vaudreuil replied that he had sent mission Indians—52 Algonkin, 30 Christian Iroquois, and 158 Abenaki—against New England. While he trusted "that consternation will be general," his allies were exasperated. In disgust, many of the Abenaki had already returned to Maine where at least they could hunt to support their families. Apparently some even settled among the Iroquois to avoid further involvement. To make matters worse, the Jesuits increasingly sympathized with Abenaki discontent. Sebastien Racle favored the migration home. He observed that drunkenness plagued his mission because it was too close to French taverns. Thoroughly discouraged in 1709 and wishing only for peace, the Abenaki still living in Canada asked if they might remain neutral for the remainder of the war. Under fire from France the governor refused, and Louis XIV later endorsed efforts to manage the Indians firmly.[74]

Denied support, chided for indifference, and seeking neutrality in their own fashion, the Abenaki left Canada in growing numbers. Although Queen Anne's War embittered them—they blamed the French for their weakened condition—the Abenaki remained close to the Jesuits who returned with them. But refusing to fight for the French did not convince the English that the tribes truly wished for peace. Prior to the war Joseph Dudley had relied on generous commercial concessions to bribe fearsome Indian tempers. At the end of the conflict he used the Abenaki's need for trade to impose his extreme demands. Dudley thus joined the French in transforming trade from a simple exchange between allies into the preferred instrument of imperial control.[75]

The Abenaki again learned that the English saw no need to placate them simply because of a European peace. In fact, when Kennebec spokesmen visited Captain Samuel Moody in January 1713 to express "a great deal of joy & Satisfaction at ye news of peace," they learned that they might be excluded from the final agreement. "What have you to do with this peace," Moody demanded, "& what if our Governr should Say you shall have no peace, what course would you take? where would you get your supply?" His questions confounded the Abenaki. Claiming that the French had deceived them, they promised to "comply with

Anything" Dudley wished. When Moody hinted that the English might still become their friends, they responded eagerly and asked for an end to war. Although Moody realized that they were "reduc'd to ye last extremity for want of provision," he told the Kennebec that he could not help them until spring.[76]

Moody browbeat the Abenaki into repudiating their alliance with the French. Governor Dudley had earlier requested Sebastien Racle to restrain the warriors, even though he himself refused to speak with them directly. The Abenaki had not attacked in the interim, but Racle would not interfere. The priest wrote to Dudley that Vaudreuil had put the hatchet in Abenaki hands and it was therefore the French governor's responsibility to remove it. By reading Racle's letter to the Abenaki, Moody tried to undermine the priest's influence. They answered only that "they were wholly ignorant of what their Minister had written and yt Monsr de Vaudreuil had nothing to do with them." They promised to "wholly renounce the French Interest" if Dudley "would receive them into favour once more."[77]

Like Moody, Governor Dudley felt little need to allay Abenaki anxieties. He informed Moody: "I will not see them nor speak further without first they deliver at your fort all the English prisoners in any of their hands." If they met this condition, they would be treated "with all kindness." Dudley added that he expected the sachems to surrender at least four children as hostages. He even ordered that they receive some English among them "to be witnesses of their good behavior." Pressed as they were, the Abenaki scorned his demands. Sebastien Racle especially disliked the idea of hostages and angrily denounced Dudley's audacity: "I had so often and so strongly talked" against surrendering hostages, the Jesuit told Vaudreuil that the Abenaki remained unyielding.[78]

Negotiations between the English and the tribes thus heralded a new era of disagreement. Governor Dudley immediately adopted a high-handed approach to the Abenaki and refused to meet the assembled peoples in Maine. Instead, he insisted that their sachems meet him in New Hampshire so that terms could be reached without complicated intra- and intertribal discussion. The governor opened the meeting forcefully. He threatened that "it will be the hardest thing to perswade the Queen of Great Britain to take them into ffriendship." The sachems ignored this threat and repudiated their alliance with the French when Dudley said he would build trading houses and personally answer "for their ffriendship and Capacity at all times." Understanding the bitter aftertaste of war, the sachems agreed that their people would remain east of Saco River: "It must have time to cool when the Iron doth lye a great while in the ffire. It must have time to cool." With this agreement Dudley permitted six commissioners to travel with the sachems to Maine so that all Abenaki could witness the treaty's ratification.[79]

When they gathered at Casco, the commissioners interpreted Dudley's promise of friendship as the old English expectation of political submission. They told the Abenaki that Dudley was willing, "notwithstanding former Breaches to receive you as her Majesty's good Subjects." Nevertheless, the commissioners failed to explain the implications of English sovereignty. Moreover, the conference transcript indicates that the Abenaki did not submit. In fact, they rejected Dudley's unstated assumption that the French had surrendered tribal lands by the Treaty of Utrecht: ". . . the French never said anything to us about it and wee wonder how they would give it away without asking us, God having at first placed us there and They have nothing to do to give it away." Although these words won them no recognition of their territorial rights, the tribes did agree that the English might resettle Maine without "molestation or claim by us or by any other Indians." The context makes clear that the Abenaki denied French power to cede their lands and that they newly asserted independence from English authority.[80]

After the signing of the Treaty of Portsmouth in 1713, the English had to discover whether commercial enticements would ease old resentments and permit Massachusetts to resettle coastal Maine. Sir William Phips had declared the Abenaki subjects in 1693 and then called them rebels when they remained at war. Governors Bellomont and Dudley continued the pretension and asserted that the tribes owed obedience. Following the peace of 1713, therefore, Massachusetts faced the challenge of assimilating the Abenaki, no easy task considering their consistent failure to build a workable alliance. The English had unilaterally assigned the tribes to a subordinate political status, a position that would be tested during the postwar years.

After 1713 the Abenaki found it increasingly difficult to reach a middle ground betwen contending English and French colonies. The Treaty of Portsmouth inaugurated an era in which the tribe was forced to reassert its independence from New France as well from New England. The Indians' exile during Queen Anne's War deepened their attachment to tribal territories and the Jesuits returned to Maine determined to buffer their missions from Euramerican contact. Within two years of Portsmouth the Abenaki and their priests were forced to weigh alliance on a scale that could balance English and French demands. English expansion on the Kennebec and Governor Dudley's failure to stabilize trade relations again disturbed the tribes. Similarly, French policy soon alerted the western tribes to the paradoxical threats of peace. Metropolitan French administrators and Governor Vaudreuil in Canada acted with little or no regard for Abenaki sentiments. The Jesuits, and Sebastien Racle in particular, forced by an untenable position between belligerent powers, lobbied for a reorientation of French policy that would bring imperial strategy in line with Indian interests. Because the tribes could not agree on how to survive yet another cycle of colonial manipulation, factionalism intensified and the Abenaki's deepest values were called into question.

# 6

# IDEALS AND ACTUALITIES

## *The Behavioral Ironies of Alliance*

From 1713 to 1727 the Abenaki found it necessary to reexamine their past in order to make sense of the violent heritage they shared with Euramericans. At one level they had extended themselves toward colonials often enough to understand that contact had created problems that begged for long-range solutions. At another level adversity prompted the tribes to look within their own communities for solutions to a crisis they knew to be of their own making. Relations with both the English and the French continued to be troublesome, but internal conflict embodied the fundamental threat to tribal integrity.

The Abenaki had fought three major wars against the English but had done so without overall coordination among themselves. While they had regularly consulted with one another and were successful in war, they invariably acted as independent tribes with separate policies. English attacks and French negligence during Queen Anne's War taught them that they had to develop a uniform policy toward all Euramericans. But before an intertribal alliance could produce unanimity in external relations, each society had to resolve its own domestic strife. The tribes planned for the future by piecing together what they could from their shattered ideals of alliance.

Competing French and English territorial claims as expressed in the
1713 Treaty of Utrecht predestined ongoing conflict. Like the Treaty of
Ryswick (1697), Utrecht ignored the Abenaki's independent role in the
colonial wars and assumed that land rights could be transferred between
European sovereigns without consulting Indians. Both the English and
French courted the tribes, but only to control their lands and satisfy
strategic needs. The Abenaki's defensive response—to preserve land,
religion, and unity—suggests that they considered most Euramericans
incapable of a positive association.[1]

The Treaty of Portsmouth (1713), which paralleled the European
agreement, accorded the tribes peace and restored them to a subordinant
status as English subjects. In this way the English pretended to
consummate a long-promised association that only tribal recalcitrance
had prevented. The tribes had proven formidable enemies and the
English were determined to pacify them. Nevertheless, despite treaty
stipulations, the English failed to meet their legal obligations. After
Queen Anne's War a single purpose predominated. The colony wished
to exploit Maine's rich resources and was determined that neither the
Abenaki nor the French would stand in its way. Massachusetts knew
that the tribes would oppose settlement but justified its actions with
powerful rationalizations: Indians were naturally treacherous, unwilling to abide by legal agreement, and susceptible to baneful French
priests.

The French were less bold but equally practical. In stripping France
of Acadia the Treaty of Utrecht left colonial boundaries undecided and
subject to local dispute. Constrained by the European accord, New
France found new reasons to nurture an alliance with the tribes. Canada
desperately sought to protect its position in the Northeast. As English
settlements pressed eastward after 1713, the French upheld Abenaki
territorial and political integrity. But there was more to their diplomacy
than the tribes' important role in Canada's defense. At least some
Frenchmen appreciated that the Abenaki resented manipulation and
that if the alliance was to be maintained Canadian authorities would
have to curry favor. The government held a powerful advantage in the
priests, traders, and military officials who lived among the tribes. These
men spoke the Abenaki's language, honored their social practices, and
shared their religious beliefs.

The Treaty of Utrecht taught the Abenaki that the French were
undependable allies. English negotiators drove a hard bargain designed

to place the tribes under Massachusetts's jurisdiction. The minister of the marine attempted to gain favorable terms at Utrecht but in the end left the Abenaki in an ambiguous position. At first, France proposed surrendering the frontier from the Kennebec to the St. John rivers in exchange for uncontested possession of the Nova Scotian peninsula. When England refused, the minister relinquished Acadia on condition that an international commission would later establish the extent of the cession. This provision would later cause intense conflict over the status of Abenaki lands.[2]

New France had a clearer sense of the issues than did the minister and worked to defuse the disastrous implications of Utrecht. Joseph Aubéry, by then a seasoned missionary, documented a French defense. He cited precedent to prove that Samuel de Champlain and other early colonials had restricted the term *Acadia* to the peninsula that the English called Nova Scotia. French officials responded enthusiastically to Aubéry's argument because it supported their contention that neither England nor Massachusetts had jurisdiction east of the Kennebec River. In this way Abenaki lands could be protected from English expansion, especially if the tribes were seen as sovereign nations freely allied with New France. Officials added a persuasive argument: Canada's historic alliance with the Abenaki demonstrated that the tribes were free and equal partners.[3]

During the negotiations at Portsmouth the Abenaki had protested the legality of the Treaty of Utrecht and thereafter maneuvered between English and French affiliations. The tribes followed their own counsel as the surest way to preserve cultural integrity and political independence. They rejected English assertions that they were subjects but contended that the Treaty of Portsmouth established what could be the minimal conditions for a cooperative alliance. In the postwar period the tribes worked toward that end, frankly expressing their complaints, welcoming English visitors, and treating humanely the many captives who chose to stay among them. Within a short time, however, it became obvious that the English refused to prevent persistent violence. Worse, the government effectively supported the settlement of western Maine, without regard to outraged Abenaki protests.

When efforts to negotiate these difficulties failed, the Abenaki responded in anger. They chose a middle course between revenge and passive resistance. Convinced that the government would never compromise over the offending settlements, the Abenaki began to destroy

English property. In their audacious defiance, the Abenaki inverted English arrogance and provoked terror on the frontier. Certain that Indians were addicted to revenge, the English recoiled from the tribes' blunt demands.

Opposing values obstructed relations between the English and the Abenaki. The resulting confrontations expressed antithetical social cultures—authoritarian English institutions contended with the tribes' consensual politics. The determined English assertion of ownership over Maine vied with the Abenaki's insistence that tribal lands could not be sold. Ultimately, the differences played themselves out in religious ideology. Even while the Abenaki found themselves hard pressed to maintain territorial integrity, the English cloaked themselves in religious ideals to pose as friends. Few in the Northeast could see that conflict was inevitable, and hope haunted every meeting.

The French, unlike the English, found a way to circumvent bureaucratic demands that Indian affairs conform to metropolitan mandate. Most English clung to the security of town and church, but many French adapted directly to the northeastern environment and to the intimate life-style of the Abenaki. They responded personally to Indians and transformed French weakness in numbers into a source of strength by coming to know and respect the Abenaki. In this way, the crucial distinction between New France and New England rested neither in Canada's small population nor in its limited use of the land. From the Abenaki perspective the French seemed remarkably willing to discuss mutual issues. A few Frenchmen mastered the Abenaki arts of persuasion and their miniscule number confirms the importance of fact-to-face relations in withstanding the tragic events of alliance.

Both economic and diplomatic conflict threatened the Abenaki. Their land and resources were too attractive to expanding New England and too strategic for weary Canada. These issues jeopardized solidarity and created the conditions for still another war. Early in the seventeenth century Abenaki communities had fractured and then reintegrated around Catholicism only to find in perennial strife with the English the seeds of vicious disagreements among themselves. These conflicts sapped tribal energies, for any compromise with colonials invariably reverberated within their own communities. Bitter intra- and intertribal polarization reflected the enormity of the Euramerican threat. Yet even in the midst of desperation, the Abenaki held to their ideal of harmony.

## POLITICS OF PROPERTY

Unsatisfactory relations between the English and Abenaki can be generally traced to a lack of candor in public conferences. As a result, the fine words reiterated at one parley after another had little effect on either people's domestic politics or on their diplomatic relations. Indian ambassadors were often forced to speak at meetings far removed from direct tribal scrutiny. They frequently failed to convey the divided opinions within their communities—a problem that had as much to do with English refusal to listen as with the envoys' polite reticence. Abenaki agents insisted that they were sent only to observe and remember so that their people could be fully informed. When they signed the Treaty of Portsmouth, the sachems declared that "all and every man here fully consents and agrees," as if insisting on their own inability to represent their respective peoples. Despite these protests, the English insisted that such men were not mediators but fully empowered "plenipotentiaries."[4]

Massachusetts officials assumed that authorized Abenaki envoys could make decisions for the tribes. Consequently, Indian spokesmen were courted with gifts, lavishly entertained, and treated deferentially. At a Boston meeting in January 1714, five Abenaki were greeted ceremoniously and two of them—Querabannit of Penobscot and Bomazeen of Kennebec—were given freshly minted coins to wear around their necks as signs of special favor. All five received Pine Tree shillings, which Governor Francis Nicholson of Nova Scotia endeavored to make a symbol of alliance, "saying they and the English should be like that Tree but One Root tho several Branches."[5]

Such courtesies seemed to win Abenaki loyalties. Bomazeen, at least, became notorious for using patronage to enrich himself. As the Kennebec learned to their sorrow, the sachem served his English benefactors. He was one of several informers who worked for John Gyles, the interpreter and truckmaster. In 1719 two English agents sent Bomazeen and another Kennebec to Boston where the council generously rewarded them. Each returned to Maine with new coats and shirts, but Bomazeen's jacket was decorated with silver thread. The tribe responded with ridicule, marking the resplendent sachem for the dupe he was.[6]

Massachusetts turned to patronage because lines of communication with the Abenaki were weak or nonexistent. Most of the irresolvable differences stemmed from that interpersonal distance. The tribes thought that peace would lead quickly to warmer relations, but the English did not share their sense of urgency. Only six months after Portsmouth, a Penobscot spokesman complained of persistent colonial unease: "The Indians do not understand why when there has been so long Peace there has been no more correspondence with us." He also said that his people hoped for friendship as it had existed "in our Grand Fathers Days."[7]

Because frontier relations lacked the trust that intimate contact might have encouraged, serious disagreements—particularly over trade and land—were discussed in ways that bore no connection to political realities. Conferences depended on public interpreters like John Gyles, Joseph Bean, and Samuel Jordan, who had only limited linguistic skill. They admitted that great idiomatic differences existed between the languages but claimed that their written conference proceedings faithfully recorded the speakers' words and meaning. In actuality, their transcripts leave much to be desired.[8]

Although the Abenaki sachems trusted the interpreters' good word, they could not judge the accuracy of the documents simply because they could not read. Much dissension stemmed from this communication problem. The difficulty of translation helps explain why both the English and the Abenaki felt that "a great many Indians told lyes." It is certain that the Abenaki suspected that some of their spokesmen were double-dealing. English officials took treaty law as an absolute contract, even when they knew that the Abenaki had not understood the real import of the text. The resulting polarized disagreements indicate that precise translation involved much more than a ready knowledge of vocabulary and grammar or a general command of idiomatic expressions.[9] While not all blame can be attributed to the interpreters' cultural bias, official documents do reveal that disjointed conversations obscured Indian statements. Basic misunderstanding—over the nature of political authority, legal responsibility, allegiance, and land ownership—largely derived from the social assumptions the interpreters unconsciously imposed on Abenaki reality. English attitudes were as frequently distorted in conference proceedings, showing that Massachusetts governors avoided frank discussion of volatile issues. Sometimes the English even felt it necessary to go beyond twisting the facts. As one Englishman told the secretary of trade: "I have been present when an article of the Peace has run in one sense in the English [language] and quite contrarie in the Indian by the Governour's express order and this has brought unnumbered mischiefs upon them."

The interpreters' accounts reflect a final problem: when faced with rigid price or angry self-interest, the Abenaki often fell silent, withholding agreement because the English refused to listen. It became an enduring tragedy of Indian-white relations that the English interpreted such giving way as dutiful acquiescence. [10]

The first confusion after 1713 concerned trade relations. The Treaty of Portsmouth had promised that Massachusetts would regulate trade and construct trading posts convenient to Abenaki villages. These stipulations stemmed from Governor Dudley's conviction that trade would keep the Abenaki properly submissive. Arguments to that effect probably account for the grudging support Dudley received when he insisted that the House of Representatives grant him executive control over the trade. The council explicitly stated English purpose in licensing traders: they were "to dispose of their goods so as to undersell the French." This goal suited the Abenaki, who wished to avoid occasions of violence and wanted good prices for their furs. [11]

Unfortunately, Dudley did not regulate the trade, and early in 1714 Abenaki spokesmen expressed tribal distress. Speaking in a garbled fashion, Bomazeen reminded the governor of his unfulfilled promises: "And [you] proposed to have a Place for Truck further Eastward than Casco Bay If the Truck Masters like not their Beaver they Kick it away The Indians are very much grieved that the Price of Beaver is so Low that its very Little Worth and Desire the Govr to putt forth the Price what it shall be sold at and they will be content." In effect, the sachem expressed urgent concerns that Dudley proceeded to sidestep. [12]

Although challenged, the governor refused to acknowledge the traders' offending behavior. As if to underscore the dependent position of the tribes, he chided the delegates for their misconduct during the previous war. As to the construction of truckhouses and regulation of commerce, Dudley said only that "That matter will have its consideration in the Great and Genll Court of this Province at their meeting appointed to be the next month." Curiously, any impatience in the Abenaki reaction to this delay is not recorded, but after the Indians returned to Maine, John Gyles transcribed two brief remarks suggesting their disappointment. Referring to the pressing needs Dudley had ignored, Bomazeen reported that his people were "sickly and out of

Provision." Wenagganet, a sachem who welcomed the delegates home, also hinted at dissatisfaction: " . . . if it might pleas we Desiear Captn Gyles might be sent to us in fourty or fivety Days & bring us Sum Necacrys that we Proposed to him for our Present supply to such time yt truck houesen be Erected."[13]

Dudley's trade policy ran into trouble in the Massachusetts House of Representatives. Although he pleaded that the Indian trade and the tribes themselves would be lost to the French, the house abrogated the Treaty of Portsmouth by voting "to admit the Indians to trade with anyone or in any part of the Province." The representatives came to oppose Dudley's authority over trade and made it impossible for the governor to regulate commercial relations. The house instituted what amounted to commercial anarchy and traders shortly plied the Abenaki with rum.[14]

Conference proceedings of July 1714 further demonstrate Dudley's inadequate response to Abenaki demands. Tribal spokesmen voiced the same complaints they had expressed the year before: the low value of furs, high prices of goods, too few trading posts, and, finally, abuse from licensed traders. They unmistakably wanted the commercial provisions of the treaty to be implemented. While some of the young men wished to trade with any of the settlers, "the solid men" wanted permanent posts where trade could be closely regulated. Dudley evaded the issue and did not tell the Abenaki that the House of Representatives had subverted the treaty. Knowing that high prices exasperated them, the governor proclaimed free trade, ostensibly to guarantee the Indians a high income from their furs. He observed that they would be free to trade wherever and with whomever they pleased.[15]

For all practical purposes Dudley was admitting that Massachusetts would not abide by the treaty terms that he himself had imposed. Moreover, he repudiated responsibility for enforcing laws against the liquor traffic and insisted that the Abenaki assume the entire burden of English lawlessness: "Wee shall punish those that abuses them with drink as it comes to Our Knowledge, but it lyes with them to avoyd such persons and if they should meet with provocation from such persons they must not revenge themselves but to apply to me for Justice and it shall be done them." In this way Dudley avoided constructing new trading posts and in effect denied the tribes any chance of submitting their complaints to Massachusetts courts. English criminals could easily escape justice. As an immediate result, relations reverted to the violence of the seventeenth century.[16]

It was one thing to dissimulate with the Abenaki; it was quite another to avoid blistering criticism from the Kennebec missionary Sebastien Racle. Furious that the English would not govern themselves, the priest wrote to Dudley regarding "disorders and Outrages committed among the Eastern Indians by Interloping Traders selling them [rum] and other Strong Liquors." The English resented this Jesuit advice and Governor Francis Nicholson of Nova Scotia compounded an already serious polarization: "I know no business a French Jesuit has with English subjects." Dudley's council did investigate the missionary's accusations but accomplished little.[17]

When the legislature annulled Portsmouth's commercial clauses, it set the stage for a more serious confrontation. In resettling the lower Kennebec the English once again expressed their contempt for Indian wishes. In May 1715 the General Court authorized settlements at Brunswick and Topsham. Then, on the very day that the council appointed a committee for the "regular prosecution of new Settlements," seven men purchased lands on the lower Kennebec. Since the original claim was based on old seventeenth-century patents received from Abenaki sachems, the purchasers at once pressed to have their titles validated. Earlier the new proprietors had asked that these lands be settled "as may make a Stronger Frontier to the Eastern Parts." No doubt because three of the purchasers sat on the land committee, the proprietors were confident of success. To further persuade committee members, they took them on an expensive tour of their lands. The confirmation of title that they won provoked ten years of violence.[18]

Incorporated on June 7, 1715, Brunswick and Topsham immediately required the council to take defensive action "upon consideration of the danger of an eruption of the Indians." In July the proprietors asked the General Court for £500 and fifteen men to reconstruct an old stone fort at Brunswick, "if not obstructed by the Indians." Early in 1716 stories swept the frontier that the Abenaki were angry, and the English sent out a scouting party "under pretence of hunting" to investigate. In May the council learned that the tribes were "assembling in great numbers," and one Abenaki, John Hegin, warned an English official on the Kennebec that "it would not be wise for him to tarry there long." In the midst of this uproar, Bomazeen and Bamegiscog arrived in Boston. Lieutenant-Governor Vaughn attempted to learn their business but discovered that they too wondered what was behind the rumors of war.[19]

Vaughn soon discovered one cause of the trouble. The Kennebec had split into two groups, one favoring the settlements, another opposing

them. Both sachems knew of this division but favored the English and
curried support. When they returned with their people's message
undelivered, Sebastien Racle wrote to repudiate them. According to the
priest, the Norridgewock sachems opposed settlement because they saw
it as the first step in driving them from their lands. He was even so
confident as to report that Governor Vaudreuil had warned the Abenaki
that the English could not be trusted. The priest also declared that no
one could buy Abenaki land because the tribes could not sell it. The land
had to be preserved for future generations. Although the English had
already armed themselves against Kennebec opposition, the council
dismissed Racle's letter as "very bold demands." The priest wrote again
to assert the illegality of English land deeds. They were unjust because
the sachems had been plied with liquor. Moreover, since the Abenaki
had thrice reconquered the territory since 1675, their ancestors' actions
had been rendered irrelevant.[20]

The Jesuit's biting words revived fears that he had instigated Abenaki
resistance, but the English clung to their claims and aggravated the
crisis. By 1717, when Samuel Shute became governor of Massachusetts,
the situation called for direct intervention and considerable finesse.
Shute traveled to the lower Kennebec and encountered the same difficulties that had troubled earlier governors. He set an antagonistic
tone, intending to overawe the Abenaki and settle their effrontery for all
time.

The new governor insisted that the Abenaki were English subjects
and cautioned them against any association with the French. He directed his interpreters to tell them that the Bible was the only guide for
their "Faith, and Worship and Life." Since the English saw the importance of undercutting French Catholic influence, they decided to support
a Protestant minister among the Kennebec. Solicitous as he felt his offer
to be, Shute thought it necessary to admonish the Abenaki to treat
Reverend Joseph Baxter "with all affection and respect." Finally, he
tried to placate the tribe by suggesting that these new settlements had
been constructed for their benefit "in having Trade brought so near
them, besides the advantage of the Neighborhood and Conversation of
the English." In short, the Abenaki could trade only if they would
accept Massachusetts's forts.[21]

The Abenaki reply drove Shute into a rage. Wiwurna, the chosen
speaker for the Kennebec and their allies, spoke bluntly. He dodged the
governor's heated interruptions with quiet pleas for "leave to go on." A

short dialogue established the contested issues. Wiwrurna insisted that English governors had consistently recognized the sovereignty of the Abenaki tribes. Still, he expressed a willingness to follow the English king—if the English would not expand their settlements. These contentions angered Shute and he insisted that "They must Desist from any Pretension to Lands which the English own."

And so the exchange went, on and on. Shute continuously interrupted while Wiwurna held his ground. "All people have a love for their Ministers," the orator explained, "and it would be strange if we should not love them that come from GOD. And as to the Bibles your Excellency mentions, We Desire to be Excused on that Point. God has given us Teaching Already, and if we should go from that we should displease God." When Shute again interjected, the speaker backed off, temporarily delaying his answer regarding the settlements.

After consulting among themselves, the Abenaki proposed a compromise midway between their assertion that they had never sold land and Shute's insistence that they accept English title. Wiwurna suggested that Massachusetts limit further expansion and in return the tribe would leave existing English settlements in place. Shute rudely cut him off: "Tell them, we desire only what is our own, and that we will have. We will not wrong them, but what is our own we will be Masters of." The orator pleaded, "It was said [in 1713], that no more Forts should be made" (a provision not included in the treaty). Mustering all the dignity he could, the governor again interposed: "Tell them the Forts are not made for their hurt, and that I wonder they should speak against them, when they are for the security of both, we being all subjects of King George." He expected "their positive Answer and Compliance in this matter, that the English be quiet in the possession of the Lands." As had happened before when met with immovable force, the Abenaki simply walked out "without taking leave and left behind their English Colours."

Racle had accompanied the Kennebec to the conference and he intervened, again by letter. The Jesuit informed Shute that inquiries had been made about the Treaty of Utrecht and that the French king held that Abenaki lands had not been ceded. Furthermore, Racle claimed that the king was prepared to offer aid if English encroachments continued. It is not surprising that Shute rejected the letter as "not worthy of his regard." He decided "not to buckle" to the tribes and the next morning "acted as if he were going away." The governor told the

Abenaki that he would again confer with them, but only "if they quitted their unreasonable Pretentions to the English Lands, and Complied with what he said."[22]

When the sachems returned, they left Wiwurna behind in evident disgrace, making it seem to the English that the Abenaki had capitulated to Shute's demands. Politely masking their exasperation, the sachems signed Shute's treaty, again in a way that embodied their reservations. The text guaranteed English possession of their land: "It was agreed in the Articles of Peace, that the English should Settle, where their Predecessors had done; And we agree to those Articles & confirm them. And desire the English may Settle as far as they ever have done." To the Abenaki's mind, therefore, the agreement expressed a conviction that settlement beyond seventeenth-century borders would not be tolerated.

The conference results more than pleased members of the Massachusetts General Court, who believed that Shute had asserted their "*just Right and Title.*" The House judged that the governor had established "a hopeful Prospect of Quiet and Safety to [the subjects of] his Majesty who are Resettling those Parts." Reporting to the Commissioners of Trade and Plantations that the Abenaki had confirmed previous treaties "and entred into some new on's," Shute claimed to have secured "the quiet and peace of these Provinces." In point of fact, he had achieved the opposite. Four years later, when the Abenaki threatened war, Chief Justice Samuel Sewall (who had sworn in the interpreters at the 1717 conference) exposed the lie: "The Indians shew a great Reluctancy against Erecting Forts higher up the River; and against the arrival of a Multitude of New Inhabitants; lest they should prove unable heartily to embrace them. They also desired the Running of a Line between the *English*, and them; and made some Proposals on their part, which were rejected: but no Proposals for fixing Boundaries, were offered to them."[23]

WARNING OFF

As Samuel Sewall feared, Shute drove the Abenaki back into the arms of their erstwhile French allies, "to the Loss and Damage of the *English.*" But it was a reluctant embrace, for the tribes' desire for peace involved them in complex and threatening forces. The Treaty of Utrecht complicated efforts to reestablish relations with the French as well as the English. The Abenaki not only learned to rue English treachery and

French faithlessness equally, they were coming to match their neighbors in manipulative cynicism.[24]

Faced with Massachusetts's refusal to regulate trade and its governor's overall inflexibility, the Abenaki turned to the French only to confront more insensitivity. Although still bitter over halfhearted French support during Queen Anne's War, after 1713 the tribes needed the help of New France. In previous wars the French had courted the Indians, but neutrality between France and England now isolated the Abenaki. France was torn between the need to maintain peace with England and Indian demands for protection. Canadian fears of English expansion produced sympathy for the Abenaki cause, but European diplomacy undercut the alliance.

While the Canadian French had to aid the Abenaki covertly, their policy rested on a firm foundation. Unlike the English, who relied almost exclusively on formal negotiations, the French enjoyed the advantage of personal relations. Even as the tribes held themselves aloof from bureaucratic manipulation, they dealt with French individuals regularly. At a diplomatic level the alliance functioned poorly. Yet in terms of the interpersonal patterns of Abenaki politics, a vital partnership had emerged. A few Frenchmen understood how the bands struggled with forces of change. Accepted as kinfolk, these individuals played a primary role in the Abenaki's cultural and political adaptation. Gabriel Druillettes set the pattern in the 1640s when he helped revitalize Abenaki religious faith. What is significant is that the Abenaki saw him also as a political leader working to ease their diplomatic and military problems.[25]

Other Jesuits who adapted to Abenaki social norms were also accepted. The most prominent of them, Sebastien Racle, was thirty-eight when he arrived in New France in 1689. Not surprisingly, he was ill-prepared to contend with Indian realities and frankly admitted shock at finding himself at "the far edge of the world." He wrote to his brother and described a bewildering variety of Indian peoples who "one may almost take for animals as for men." Such sentiments were common among Euramericans of the day, but Racle soon found that such impressions widely missed the mark.[26]

The priest's particular intellectual skills eased his adaptation. A professor of rhetoric, Racle was well prepared to learn the structure of Indian languages. As he became fluent, the missionary began absorbing the behavioral rules and values of the Abenaki world and found himself at the center rather than on the fringes of human cultural order. By 1689 the tribes were already largely Catholic and so Racle could easily appreciate their moral character. Racle understood that their eloquence in speech indicated intellectual and moral vigor. In these qualities the Abenaki were as sophisticated as he could wish, and the priest's admiration drew him into the intimacy of their social life.

Racle studied with an extended Abenaki family that treated him hospitably. At the end of his education he referred to them as "those of my cabin" and baptized one child with his own name. The elegant directness of their speech engaged Racle's professional regard, but their behavior won his personal loyalty. When he was recalled to the Jesuit seminary at Quebec, the Abenaki missed him. The mother of "little Sebastien" followed and urged him to remain. "You love us," she pleaded, "and you were of our cabin, and you were our father. Why then did you leave us?" Racle again wrote his brother, "I swear to you that I could not respond to them except through my tears." In apprenticeship Racle had wholly submitted himself to Abenaki tutors and in openness was transformed. "As for what concerns me personally, I assure you that I see, that I hear, that I speak, only as a savage." Racle's personal identification with the Abenaki exposes the level of alliance that truly worked.

As years passed the Jesuits identified more and more with Abenaki interests and did what they could to protect the integrity of tribal life. As early as King William's War the priests used Abenaki political techniques to lobby for common interests. They realized that it would be a serious mistake to allow arbitrary government dictates to thwart their efforts. During the war Jesuits and Abenaki carefully discussed how troublesome issues might be handled. The official criticism they suffered after the Treaty of Ryswick indicates just how gingerly the priests dealt with commercial issues and international politics. Some of them actually supported peace between the Abenaki and the English. The tribes would have been in even greater jeopardy during Queen Anne's War had the priests not been there to lend advice and aid. The Jesuits understood the economic crisis that conflict created and offered the tribes a haven, unsatisfactory as it became. Perhaps most important, the missionaries accepted the Abenaki's decision to return to Maine when French negligence grew intolerable.

The Treaty of Portsmouth threw additional responsibility onto these few French representatives and they increasingly spoke in defense of Abenaki interests. French administrators began another cycle of manipulation, this time to strengthen their new stronghold at Louisbourg, northeast of Nova Scotia. Governor Vaudreuil returned to Canada having agreed with the minister of marine's desire to move the northeastern Algonkians to Cape Breton Island. The priests contemptuously criticized the plan. It showed, Father Pierre LaChasse said, that French authorities "must be ignorant of the extreme attachment that these Indians bear their country." He urged the king to concentrate on settling Canada's southern boundary in order to protect Abenaki territory.[27]

The Jesuits understood, as French officials did not, Abenaki reactions to the Treaty of Utrecht. When the English claimed that the treaty had surrendered the Indians' lands, the sachems asked the priests, "By what right did the King of France dispose of their Country?" Had the Jesuits not appeased the tribes and squelched plans to move them, the alliance would have ended at once. The impact of the English claim, said Father Charlevoix, "can be conceived, only when it is known [to] what a point these nations are jealous of their liberty and independence." Put on the spot, Racle and LaChasse replied truthfully to the sachems that "an ambiguous expression" in the treaty had deceived the English. They added less candidly that Abenaki territory "was not included in that which had been ceded to the English." In this way the Jesuits encouraged Abenaki resistance but unintentionally planted the seeds for continuing exasperation with the French, who could not openly take sides.[28]

As a sign of friendship the Jesuits implied that the Abenaki might expect Canadian aid. In continuing to provide funds for their support and in paying for new chapels on the Kennebec, Penobscot, and St. John rivers, the king seemed to reinforce these promises. Eager themselves to trust in the king's good favor, the Jesuits reported the strategic importance of Abenaki resistance. Indeed, after 1717 the priests attempted to direct metropolitan policy concerning the international boundary, the Abenaki's political status, and, most important, the necessity of encouraging tribal resistance.[29]

The priests also compromised over Abenaki efforts to deal with the English. In 1718, for example, when two Englishmen killed a Penobscot, the tribe resolved to placate settlers' fears by calling the death "an accident." Fearing that this effort to reassure the skittish English would be taken for submission, Father Étienne Lauverjat advised the tribe to wait for Massachusetts governor Shute's reaction. But the Penobscot insisted that the priest write immediately to the English explaining their nonviolent intent. Vaudreuil later criticized the priest, even when

Lauverjat explained that had he refused, the Penobscot would have asked the Protestant minister Joseph Baxter to write for them.

Lauverjat noted that the Abenaki disagreed among themselves and acted to avoid any further domestic split. When the Penobscot discussed the killing, the young men favored war. Cooler heads warned: "If you do so, you will do ye Devils work & the Devil will take you." Most "were afraid at this time of a new war. The old men were loath to quit their villages. . . where they lived at ease." At the young men's insistence, however, Shute was asked to remove "all those capable of setting them at variance."[30]

Sebastien Racle was less temperate than Lauverjat and heedlessly provoked English anger. He soon quarreled with Joseph Baxter for having the audacity to attack Catholic doctrine. The Jesuit wrote a long letter defending his church, and in a rapid exchange of notes the two clerics vilified each other. Racle faulted Baxter's Latin, while the minister disparaged the priest's choleric personality. Affronted when Racle reminded him of the Abenaki's "warlike and terrible genius," Shute entered the fray to protect his protégé. The governor contended that Racle's conduct was not in accord with the Apostle's exhortation: "Notwithstanding every way, whether in pretence or in truth, Christ is preached, and I therein rejoyce, yea and I will rejoyce." Failing to take his own advice, Shute enclosed a copy of the law banning Roman Catholic priests from Massachusetts, which, he advised, Racle would "do well to consider of."[31]

Religious rivalry with Joseph Baxter made the Jesuits even more devoted to Abenaki interests. As the English pressed forward with settlement and as the liquor traffic increased, the Abenaki began killing English cattle to convey their resentment. When the settlers called for compensation, the Abenaki replied vigorously: "Complain all you want to the Governor, he is not my judge. And as for the payment for the cattle, ask whoever told you to settle there." Since the English ignored Racle's warnings, the priest turned his attention to French authorities, alerting them to the crisis. He advised that only prompt settlement of the boundary could prevent certain war.[32]

Canadian officials responded to Racle's pleas, less out of love for the Abenaki than out of fear for Canada's defense. Vaudreuil informed the Council of Marine that he could not refuse to aid the tribes if they were attacked. Intendant Michel Begon begged metropolitan authorities to negotiate with England. He claimed that should Massachusetts gain Abenaki territory, the angry tribes could easily become the scourge of

New France. Instigated by Jesuit outrage, these shrill alarms woke the Council of Marine. Contending that English pretensions to Abenaki territory "are exorbitant," the council indecisively informed Canadian officials that until a boundary commission could be set up, they might encourage the Abenaki to halt English settlement. Vaudreuil was told, however, not to disturb the French alliance with England.[33]

Limited as these equivocal reactions were, they encouraged Racle. The missionary sent two Kennebec sachems to assure Vaudreuil that the Abenaki would oppose the settlers. The priest daily grew more strident—so much so that the English called him an "Incendary of mischeif." Racle spat back that the Canadian Abenaki chided the Kennebec "that in giving away their lands, they kild themselves and them to, and that they were Obliged to assist them in case of any injustice done them by the English." Although many Kennebec did not agree with Racle's unyielding position, the tribe continued to destroy English property and claimed that Massachusetts land deeds were invalid. English commissioners concluded only that Vaudreuil and the "Cunning Insinuations" of Racle encouraged the Abenaki to resist.[34]

Knowing full well that the English blamed him, Racle again intervened. This time he insisted that the Kennebec retained their territorial rights and rejected the terms of Shute's 1717 treaty, which had convinced the Abenaki that English demands were unreasonable. The tribe had generously offered to compromise, but Shute refused to negotiate. Racle declared, "If the Indians kill Cattle below the Mill towards the seaside they must absolutely pay for them." But he added: "Any treaty. . .is Null, If I don't approve it, though the Indians have consented, for I bring them so many reasons against it that they absolutely condemn what they have done." Calling Shute a "Warrior," the Jesuit advised the governor to recall all the settlers "for assuredly, there shall not one remain there." He promised to write a book telling the world how "the English treat the Indians" and how the English rejected the Indians' legitimate demands by insisting that the Jesuit "bid you say it." But in assuring the Kennebec that they might make war to protect their lands, Racle confirmed the worst of English impressions.[35]

For a time following Racle's letter, Massachusetts seemed conciliatory. Shute finally admitted that the treaties did require that the English construct trading houses. He even asked the General Court to establish a boundary to quell Kennebec agitation. Characteristically, however, the house insisted that Massachusetts's pretended rights took precedence over those of the Indians and insisted that the treaties had already established boundaries. Even when the Abenaki petitioned to ask for official approval of Shute's new moderate policies, the house refused to bend. Fearing this legislative defeat would provoke hostilities, the council assured the settlers that they would be protected.[36]

By 1720 the house concluded that Governor Shute and his council could not manage the Abenaki and so it again intervened. The impatient representatives resolved "That it is deragatory to his Majesties Honour and very injurious to this Province, that Monsieur Ralle a French Jesuit and Missionary should in defiance of the Law, Reside in any part of this Province." The house demanded that two hundred men be sent to arrest Racle and insisted that the Abenaki make immediate restitution for damaged English property. More arguments within the government followed, but commissioners were finally sent to meet the Kennebec.[37]

The resulting conference of November 1720 satisfied no one. The crisis had reached ominous proportions. The Kennebec insisted that settlers withdraw and the commissioners demanded restitution "for ye Wrongs done us." The English got their way, but only after adamantly refusing to compromise on land ownership. Although Kennebec spokesmen argued to the last, they surrendered four sachems as a hostage for their promise to pay 200 beaver skins in damages. Even this did not end opposition. The spokesmen, who dreaded impending war and acted without their people's consent, loudly expressed Kennebec determination to be rid of English settlers. Under such circumstances the capitulation soon embarrassed the English as well as the Abenaki. The Kennebec almost at once regretted their sachems' submission, and, as if aware of the agreement's fragility, the English feared that any compromise with the tribes would be seen as a fatal sign of weakness.[38]

To compound an already tense situation, the conference all but shattered the alliance between the Kennebec and New France. When the tribe approached Governor Vaudreuil for aid, they discovered that Racle had misled them. Vaudreuil cautiously assured them that "he should never fail them in time of need" and promised to send them hatchets, powder, and lead secretly. Since the Kennebec had expected the French to join in war, Vaudreuil's refusal angered them: "Is this the way, then, the Indians retorted, that a Father aids his children, and was it thus we assisted you? A father, they added, when he see his son engaged with an enemy stronger than he, comes forward, extricates his son and tells the enemy that it is with him he has to do." The governor immediately perceived his mistake and promised that he would encourage Canadian Indians to assist them. His cautious neutrality only further exasperated the Kennebec: "At these words the deputies retorted with an ironical laugh—Know, that we all who inhabit this vast continent, will, whensoever we please, as long as we exist, unite to expel all foreigners from it, be they who they may."[39]

Afraid to offend New England, Vaudreuil lost stature among the Abenaki. He sensed his faltering influence and, along with Intendant Begon, worried that the Kennebec would entirely succumb to Massachusetts. Begon knew better than to judge the divided "Abenaquis of the present day by the Abenaquis of former times." The Kennebec were so splintered that even Sebastien Racle's life was in danger. Yet as an ultimate irony, the difficult task of reuniting the tribe rested in his hands. The English thought that the Jesuits were French agents. Even Father Charlevoix claimed that only the missionaries could persuade the Abenaki to submit to Vaudreuil's will. The governor did not understand the extent to which the Jesuit's loyalties had aligned with the Indian cause. Far from imposing his own will, the governor had no choice except to follow Racle's lead in appeasing the Abenaki.[40]

The priest instantly took advantage of Kennebec resentment. Aware that the tribe could not endure endless factionalism, Racle determined to drive the settlers from Merrymeeting Bay. When the English demanded that the Abenaki meet them and give evidence of their missionary's dismissal, they sealed their fate for Racle met force with force. The missionary simply decided to undermine what he perceived as the pro-English faction among the Abenaki and pack the conference. He sent six Kennebec to invite Canadian Abenaki to join them and at his behest Vaudreuil hastened to those villages to ensure that they accept the invitation.[41]

The missionary was afraid that if the Kennebec wasted time arguing over his advice they would lose their lands. He told Vaudreuil how to handle the tribal spokesmen and the governor complied. "I think you will find," Begon reported, that the governor's speech was "in the Sense proposed by you." Vaudreuil decided not to write an angry note to Shute. Instead, he again accepted Racle's advice: the Abenaki must remain on their land, and they must unite in "Speaking Firmly to the Englishmen." Nevertheless, Canadian officials distrusted the Jesuit's intensity. Begon warned the priest three times of "the prudence with which we Deem ourselves obliged To act toward the English, so that we may not Commit ourselves." The governor also sent Father Pierre

LaChasse to restrain Racle "until the Council of Marine has Explained Whether The King's Intention is that the French should join the Savages. . . or whether he will Content himself with supplying them with Munitions of War."[42]

Racle's program, a calculated gamble, proved at least a temporary success. Captain Samuel Moody reported from the frontier that the Abenaki refused to dismiss their priest and demanded the release of the Indians held as prisoners. In July 1721 Racle and the Kennebec inquired "dayly after their Men." Faced with nearly two months of official silence, 200 Abenaki along with Sebastien Racle, Pierre LaChasse, and Joseph d'Abbadie de Saint Castin (the half Penobscot fifth baron and son of Jean Vincent) accosted the English. In Vaudreuil's words, "The Indians then threw down two hundred beavers, which they had promised for the cattle that had been killed, and demanded, at the same time, where were the four men they had conveyed to Boston as hostages for this payment." When the English replied that the captives would not be freed, LaChasse read a prepared letter from the Abenaki: "Is it to live in peace with me to take my land despite me?" They added:

> Consider Great Captain that I have frequently told thee to retire off from my lands, and I repeat to thee now for the last time. . . . It is not thine by gift; the King of France, thou sayst has given it to me; but has he power to give it to thee? Am I his subject? The Indians have given it to thee. Some Indians that thou has overreached by making them drink, have they the power to give it to thee to the prejudice of all their nation?

Like other Racle-inspired petitions, this one ended with a terrible threat: "I will wait then thy reply within three Sabbath days; if within this time thou doest not write me, that thou has retired from my land, I will not tell thee again."[43]

The result was heightened tension. Massachusetts strengthened its militia, demanded the immediate surrender of Racle and Saint Castin, and prohibited trade. In short, the colony considered itself at war, although without a formal declaration. Writing to Racle, Vaudreuil fueled the fire: "For my part, I am of the opinion that, if they have taken a Sincere resolution not to allow The English On Their Land, they Must not hesitate to Drive them Therefrom as Soon as Possible." To prod metropolitan officials, the governor claimed that Abenaki would ally themselves with the English if their demands for French soldiers were refused. He complained in vain.

Had they understood the situation, the English could have used the French king's refusal to join the Kennebec as a means of winning over the tribe. But Massachusetts did not perceive its opportunity. Turning instead to aggression, the English captured Saint Castin, citing him for rebellion. The English thereby forced his Penobscot kin to support the Kennebec cause. Then in the winter of 1722 Massachusetts sent a force against the village at Norridgewock and seized the correspondence between Racle and Vaudreuil. Newly convinced of French conspiracy, the English accused the Canadian governor of "instigating the Indians to commit hostilities."[44]

In the face of these aggressions the Abenaki remained quiet until summer. Then, after planting their crops, they descended on the lower Kennebec and captured sixty-five settlers. In a final attempt to force the release of their sachems, they freed all but five of the English. Their actions had an immediate effect. Both the house and council rejected plans to attack Norridgewock, and in alarm the house finally suggested that Abenaki captives be swapped for English prisoners. Such pacific measures had come too late. By mid-July the Kennebec had burnt Brunswick and eighteen warriors had been killed. No longer able to evade the quarrel he had done so little to resolve, Governor Shute declared war on July 25 against Abenaki "rebels, Traitors and Enemies."[45]

### REDEFINING RELATIONS

The war of 1722−27 represents a turning point in Abenaki history. Massachusetts chastized the tribes as never before, repeatedly marching on Abenaki villages, destroying the Kennebec village of Norridgewock, and killing Sebastien Racle in August 1724. The tribes inflicted reprisals, but after the loss of their village the surviving Kennebec took refuge in Canada. The war ultimately showed the Abenaki that Massachusetts could not be defeated without French military support. As a result, the Abenaki were forced to take stock of fifty years of conflict and to reevaluate the political ties that bound them to one another.

The attack on Norridgewock came to symbolize the difficulties of alliance in the Northeast. The English saw the battle as the high point in a religious crusade. Their forces were welcomed in Boston with "great Shouting and Triumph," for they carried with them the scalp of the Jesuit who had fought, gun in hand, to the very end. Chief Justice Samuel Sewall, who alone had supported Abenaki demands before the war, muttered in awe: "The Lord help us to rejoice with trembling." Reverend Benjamin Colman preached that the victory "was the singular work of God." But a more accurate assessment of the excitement was secular in tone. In his contemporary history of the war Samuel Penhallow observed that the fall of Norridgewock was "the greatest victory we have obtained in three of four last wars: and it may be as noble an exploit (all things considered) as ever happened in the time of king Philip."[46]

The Abenaki defeat created a crisis for the French. Recognizing that English power had begun to hedge them in, the French took refuge in indignation, making Racle a martyr for the faith. Father Charlevoix eulogized him as a hero and claimed with some truth that "the English seemed to wage war only to get rid of one man, to whom alone they ascribed the opposition." Charlevoix's account of the attack closely follows the reports of fleeing Kennebec. When they returned to their village they found Racle's body. Not much else remained because the English had burned Norridgewock as they departed. The survivors concluded that Racle met his death with humility. They told the French that just as the attack began, he fearlessly met the assailants. Rushing to a large crucifix, he was killed along with seven sachems who tried to protect him: "They found him pierced with a thousand blows, his scalp torn off, his skull crushed by hatchets, his mouth and eyes full of mud, his leg bones broken, and all his members mutilated in a hundred different ways."[47]

In fact, the attack had dimensions that escaped both the English and the French. Early on the morning of the raid, a war party returned to Norridgewock with a warning that two hundred men were coming to "drive them out of their camp." Racle thought the possibility remote. He argued that the English were on the defensive and observed that they had never attacked the Abenaki in the summer because their troops quickly fell sick. But, as Racle wrote to his superior just before the attack began, the Kennebec listened to all his reasons "but follow their own." They decided, and the priest reluctantly agreed, to abandon the village and move farther up river. Had another day passed, the disaster would have been averted.[48]

An Abenaki oral tradition adds details to Racle's account. It points to the factional dispute that surrounded the priest and suggests that neither the English nor French understood the Kennebec's complex relations with him. Apparently many Abenaki resented Racle's interference in village politics and distrusted him. Some bitter survivors of Norridgewock said that Racle had ridiculed a shaman who warned of the English approach. Their story has it that the old priest sold the lives of Kennebec people for a bag of gold. As improbable as this folk memory may seem, it does indicate that even before the loss of Norridgewock, political division plagued the tribe. All of the Abenaki tribes had to resolve such tensions in the postwar years.[49]

Finally, the destruction of Norridgewock had a profound impact on international politics. Emboldened by victory, Massachusetts lieutenant-governor William Dummer answered Vaudreuil's offer to mediate the conflict by accusing him of causing the war. Dummer also sent commissioners to demand Vaudreuil's neutrality. The Jesuits, however, supported Abenaki demands that the English "quit their lands, restore their prisoners, rebuild their Church, and indemnify them for. . . killing Father Rasle, and for the expenses of the war." It is odd that Vaudreuil reported to the minister of marine that he was convinced that the English governor was "extremely anxious for peace."[50]

In the end the Abenaki could not maintain unity against the English. While the Penobscot and other tribes had supported the Kennebec's defense of their lands, the destruction of Norridgewock signaled the end of effective resistance. Early in 1725 the Penobscot, whose village had been attacked not long before, responded to Dummer's promise "to receive their Submission & let them live in Peace." Although the English governor doubted "whether wee shall ever make a good & honorable Peace," the Indians sent delegates to Boston and asked for a cease-fire.[51]

The Penobscot wanted to satisfy Massachusetts and assumed responsibility for convincing other Abenaki to submit as well. Led by Loron Sauguaaram, ten spokesmen traveled to Quebec and asked Vaudreuil, the Canadian Abenaki, and other mission Indian allies to accept Dummer's terms. Vaudreuil feigned indifference, irritated because the Penobscot had reneged on their promise not to negotiate except in his presence. The Canadian Abenaki and the surviving Norridgewocks continued to harrass the English. Not in the least deterred by this unanimous opposition, the Penobscot negotiated an agreement with Dummer, assuring him that the other tribes had empowered them to do so on their behalf. In actuality, they dissembled in hopes that the treaty would demonstrate English good faith to the hostile tribes. Sauguaaram did emphasize his limited authority and insisted that a meaningful peace required the resolution of the issues that had caused the war. English misconceptions once again predestined the failure of the treaty.[52]

Dummer's Treaty reflected old assumptions and made new demands. According to the text read to them, the Penobscot acknowledged English sovereignty and accepted Massachusetts' jurisdiction. As in the Treaty of Portsmouth, this treaty stipulated that the English be responsible for regulating trade and that the Abenaki recognize English land titles. Finally, the Indians agreed to join their warriors with the English military forces in the event that any "Tribes of Indians intended to be included in this Treaty" refused to submit. But in admitting the futility of war, the Penobscot had not forgotten their allies' grievances and worked toward a united Abenaki diplomacy.[53]

Speaking for the Penobscot, Sauguaaram countered English proposals: "We think it would be better to come wholly upon a new Footing, for all those former Treaties have been broke because they were not upon a good Footing." He suggested that English settlements be confined to southern Maine, fearing inevitable misunderstandings from "the English settling to nigh us." The spokesman promised that the Abenaki would then accept peace: "It is the Mind of all the Tribes That if [the English removed their two forts], they would all think that the English were hearty and in earnest for a lasting peace." When Dummer balked, Sauguaaram backed off but declared that he was not empowered to accept the validity of English land titles. Despite this fundamental disagreement, four Penobscot delegates signed a provisional treaty, to be ratified later by all of the tribes.[54]

Dummer's demands undermined negotiations. The English believed that the time had come for the Abenaki to submit to Massachusetts's just demands and Dummer addressed the delegates from a position of strength. It seemed enough to him to assure the Indians that their lands would not be unfairly appropriated. Not realizing that the Penobscot cared nothing for the niceties of property law, the English could not understand why Sauguaaram questioned their motives. A Mr. Delafaye caught something of the dilemma when he declared to Governor Burnet: "I wish our own people may not be in some measure be the aggressors by dealing unjustly or roughly with the Indians, for I doubt our planters are too apt to overvalue themselves, and to imagine those creatures are not to be treated as rational beings like themselves."[55]

The agreement went up in smoke almost immediately. When Étienne Lauverjat translated the treaty from English into Abenaki,

Sauguaaram wrote to Dummer denouncing the document as "entirely defferring from what we have said in presence of one another." He added: " 'Tis therefore to disown them that I write this letter unto you." He protested that he had not submitted to the English sovereign, "butt only that I own'd that He was king in His kingdom as the king of France is king in His." Nor had he agreed that the Penobscot would force other Abenaki to submit: "I told you we would do on our side all we could to bring them back butt I have given you notice att the same time that I did not understand that we should strike on them, or that we should joyn our forces to yours to march against them." Sauguaaram concluded that the Penobscot had suspended negotiations now that "I have had the confusion to see that my words have been taken in a quite contrary sense."[56]

The Penobscot nonetheless continued to urge compromise. At a conference in the summer of 1726, Sauguaaram tried to explain why only the Penobscot were present to ratify the treaty. Had the English removed the two offending forts "we with the other Indians should all have come into a Peace before now." Dummer demanded that English rights be recognized and asked Sauguaaram if he understood what that meant. "Everything of the Treaty is very plain to us, and there is nothing in the way excepting the two [forts]." The spokesman continued: "It would be but a small matter for the Government to make Allowance for them, and give them up." Trying uselessly to convince Dummer that the tribes were adamant, Sauguaaram repeated his case: "We insist upon the removal of these two Houses. . . and if they were removed there would be no difficulty among the tribes."[57]

Refusing compromise, the governor introduced the Penobscot to the committee on land claims, which read them twenty-nine deeds validating English title. "They had been shewn Deeds & papers enough," the Penobscot exclaimed, "to last them to the fall of the year, and that they did not desire to see any more." In effect, the Indian delegates collapsed under the barrage of paper and yet warned that misunderstandings would continue because the other tribes resented Penobscot negotiations. Still, Sauguaaram promised to work toward peace.[58]

While the Kennebec, Androscoggin, and Canadian Abenaki continued to attack the frontier, they too were tired of the war. The Penobscot carefully informed Dummer of this change of heart. In May 1727 the Penobscot even halted Canadian Abenaki warriors, warning them that "if they Did any harm to ye English, they should Neiver Return to Caneday a Livef." At the same time, however, the Penobscot disputed the meaning of the treaty they had ratified the previous summer. They discussed every article with the returning Abenaki, informing them that the interpreters had misconstrued the treaty's terms. When the united Abenaki met Dummer in July they told him as much: "We desire the interpreters would be very careful. . . that they would not lean to one side nor the other during the Conference." Despite their distrust, all of the tribes ratified Dummer's Treaty on July 21, 1727.[59]

While the English thought the treaty resolved all differences, the Abenaki steeled themselves to a new kind of politics which recognized that Massachusetts had to be managed carefully. The Abenaki realized that the interpreters had again distorted the meaning of the treaty. Instead of saying that the Abenaki submitted to English sovereignty, as the text had it, Sauguaaram asserted that the interpreters had actually said that the tribes had come to salute Dummer, to make peace with him, and to renew their ancient friendship. Sauguaaram explained the Abenaki response to the French. What could he do when, as he said, "the Englishman himself disavows [his words] in my presence, when he reads and interprets them to me himself." Reviewing the history of Penobscot negotiations that he had led, Sauguaaram repudiated the treaty, clause by clause: "If, then, any one should produce any writing that makes me speak otherwise, pay no attention to it, for I know not what I am made to say in another language, but I know well what I say in my own."[60]

The Penobscot led the Abenaki into an new era of cautious relations with Euramericans. Their new politics admitted that English settlers could not be removed, but united the tribes to hold the line on further expansion. They also refurbished their alliance with Quebec. The Abenaki continued to welcome the Jesuits but asserted independence from French politicians. After 1725 the Abenaki were mindful of the political motives that colored all aspects of French policy. Most important the Penobscot helped to form an intertribal consensus on relations with both English and French. Penobscot emissaries became familiar figures, traveling from the Micmac in Nova Scotia to the mission villages of New France. Faced with English refusal to resolve their grievances, the Abenaki developed an intertribal diplomacy that recognized the vagaries of both French and English politics.[61]

### THE ELUSIVE IDEAL

The colonial period had begun with the Abenaki divided. From a European perspective that disunity proved that Indians were culturally backward peoples. In fact, the tribes valued their small, independent communities but came to understand that political fragmentation worked to the advantage of the colonists. Events of the seventeenth century gradually pushed the Abenaki to resolve their differences. They knew that their survival required the strength of an intertribal alliance and a realistic assessment of Euramericans. The tribes drew together around a reinvigorated religious tradition, sharing the tribulations of war and the challenges of peace.

By the end of Queen Anne's War the Abenaki had not achieved a uniform policy that allowed them to fend off the two great colonial powers. Massachusetts was determined to settle Kennebec lands, and New France was equally intent on using the tribes as a buffer to protect its vulnerable southern flank. In the very act of resisting and in the persistent efforts to communicate their dissatisfaction, the Abenaki came to understand that the complexities of alliance were more and more being defined in Boston, Quebec, and Europe. Kennebec opposition to foreign authority after 1713 began to show the tribe the great cultural distance that separated them from Euramericans.

Nonetheless, as the Abenaki understood it, intra- and intertribal conflict posed the fundamental challenge of alliance. Divisiveness made the separate tribes particularly vulnerable to Euramerican manipulation. Time and again, individual sachems acquiesced to French and English demands, placing their peoples in jeopardy. Bitter polarization was the eventual result. The Kennebec bore the brunt of contact with Massachusetts but remained so intent on establishing a constructive association that great arguments emerged among members of the tribe. Important as it was to resist expansion, some of the Kennebec still felt that accommodation might be possible. War weariness urged the tribe to compromise with English demands, but, more important, a few leaders continued to believe in the ideal of alliance. Even those who felt that the English could not be trusted would have remained at peace if Massachusetts had been willing to bend.

As the confrontation reached an impasse, it became clear that the French were undependable allies. Sebastien Racle tried to alert the Kennebec to the long-range implications of dispossession, but in the process he aggravated tribal disharmony. Ironically, his attachment to the Kennebec cause, and his strident opposition to Massachusetts, worsened the tribe's predicament. Those Kennebec who hoped to compromise with Massachusetts opposed the priest, and dissension weakened the tribe. Faced with Kennebec factionalism and denied official French support, Racle was pushed to advocate violent reprisal.

The refusal of administrators in Quebec and Versailles to aid the Kennebec (even while they urged the tribe to war) forced the Abenaki to recognize that the French as well as the English had to be managed firmly. It was apparent to the tribes, however, that they could not deal with either colonial power until they had developed a consensus on the tribal level. Nor could they wage defensive war without intertribal unity. If peace made the task difficult, war with Massachusetts made it imperative. Since the Abenaki fought Dummer's War with little French support, they moved to consolidate forces and finally achieved a workable intertribal alliance.

The Abenaki's unfailing attempts to compromise with Euramericans cast light on the inherent contradiction between the ideal of alliance and its violent actuality. From the point of view of the Abenaki, the English epitomized the problem: their arrogant ethnocentrism and will to power were the roots of frontier disorder. Certain that the northeastern wilderness had to be economically transformed and politically subdued, settlers planted themselves where they pleased, without concern that their farms and lumbering operations disrupted the Indians' seasonal use of sea and river shores. They relegated the Abenaki to subhuman status and relied on power politics to resolve disagreements between themselves and the tribes. Colonial Englishmen resented Indian resistance, unwittingly provoked anger, and punished it when all else failed. In short, settlers did not relate to Indians humanely and could not fathom their own responsibility for endemic hostilities.

Although French policy also threatened the tribes, Canada enjoyed one crucial advantage: some Frenchmen met the tribes directly. Despite the Jesuits' sometimes disruptive influence, the Abenaki remained closely attached to their priests. Their devotion suggests that the missionaries were usually seen as trusted allies rather than as French agents. During Dummer's War and after, the Abenaki welcomed the Jesuits but grew increasingly blunt with the Canadian government. Determined to balance the competing demands of the two colonial powers, the Penobscot declared their independence even from New France. At the same time the Jesuit missions in Canada continued to provide all the tribes with a temporary refuge. Moreover, the permanent Abenaki population near Quebec brought a healthy diversity to intertribal diplomacy. In this way an alliance endured among all of the Abenaki, and in times of need the Maine tribes found they could still enlist French support. When Massachusetts drove the tribes to war in the 1740s and again in the 1750s, the independent Abenaki had friends to rely on.

Abenaki responses to Euramericans depart considerably from the general character of colonial Indian-white relations. It is true that along with other Indian peoples the Abenaki faced expansionistic settlers, suffered the deadly impact of disease, trade, and liquor, fought defensive wars, and finally adapted to the new Euramerican world order. But none of these factors put the Abenaki in a passive position. Violence became commonplace, but the Abenaki did more than resist. In fact, they invested most of their energy in attempting to forestall hostilities, repeatedly seeking to communicate and negotiate their differences.

At the opening of the eighteenth century Abenaki efforts to reconcile themselves to the realities of English and French diplomacy proved unacceptable to both governments. Queen Anne's War impressed on the tribes that all Euramericans promised more than they could or would deliver. So when the Abenaki were forced to assert their own sovereignty after 1713, they were declaring something more than a simple defiance of colonial dominance. They were stating their conviction that only an alliance between equal partners would be tolerated. Even Dummer's War, which was primarily fought to defend their territory and resources, found the Abenaki holding to that ideal. In the Kennebec's persistent efforts to negotiate before the war and in the Penobscot's cautious diplomacy afterward, the tribes expressed an unswerving desire to put association with Euramericans on a positive footing.

The history of Abenaki attempts to relate productively to the English and the French thus exposes the moral parameters of alliance. Although French advice was not always in the best interest of the Abenaki, the mutuality of their decision-making process—whether the issue was an Abenaki or French one—provided the motive force of the relationship. Destructive as the affiliation with French Canada sometimes was and divided among themselves as the Abenaki often were, seldom have relations between American Indians and Euramericans been more positive. The Abenaki's history unmistakably establishes the social, religious, and political conditions that made alliance not only possible but a historic reality.

# ABBREVIATIONS

| | |
|---|---|
| *AA* | *American Anthropologist* |
| *AC* | Archives des Colonies, Ottawa: Public Archives of Canada |
| *Acts & Resolves* | *The Acts and Resolves, Public and Private of the Province of the Massachusetts Bay.* 4 vols. Boston: Wright and Potter, 1869—1922. |
| *Bax. Mss.* | Baxter, James Phinney, ed. *Baxter Manuscripts, Documentary History of the State of Maine.* 24 vols. Portland: Maine Historical Society, 1869—1916. |
| *CHR* | *Canadian Historical Review* |
| *Coll. de Mss.* | *Collection de Manuscripts contenant lettres, Mémoires, et autres documents historiques relatifs à la Nouvelle-France.* 4 vols. Québec: Législature de Québec, 1883—1885. |
| *CSP* | *Calendar of State Papers, Colonial Series, 1574—1733.* 40 vols. NCR Microcard Editions, 1965. |
| *DCB* | Brown, George W., et al., eds. *Dictionary of Canadian Biography.* Vols. 1—3. Toronto: University of Toronto Press, 1966—. |
| *JAFL* | *Journal of American Folklore* |
| *JR* | Thwaites, Reuben Gold, ed. *The Jesuit Relations and Allied Documents.* 73 vols. New York: Pageant, 1959. |
| Mass. Arch. | Massachusetts State Archives, Boston, Massachusetts |

| | |
|---|---|
| Mass. His. Soc. | Massachusetts Historical Society, Boston, Massachusetts |
| Me. His. Soc. | Maine Historical Society, Portland, Maine |
| *Min. Aff. Étr.* | Ministère des Affaires Étrangères. Ottawa: Public Archives of Canada |
| *NYCD* | O'Callaghan, E. B., ed. *Documents Relative to the Colonial History of New York.* 15 vols. Albany: Weed, Parsons, 1855–1861. |
| *RSUS* | Library of Congress, Records of the States of the United States: A Microfilm Compilation |
| *W&MQ* | *William & Mary Quarterly* |

# NOTES

## INTRODUCTION

1. Kenneth M. Morrison, "Sebastien Racle vs. New England: A Case Study of Frontier Conflict" (M.A. thesis, University of Maine, Orono, 1970); "Sebastien Racle and Norridgewock, 1724: The Eckstorm Conspiracy Thesis Reconsidered," *Maine Historical Society Quarterly* 14 (1974): 76—97.

2. In addition to presenting a narrative history of Abenaki relations with Euramericans, my dissertation also explored the nature of the tribes' world view and argued that a study of interpersonal interaction was a productive approach to Indian-white relations. See Kenneth M. Morrison, "The People of the Dawn: The Abnaki and Their Relations with New England and New France, 1600—1727" (Ph.D. diss., University of Maine, Orono, 1975).

3. No one has better explored the tenacity of Eurocentric ideas in American estimations of Indian culture and history than Robert Berkhofer, *The White Man's Indian: Images of the Indian from Columbus to the Present* (New York: Alfred A. Knopf, 1978); and see Robert A. Nisbet, *Social Change and History: Aspects of the Western Theory of Development* (New York: Oxford University Press, 1969); Roy Harvey Pearce, *Savagism and Civilization: A Study of the Indian and the American Mind* (Baltimore: Johns Hopkins Press, 1953; rev. ed., 1965); Robert Redfield, *The Primitive World and Its Transformation* (Ithaca, N.Y.: Great Seal Books, 1953); Bruce Trigger, *The Children of Aataentsic: A History of the Huron People to 1660*, 2 vols. (Montreal: McGill-Queens University Press, 1976), 1:1—26.)

4. For an introduction to the methodological literature on ethnohistory and a survey of its practice, see James Axtell, "The Ethnohistory of Early America: A Review Essay," *W&MQ* 35 (1978): 110—144. And see William N. Fenton, Lyman H. Butterfield, and Wilcomb E. Washburn, *American Indian and White Relations to 1830: Needs and Opportunities for Study* (Chapel Hill: University of North Carolina Press, 1957); Bernard W. Sheehan, "Indian-White Relations in Early America: A Review Essay," *W&MQ* 26 (1969): 267—286; Robert M. Carmack, "Ethnohistory: A Review of Its Development, Definition, Methods, and Aims," *Annual Review of Anthropology* 1 (1972): 227—246.

5. For theoretical orientations see Everett H. Hughes and Ellen M. Hughes, *Where Peoples Meet: Racial and Ethnic Frontiers* (Glencoe, Ill.: The Free Press, 1952); Jack D. Forbes, "Frontiers in American History and the Role of the Frontier His-

torian," *Ethnohistory* 15 (1968): 203–235; Walter B. Miller, "Two Concepts of Authority," *AA* 57 (1955): 271–289; Robert H. Lowie, "Empathy, or 'Seeing from Within,' " in *Culture in History: Essays in Honor of Paul Radin*, ed. Stanley Diamond (New York: Columbia University Press, 1960), pp. 145–167; Dell Hymes, "Toward Ethnographies of Communication: The Analysis of Communicative Events," *AA* 66 (1964): 12–25; Walter Goldsmidt, "An Ethnography of Encounters: A Methodological Enquiry into the Relation between the Individual and Society," *Current Anthropology* 13 (1972): 59–78; Social Science Research Council, "Acculturation: An Exploratory Formulation," *AA* 56 (1954): 973–1002; Edward H. Spicer, ed., *Perspectives in American Indian Culture Change* (Chicago: University of Chicago Press, 1961).

6. Clyde Kluckhohn, "Values and Value Orientations in the Theory of Action: An Exploration in Definition and Classification," in *Toward a General Theory of Action*, ed. Talcott Parsons and Edward Shils (Cambridge, Mass.: Harvard University Press, 1951), pp. 88–433; James K. Feibleman, "Toward an Analysis of the Basic Value System," *AA* 56 (1954): 421–432; A. Irving Hallowell, "Values, Acculturation, and Mental Health," in his *Culture and Experience* (Philadelphia: University of Pennsylvania Press, 1955), pp. 358–366; Florence R. Kluckhohn, "Dominant and Variant Value Orientations," in *Personality in Nature, Society and Culture*, 2d ed., rev. ed. Clyde Kluckhohn and Henry S. Murray (New York: Alfred A. Knopf, 1967), pp. 342–357; Florence R. Kluckhohn and Fred L. Strodtbeck, *Variations in Value Orientations* (Evanston, Ill.: Row, Peterson, 1961); Leslie A. White, "Values and Cultural Systems," in his *The Concept of Cultural Systems: A Key to Understanding Tribes and Nations* (New York: Columbia University Press, 1975), pp. 141–146.

7. For a consensual definition of the concept of culture, see James Axtell, "The Ethnohistory of Early America," pp. 114–116. See also Gary B. Nash, *Red, White, and Black: The Peoples of Early America* (Englewood Cliffs, N.J.: Prentice-Hall, 1974), pp. 4–5; Anthony F. C. Wallace, *Culture and Personality*, especially chap. 4, "The Psychology of Culture Change" (New York: Random House, 1961), pp. 120–163; Robert Berkhofer, *A Behavioral Approach to Historical Analysis* (New York: The Free Press, 1969).

8. For basic ethnological information on the Abenaki societies, see the articles by Philip K. Bock, Vincent O. Erikson, Dean R. Snow, and Gordon M. Day in *Handbook of North American Indians, XV Northeast*, ed. Bruce G. Trigger (Washington: Smithsonian Institution, 1978), pp. 109–159; Dean R. Snow, "The Ethnographic Baseline of the Eastern Abenaki," *Ethnohistory* 23 (1976): 291–306; Lucien Campeau, *Monumenta Novae Franciae, I, La Première Mission d'Acadie (1602–1616)* (Québec: Les Presses de l'Université Laval, 1967), pp. 55*–276*; P.-André Sévigny, *Les Abénaquis: habitat et migrations (17$_e$ et 18$_e$ siècles* (Montréal: Cahiers d'Histoire des Jésuites, 1976); Gordon M. Day, *The Identity of the Saint Francis Indians*, Canadian Ethnology Service, Paper no. 71 (Ottawa: National Museums of Canada, 1981). For bibliographical resources see W. D. Hamilton and W. A. Spray, *Source Materials Relating to the New Brunswick Indians* (Fredericton, N.B.: Hamroy Books, 1977);

Michael R. P. Herisson, *An Evaluative Ethnohistorical Bibliography of the Malecite Indians* (Ottawa: National Museum of Man, 1974); Roger B. Ray, *The Indians of Maine and the Atlantic Provinces* (Portland: Maine Historical Society, 1977); Elizabeth Tooker, *The Indians of the Northeast: A Critical Bibliography* (Chicago: Newberry Library Center for the History of the American Indians and Indiana University Press, 1978); Eunice Nelson, *The Wabanaki: An Annotated Bibliography* (Cambridge, Mass.: Maine Indian Program, American Friends Service Committee, 1982).

9. Scholars have long called for the study of Indian-Indian relations, but the approach is still largely undeveloped methodologically and remains a major frontier in American Indian history. For general orientations see Alfonso Ortiz, "Some Concerns Central to the Writing of 'Indian' History," *The Indian Historian* 10 (1977): 17–22; Robert Berkhofer, "The Political Context of the New Indian History," *Pacific Historical Review* 40 (1971): 357–382; Wilcomb Washburn, "The Writing of American Indian History: A Status Report," *Pacific Historical Review* 40 (1971): 261–281; Gary B. Nash, "Whither Indian History?" *Journal of Ethnic Studies* 4 (1976): 69–76; Russell Thornton, "American Indian Studies as an Academic Discipline," *American Indian Culture and Research Journal* 2 (1978): 10–19; Edward Spicer, *A Short History of the Indians of the United States* (New York: Van Nostrand, 1969); Eleanor B. Leacock and Nancy O. Lurie, *North American Indians in Historical Perspective* (New York: Random House, 1971).

10. For pioneer applications of mythology and folklore to Indian history, see Anthony F. C. Wallace, *Death and Rebirth of the Seneca* (New York: Alfred A. Knopf, 1969); Father Peter J. Powell, *Sweet Medicine: The Continuing Role of the Sacred Arrows, the Sun Dance, and the Sacred Buffalo Hat in Northern Cheyenne History*, 2 vols. (Norman: University of Oklahoma Press, 1969); Father Peter J. Powell, *People of the Sacred Mountain: A History of the Northern Cheyenne Chiefs and Warrior Societies, 1830–1879*, 2 vols. (San Francisco: Harper and Row, 1981); Gordon M. Day, "Oral History as Complement," *Ethnohistory* 19 (1972): 99–108; Alfred G. Bailey, *The Conflict of European and Eastern Algonkian Cultures, 1504–1700: A Study in Canadian Civilization* (St. John: The New Brunswick Museum, 1937), 2d ed. (Toronto: University of Toronto Press, 1969).

11. For important orientations to the study of myth and oral tradition, see Bernard L. Fontana, "American Indian Oral History: An Anthropologist's Note," *History and Theory* 8 (1969): 366–370; Alfonso Ortiz, "Some Concerns Central to the Writing of 'Indian' History," pp. 17–22; A. Irving Hallowell, "Myth, Culture and Personality," *AA* 49 (1947): 544–556; Kees W. Bolle, *The Freedom of Man in Myth* (Nashville, Tenn.: Vanderbilt University Press, 1968); Mircea Eliade, *The Sacred and the Profane* (New York: Harcourt, Brace, 1959); Mircea Eliade, *Myth and Reality* (New York: Harper and Row, 1963); Anthony F. C. Wallace, *Religion: An Anthropological Approach* (New York: Random House, 1966); Clifford Geertz, *The Interpretation of Cultures: Selected Essays* (New York: Basic Books, 1973); G. Van Der Leeuw, *Religion in Essence and Manifestation* (Gloucester, Mass.: Peter Smith, 1967), 2:591–670. For extended studies that examine how myth and folkloric texts can be used to establish

world-view postulates, see the special issue of *Parabola* 4 (1979): "Myth and the Quest for Meaning"; Alan Dundes, "From Etic to Emic Units in the Structural Study of Folktales," *Journal of American Folklore* 75 (1961): 95−105; Thomas C. Blackburn, *December's Child: A Book of Chumash Oral Narratives* (Berkeley, Los Angeles, London: University of California Press, 1975); Alan Dundes, *The Study of Folklore* (Englewood Cliffs, N.J.: Prentice-Hall, 1965); Melville Jacobs, *The Content and Style of an Oral Literature: Clackamas Chinook Myths and Tales* (Chicago: University of Chicago Press, 1959); Katherine Spencer, *Mythology and Values: An Analysis of Navaho Chantway Myths* (Philadelphia: University of Pennsylvania Press, 1957); Victor Barnouw, *Wisconsin Chippewa Myths and Tales and Their Relation to Chippewa Life* (Madison: University of Wisconsin Press, 1977); Mac Linscott Ricketts, "The North American Indian Trickster," *History of Religions* 5 (1966): 327−350. For studies of American Indian religions, see Sam D. Gill, "Native American Religions: A Review Essay," *Religious Studies Review* 5 (1979): 251−258; Sam D. Gill, *Native American Religions: An Introduction* (Belmont, Calif.: Wadsworth, 1982; Sam D. Gill, *Native American Traditions* (Belmont, Calif.: Wadsworth, 1983); Äke Hultkrantz, "North American Indian Religion in the History of Research: A General Survey," *History of Religions* 6 (1966): 91−107, 208−235; 7 (1967): 13−34, 112−148; Äke Hultkrantz, *The Religions of the American Indian*, trans. Monica Setterwall (Berkeley, Los Angeles, London: University of California Press, 1979); Werner Muller, "North America," in *Pre-Columbian American Religions*, ed. Walter Krickeberg (London: Weidenfeld and Nicolson, 1968).

12.   Julian H. Steward, "The Direct Historical Approach to Archaeology," *American Antiquity* 7 (1942): 337−343; J. V. Wright, "The Application of the Direct Historical Approach to the Iroquois and the Ojibwa," *Ethnohistory* 15 (1968): 96−111.

13.   There are a number of studies of the influence of myth on European behavior, and especially on colonial Puritans, but little has been done on either the French or the
· northeastern Algonkian. For good examples (among many others) see Edward Dudley and Maximillian E. Novak, eds., *The Wild Man Within: An Image in Western Thought from the Renaissance to Romanticism* (Pittsburg: University of Pittsburg Press, 1972); Richard Slotkin, *Regeneration through Violence: The Mythology of the American Frontier, 1600−1860* (Middletown, Conn.: Wesleyan University Press, 1973); Sacvan Bercovitch, *The American Jeremiad* (Madison: University of Wisconsin Press, 1978).

14.   There is no better critical study of this view than Francis Jennings, *The Invasion of America: Indians, Colonialism, and the Cant of Conquest* (Chapel Hill: University of North Carolina Press, 1975). To my mind, however, an overemphasis on materialistic factors mars Jennings's study. Much of the history of New England Indians is confused on this issue. Ironically, in failing to account for Indian senses of historical causality, Jennings does not depart significantly from an older study that he criticizes: Alden Vaughn, *New England Frontier: Puritans and Indians, 1620−1675* (Boston: Little, Brown, 1965); also see the new introduction to Vaughn's work in

which he discusses the developing historiography of Indian-white relations: rev. ed. (New York: W. W. Norton, 1979). See also James P. Ronda, "Beyond Thanksgiving: Francis Jennings' *The Invasion of America," Journal of Ethnic Studies* 7 (1979): 88 — 94. For the theme of dispossession and cultural destruction in colonial Canadian history, see Alfred G. Bailey, *Conflict of European and Eastern Algonkian Cultures*; Cornelius Jaenen, *Friend and Foe: Aspects of French Amerindian Cultural Contact in the Sixteenth and Seventeenth Centuries* (Toronto: McClelland and Stewart, 1979); and especially L. F. S. Upton, *Micmacs and Colonists: Indian-White Relations in the Maritimes, 1713—1867* (Vancouver: University of British Columbia Press, 1979).

15. For a solid overview of the social implications of scale see Fredrik Barth, ed., *Scale and Social Organization* (Oslo: Universitetsforlaget, 1978); and see Robert Redfield, *The Little Community: Viewpoints for the Study of a Human Whole* (Chicago: University of Chicago Press, 1955); Ruth E. Sutter, *The Next Place You Come To: A Historical Introduction to Communities in North America* (Englewood Cliffs, N.J.: Prentice-Hall, 1973); Marshall McLuhan, *Understanding Media: The Extensions of Man* (New York: McGraw-Hill, 1964); and Jacques Ellul, *The Technological Society* (New York: Alfred A. Knopf, 1964).

16. A. Irving Hallowell, "Temporal Orientations in Western Civilization and in a Pre-literate Society," *AA* 39 (1937): 647 — 670; David Reisman, "The Oral and Written Traditions," *Explorations* 6 (1956): 22 — 28; Marshall McLuhan, *The Gutenberg Galaxy: The Making of Typographic Man* (Toronto: University of Toronto Press, 1962); Elizabeth L. Eisenstein, "Some Conjectures about the Impact of Printing on Western Society and Thought: A Preliminary Report," *The Journal of Modern History* 40 (1968): 1—56; Elizabeth Eisenstein, *The Printing Press as an Agent of Change* (Cambridge: Cambridge University Press, 1978); Jack Goody, *The Domestication of the Savage Mind* (Cambridge: Cambridge University Press, 1977); Vine Deloria, *God Is Red* (New York: Grosset and Dunlap, 1973).

17. Francis Jennings, *The Invasion of America*, pp. 3—14.

18. James Axtell, "The White Indians of Colonial America," *W&MQ* 32 (1975): 55 — 88; A. Irving Hallowell, "The Impact of the American Indian on American Culture," *AA* 59 (1957): 201—217; A. Irving Hallowell, "The Backwash of the Frontier: The Impact of the Indian on American Culture," in his *Contributions to Anthropology: Selected Papers of A. Irving Hallowell* (Chicago: University of Chicago Press, 1976), pp. 481—497.

19. My view of the relationship between culture and human behavior derive from scholars who emphasize how people struggle to create communities against the restrictiveness of established social structures. They include Martin Buber, *I and Thou*, 2d ed., trans. R. B. Smith (New York: Charles Scribner's Sons, 1958); Martin Buber, *Between Man and Man* (New York: Macmillan, 1965); Victor Turner, *Dramas, Fields, and Metaphors: Symbolic Action in Human Society* (Ithaca, N.Y.: Cornell University Press, 1974); Marshall Sahlins, *Culture and Practical Reason* (Chicago: University of Chicago Press, 1976).

1: FISH, FUR, AND DISCORD

1. Harold Innis, *The Cod Fisheries: The History of an International Economy* (New Haven: Yale University Press, 1930); Samuel Eliot Morison, *The European Discovery of America: The Northern Voyages, A.D. 500–1600* (Boston: Little, Brown, 1972), p. 272.

2. See Introduction, notes 1, 2, 7, 9, 10, 14.

3. For statements of the older view see George T. Hunt, *The Wars of the Iroquois: A Study in Intertribal Trade Relations* (Madison: University of Wisconsin Press, 1940); Francis Jennings, *The Invasion of America: Indians, Colonialism, and the Cant of Conquest* (Chapel Hill: University of North Carolina Press, 1975), p. 49; and Harold Hickerson, "Fur Trade Colonialism and the North American Indians," *Journal of Ethnic Studies* 1 (1973): 15–44. Recent literature on the impact of trade is more sensitive to the subtle social influences it had on Indian life at particular times. See, for a few examples, E. E. Rich, "Trade Habits and Economic Motivation among the Indians of North America," *Canadian Journal of Economics and Political Science* 26 (1960): 35–53; Charles A. Bishop, *The Northern Ojibwa and the Fur Trade: An Historical and Ecological Study* (Toronto: Holt, Rinehart, and Winston, 1974); Arthur J. Ray, *Indians in the Fur Trade: Their Roles as Trappers, Hunters, and Middlemen in the Lands Southwest of Hudson Bay, 1660–1870* (Toronto: University of Toronto Press, 1974); John Phillip Reid, *A Better Kind of Hatchet: Law, Trade, and Diplomacy in the Cherokee Nation during the Early Years of European Contact* (University Park: Pennsylvania State University Press, 1976); Calvin Martin, *Keepers of the Game: Indian-Animal Relationships and the Fur Trade* (Berkeley, Los Angeles, London: University of California Press, 1978); Jennifer Brown, *Stranger in Blood: Fur Trade Company Families in Indian Country* (Vancouver: University of British Columbia Press, 1980); Sylvia Van Kirk, *"Many Tender Ties": Women in Fur Trade Society, 1670–1870* (Winnipeg: Watson and Dyer, 1980).

4. James P. Howley, *The Beothucks, or Red Indians, the Aboriginal Inhabitants of Newfoundland* (Cambridge: Cambridge University Press, 1915), p. 5; H. P. Biggar, *The Precursors of Jacques Cartier, 1497–1534* (Ottawa: Public Archives of Canada, 1911), pp. xxiii, 100; S. E. Morison, *Northern Voyages*, pp. 215, 230–231; Gustave Lanctot, *A History of Canada*, 3 vols. (Cambridge, Mass.: Harvard University Press, 1963–65), 1:79; Wendall Oswalt, *This Land Was Theirs: A Study of the North American Indian* (New York: John Wiley and Sons, 1966), pp. 65–80; L. F. S. Upton, "The Extermination of the Beothucks of Newfoundland," *CHR* 58 (1977): 133–153; David B. Quinn, "The Argument for the English Discovery of America between 1480 and 1494," *The Geographical Journal* 127 (1961): 277–285.

5. Lawrence C. Wroth, *The Voyages of Giovanni da Verrazzano, 1524–1528* (New Haven: Yale University Press, 1970), p. 140–141; George Parker Winship, ed., *Sailors' Narratives of Voyages along the New England Coast, 1524–1624* (Boston: Houghton Mifflin, 1905), p. 21–22; Neal Salisbury, *Manitou and Providence: Indians,*

*Europeans, and the Making of New England, 1500 — 1643* (New York: Oxford University Press, 1982), pp. 52 — 54.

6. Lawrence C. Wroth, *Voyages of Giovanni da Verrazzano*, pp. 88 — 89, 141; Marcel Trudel, *The Beginnings of New France, 1524 — 1603* (Toronto: McClelland and Stewart, 1973), p. 8; S. E. Morison, *Northern Voyages*, pp. 308 — 313, 329, 331; L. A. Vigneras, "Estevão Gomes," *DCB*, 1:342 — 343; and see Jacques Habert, *La Vie et les Voyages de Jean de Verrazine* (Ottawa: La Circle de Livre de France, 1964), pp. 137 — 405; Bernard G. Hoffman, *Cabot to Cartier* (Toronto: University of Toronto Press, 1961), pp. 116 — 117.

7. H. P. Biggar, ed., *The Voyages of Jacques Cartier* (Ottawa: Public Archives of Canada, 1924), pp. 52 — 53; Marc Lescarbot, *The History of New France*, ed. H. P. Biggar (Toronto: Champlain Society, 1907 — 14), 3:158.

8. H. P. Biggar, ed., *Voyages of Jacques Cartier*, pp. 60, 65 — 67.

9. H. P. Biggar, *Early Trading Companies of New France* (Toronto: University of Toronto Press, 1901), pp. 21 — 22; S. E. Morison, *Northern Voyages*, p. 378.

10. Harold Innis, *The Fur Trade*, pp. 11 — 12; Gustave Lanctot, *A History of Canada*, 1:79; George MacBeath, "The Atlantic Region," *DCB*, 1:22; Marcel Trudel, *Beginnings of New France*, p. 57 — 58; D. B. Quinn, "The Voyage of Etienne Bellenger to the Maritimes in 1583: A New Document," *CHR* 43 (December 1962): 328 — 343; "Etienne Bellenger," *DCB*, 1:87 — 89; Bernard G. Hoffman, *Cabot to Cartier*, p. 33.

11. As quoted in Gilliam T. Cell, *English Enterprise in Newfoundland, 1577 — 1660* (Toronto: University of Toronto Press, 1969), pp. 22 — 24, 40, 48; Richard Hakluyt, "Discourse on Western Planting, 1584," *Bax. Mss.*, 2:34; Bernard G. Hoffman, *Cabot to Cartier*, pp. 120 — 121.

12. Gilliam T. Cell, *English Enterprise*, pp. 24, 48; S. E. Morison, *Northern Voyages*, p. 479.

13. Gustave Lanctot, *A History of Canada*, 1:79.

14. "Jacques Noel," *DCB*, 1:520; Marcel Trudel, *Beginnings of New France*, p. 58.

15. H. P. Biggar, *Early Trading Companies*, p. 33; S. E. Morison, *Northern Voyages*, pp. 464 — 469; "Charles Leigh," *DCB*, 1:450; "Sylvester Wyet," *DCB*, 1:671 — 672; David B. Quinn, "England and the St. Lawrence, 1577 to 1602," in *Merchants and Scholars: Essays in the History of Exploration and Trade*, ed. John Parker (Minneapolis: University of Minnesota Press, 1965), pp. 119 — 143; Gilliam T. Cell, *English Enterprise*, pp. 49 — 57; "Stevan de Bocall," *DCB*, 1:306, 671, 672.

16. D. B. Quinn, "Voyage of Etienne Bellenger," pp. 328 — 343, quotations at 341; Marc Lescarbot, *History of New France*, 3:125, 207; S. E. Morison, *Northern Voyages*, pp. 464 — 465; A. G. Bailey, *The Conflict of European and Eastern Algonkian Cultures, 1504 — 1700*, 2d ed. (Toronto: University of Toronto Press, 1969), pp. 8, 18 — 19; Marcel Trudel, *Beginnings of New France*, p. 57; *JR*, 5:113 — 115; Henry Harrisse, *Découverte et Evolution Cartographique de Terre-Neuve et des Pays Circonvoisins, 1497—1501—1769* (London: Henry Stevens, Son and Stiles, 1900), p. lxiii; Douglas R. McManis, *European Impressions of the New England Coast, 1497 — 1620*

(Chicago: University of Chicago, 1972), pp. 49–67; T. N. Marsh, "An Unpublished Hakluyt Manuscript?" *The New England Quarterly* 35 (1962): 247–252; Dean R. Snow, "Abenaki Fur Trade in the Sixteenth Century," *The Western Canadian Journal of Anthropology* 6 (1976): 3–11; Selma Barkham, "The Basques: Filling a Gap in Our History between Jacques Cartier and Champlain," *Canadian Geographical Journal* 96 (1978): 8–19.

17. "Pierre de Chauvin de Tonnetuit," *DCB*, 1:209–210; Marcel Trudel, *Histoire de la Nouvelle France, I, Les Vaines Tentatives, 1524–1603* (Montréal: Fides, 1963); "Francois Gravé du Pont," *DCB*, 1:345–346.

18. H. P. Biggar, ed., *The Works of Samuel de Champlain*, 6 vols. (Toronto: Champlain Society, 1922–36), 1:98–100; H. P. Biggar, *Early Trading Companies*, p. 32.

19. H. P. Biggar, ed., *The Works of Samuel de Champlain*, 1:100.

20. H. P. Biggar, ed., *The Works of Samuel de Champlain*, 1:101, 103, 107, 141, 160, 170; Harold Innis, *The Fur Trade in Canada: An Introduction to Canadian Economic History* (New Haven: Yale University Press, 1930), p. 15. For early Iroquois-Micmac relations see H. P. Biggar, *Voyages of Jacques Cartier*, pp. 177–178; "Tessouat," *DCB*, 1:638.

21. H. P. Biggar, ed., *The Works of Samuel de Champlain*, 1:123–124, 166. For discussion of this Iroquoian-Algonkian war see Bruce G. Trigger, "Archaeological and Other Evidence: A Fresh Look at the 'Laurentian Iroquois,' " *American Antiquity* 33 (1968): 429–440; Bruce G. Trigger, "Who Were the 'Laurentian Iroquois,' " *The Canadian Review of Sociology and Anthropology* 3 (1966): 201–213; Bruce G. Trigger, "Trade and Tribal Warfare on the St. Lawrence in the Sixteenth Century," *Ethnohistory* 9 (1962): 240–256; A. G. Bailey, "The Significance of the Identity and Disappearance of the Laurentian Iroquois," *Transactions of the Royal Society of Canada* 27 (1933): 97–108; Bernard G. Hoffman, "The Souriquois, Etechemin and Kwedech: A Lost Chapter in American Ethnography," *Ethnohistory* 2 (1955): 65–87; A. G. Bailey, "Social Revolution in Early Eastern Canada," *CHR* 19 (1938): 265; A. G. Bailey, "Reappraisals," in *Conflict of Cultures*, pp. xi–xxiii; A. G. Bailey, "Vanished Iroquoians," in his *Culture and Nationality* (Toronto: McClelland and Stewart, 1972), pp. 14–28; see also James F. Pendergast and Bruce G. Trigger, *Cartier's Hochelaga and the Dawson Site* (Montreal: McGill-Queen's University Press, 1972).

22. John Brereton, "Briefe and True Relation of the Discoverie of the North Part of Virginia in 1602," in *Early English and French Voyages Chiefly from Hakluyt, 1534–1608*, ed. Henry S. Burrage (New York: Charles Scribner's Sons, 1906), pp. 325–340; Martin Pring, "A Voyage set out from the citie of Bristol, 1603," in *Early Voyages*, ed. Henry S. Burrage, p. 348; David B. Quinn, *England and the Discovery of America, 1481–1620* (New York: A. A. Knopf, 1974); A. L. Rowse, *The Elizabethans and America* (London: Macmillan, 1959), pp. 89–97.

23. James Rosier, "A True Relation of the Voyage of Capitaine George Waymouth, 1605," in *Early Voyages*, ed. Henry S. Burrage, pp. 347, 372–373, 376; see

Henry S. Burrage, *Gorges and the Grant of the Province of Maine, 1622: A Tercentenary Memorial* (Augusta, Me., 1923), pp. 39—75.

24. James Rosier, "True Relation," in *Early Voyages*, ed. Henry S. Burrage, p. 377—379; Henry S. Burrage, *The Beginnings of Colonial Maine, 1602—1658* (Portland, Me.: Marks Printing House, 1914), p. 44; Carolyn T. Foreman, *Indians Abroad, 1493—1938* (Norman: University of Oklahoma Press, 1943), pp. 15—16.

25. James P. Baxter, ed., *Sir Ferdinando Gorges and His Province of Maine*, 3 vols. (Boston, 1890), 2:8—9; A. L. Rowse, *Elizabethans and America*, pp. 95—97, 102; Richard A. Preston, *Gorges of Plymouth Fort* (Toronto: University of Toronto Press, 1953); Charles M. Andrews, *The Colonial Period of American History*, 4 vols. (New Haven: Yale University Press, 1934), 1:78—97.

26. Henry O. Thayer, ed., *The Sagadahoc Colony* (Portland, Me., 1892), pp. 42, 56—60; "A Relation of a Voyage to Sagadahoc, 1607—1608," in *Early Voyages*, ed. Henry S. Burrage, pp. 399—419; Henry S. Burrage, *Gorges*, pp. 79—98. On Skidwarres's and Nahanada's refusal to cooperate see Richard A. Preston, *Gorges of Plymouth Fort*, p. 147.

27. Lucien Campeau, *Monumenta Novae Franciae, I, La Première Mission d'Acadie (1602—1616)* (Québec: Les Presses de l'Université Laval, 1967), p. 246; William I. Roberts, "The Fur Trade of New England in the Seventeenth Century" (Ph.D. diss., University of Pennsylvania, 1958), pp. 10—11.

28. *JR*, 2:45—47; Gorges letter, February 7, 1607, in James P. Baxter, ed., *Gorges*, 3:161.

29. H. P. Biggar, *Early Trading Companies*, pp. 53—55, 63.

30. H. P. Biggar, ed., *The Works of Samuel de Champlain*, 1:238—296.

31. "The Third Voyage of Henry Hudson," in *Sailors' Narratives*, ed. George Parker Winship, pp. 181—182; John Smith, *A Description of New England; Or, Observations and Discoveries in North America, 1616*, in *Travels and Works of Captain John Smith*, ed. Edward Arber (Edinburgh: John Grant, 1911), 2:698; *JR*, 2:127, 179.

32. "Jesse Fléché," *DCB*, 1:307; Marc Lescarbot, "La Conversion des Sauvages," in Lucien Campeau, *Monumenta Novae Franciae*, 1:61—93; *JR*, 1:163—165; 2:41—43, 51, 89; 3:147, 245.

33. Lucien Campeau, *Monumenta Novae Franciae*, 1:287—288, 296—298, 394—396, 409—412, 415—419, 435—439, 443—449, 569—589; P. F. X. de Charlevoix, *History and General Description of New France*, ed. J. G. Shea, 6 vols. (New York: Francis P. Harper, 1900), 1:260—283; Charles M. Andrews, *The Colonial Period*, 1:148—149; John Bartlet Brebner, *New England's Outpost, Acadia before the Conquest of Canada* (New York: Columbia University Press, 1927), pp. 19—20.

34. William Durkee Williamson, *The History of the State of Maine* (Hallowell, 1832), 1:220—260; Lucien Campeau, *Monumenta Novae Franciae*, 1:663—664; George F. Willison, *Saints and Strangers* (New York: Time, 1964), pp. 263—305; "Charles de Saint-Etienne de la Tour," *DCB*, 1:593—594; William J. Eccles, *The Canadian Frontier: 1534—1760* (New York: Holt, Rinehart, and Winston, 1969),

pp. 1—34; Marcel Trudel, *The Beginnings of New France, 1524—1603* (Toronto: McClelland and Stewart, 1973), pp. 163—180; Gustave Lanctot, *A History of Canada*, 1:128—147; "Charles de Biencourt de Poutrincourt," *DCB*, 1:99—102.

35. For another view see A. G. Bailey, *Conflict of Cultures*, pp. 12—13, 57—58.

36. Bernard G. Hoffman, *Cabot to Cartier*, p. 112; Neal Salisbury, *Manitou and Providence*, pp. 50—60; Patrick M. Malone, "Changing Military Technology among the Indians of Southern New England, 1600—1677," *American Quarterly* 25 (1973): 50; T. J. Brasser, "Early Indian-European Contacts," in *Handbook of North American Indians, XV, Northeast*, ed. Bruce G. Trigger (Washington: Smithsonian Institution, 1978), pp. 78—88; Bert Salwen, "Indians of Southern New England and Long Island: Early Period," in *Handbook of North American Indians*, ed. Bruce G. Trigger, 15:166; A. G. Bailey, *Conflict of Cultures*, p. 136; William Wood, *New England Prospect* (London, 1634), p. 78; James P. Howley, *The Beothucks*, p. 3; Calvin Martin, "The Four Lives of a Micmac Copper Pot," *Ethnohistory* 22 (Spring 1975): 111—133.

37. *JR*, 3:105—109; Marc Lescarbot, *History of New France*, 3:168, 219—220; John Smith, *Description of New England; Or, Observations and Discoveries in North America*, in *Tracts and Other Papers, Relating Principally to the Origin, Settlement, and Progress of the Colonies in North America, From the Discovery of the Country to the Year 1776*, ed. Peter Force (Gloucester, Mass.: Peter Smith, 1963), 2:17; *JR*, 1:69, 83; Chretien LeClercq, *New Relation of Gaspesia, With the Customs and Religion of the Gaspesian Indians*, ed. William F. Ganong (Toronto: Champlain Society, 1910), pp. 110, 111, 139; Lucien Campeau, *Monumenta Novae Franciae*, 1:483—487; H. P. Biggar, ed., *The Works of Samuel de Champlain*, 1:273—274.

38. *JR*, 1:77; 3:83; H. P. Biggar, ed., *The Works of Samuel de Champlain*, 1:292, 308; Bernard G. Hoffman, *Cabot to Cartier*, p. 116; Bruce J. Bourque, "Aboriginal Settlement and Subsistence on the Maine Coast," *Man in the Northeast* 6 (1973): 6; John Josselyn, "An Account of Two Voyages to New England," *Mass. His. Soc., Coll.*, 3d ser., vol. 3 (Cambridge, 1833), p. 298; H. P. Biggar, *Precursors*, p. 193.

39. For territoriality and seasonality see Lucien Campeau, *Monumenta Novae Franciae*, 1:79, 114—115, 488 (emphasis in original); H. P. Biggar, ed., *The Works of Samuel de Champlain*, 1:329; 3:376; M. de Villebon to M. de Pontchartrain, August 20, 1694, *NYCD*, 9:575; John M. Cooper, "The Culture of Northeastern Indian Hunters: A Reconstructive Interpretation," in *Man in America*, ed. Frederick Johnson (Andover, Mass.: Phillip's Academy, 1946), p. 287; Wilson D. Wallis and Ruth S. Wallis, *The Malecite Indians of New Brunswick* (Ottawa: Ministry of Northern Affairs and National Resources, 1957), p. 25; David Sanger, "Passamaquoddy Bay Prehistory: A Summary," *Maine Archaeological Society* 11 (1971): 14—20. For views that argue that contact was destructive, see A. G. Bailey, *Conflict of Cultures*, p. 88; T. J. Brasser, "Early Indian-European Contacts," in *Handbook of North American Indians*, ed. Bruce G. Trigger, 15:83—84; Dean R. Snow, "Wabanaki 'Family Hunting Territories,' " *AA* 70 (1965): 1143—1151.

40. *JR*, 2:81, 477—478; 3:81, 212—213, 253; Marc Lescarbot, *History of New France*, 3:212—213; Nicholas Denys, *The Description and Natural History of the Coasts of*

*North America (Acadia)*, ed. William F. Ganong (Toronto: Champlain Society, 1908), pp. 477–478; John Brereton, "Briefe and True Relation of the Discoverie of the North Part of Virginia in 1602," in *Early Voyages*, ed. Henry S. Burrage, pp. 336–337.

41. *JR*, 3:88–89; 50:75–77; A. Irving Hallowell, "The Nature and Function of Property as a Social Institution," in *Culture and Experience* (Philadelphia: University of Pennsylvania Press, 1955), pp. 236–249; Marshall David Sahlins, *Stone Age Economics* (Chicago: Aldine, Atherton, 1972); John A. Price, "Sharing: The Integration of Intimate Economies," *Anthropologica* 17 (1975): 3–27; for pertinent ethnological discussion see John H. Dowling, "Individual Ownership and the Sharing of Game in Hunting Societies," *AA* 70 (1968): 502–507; F. G. Speck, "Ethical Attributes of the Labrador Indians," *AA* 35 (1933): 559–594; Julius Lips, "Public Opinion and Mutual Assistance among the Montagnais-Naskapi," *AA* 39 (1937): 222–228; for a discussion of viewpoints among economic anthropologists see Calvin Martin, *Keepers of the Game*, pp. 1–21.

42. *JR*, 1:75–77; 2:73, 354–355; Marc Lescarbot, *History of New France*, 3:214; Christopher Levett, "A Voyage to New England," in *Sailors' Narratives*, ed. George Parker Winship, p. 284 (emphasis in original); Nicholas Denys, *Description and Natural History*, pp. 195–196; James Rosier, "True Relation," in *Early Voyages*, ed. Henry S. Burrage, p. 371; Chretien LeClercq, *New Relation*, pp. 172–173, 245. For interpretations see A. G. Bailey, "Social Revolution," p. 272; Alvin Morrison, "Dawnland Decisions: Seventeenth-century Wabanaki Leaders and Their Response to the Differential Contact Stimuli in the Overlap Area of New France and New England" (Ph.D. diss., State University of New York, 1974).

43. James Rosier, "True Relation," in *Early Voyages*, ed. Henry S. Burrage, pp. 371, 391; Marc Lescarbot, *History of New France*, 2:322; Chretien LeClercq, *New Relation*, p. 246.

44. See Introduction, note 8.

45. Chretien LeClercq, *New Relation*, p. 95; Marc Lescarbot, *Nova Francia: A Description of Acadia, 1606*, trans. P. Erondelle (London: George Routledge and Sons, 1928), pp. 211–212; Roger Williams, "Key to the Indian Language," *Rhode Island His. Soc., Coll.*, 1:135; Gaby Pelletier, "From Animal Skins to Polyester," *Journal of the New Brunswick Museum* (1978), pp. 118–130; Ruth Holmes Whitehead, *Elitekey: Micmac Material Culture from 1600 A.D. to the Present* (Halifax: Nova Scotia Museum, 1980).

46. H. P. Biggar, ed., *The Works of Samuel de Champlain*, 1:338, 353; John Smith, *Description of New England*, in *Tracts*, ed. Peter Force, 2:16.

47. H. P. Biggar, ed., *The Works of Samuel de Champlain*, 1:299, 321, 329; 3:370; *JR*, 1:105; Marc Lescarbot, *History of New France*, 2:169.

48. H. P. Biggar, ed., *The Works of Samuel de Champlain*, 1:272.

49. Ibid., 1:311–316, 357, 363–364.

50. Marc Lescarbot, *History of New France*, 2:323–324; H. P. Biggar, ed., *The Works of Samuel de Champlain*, 1:181, 278, 381, 394–398.

51. Marc Lescarbot, *History of New France*, 2:323−324.

52. Ibid., 2:324−325; H. P. Biggar, ed., *The Works of Samuel de Champlain*, 1:396.

53. Wendell S. Hadlock, "War among the Northeastern Woodland Indians," *AA* 49 (1947): 204−221; "Membertou," *DCB*, 1:500; Alvin Morrison "Membertou's Raid on Chouacoet 'Almouchiquois'—The Micmac Sack of Saco in 1607," in *Papers of the Sixth Algonquian Conference, 1974*, ed. William Cowan (Ottawa: Carleton University, 1975), pp. 141−158; Neal Salisbury, *Manitou and Providence*, pp. 60−72.

54. H. P. Biggar, ed., *The Works of Samuel de Champlain*, 1:311−312, 457−458; for Panounias see H. P. Biggar, ed., *The Works of Samuel de Champlain*, 1:311, 316, 435−436, 442−446, and *DCB*, 1:529−530; Marc Lescarbot, *History of New France*, 3:263−272; *JR*, 3:93−95; Lucien Campeau, ed., *Monumenta Novae Franciae*, 1:489−491.

55. H. P. Biggar, ed., *The Works of Samuel de Champlain*, 1:445, 457; John E. Godrey, "Bashaba and the Tarrantines," *Me. His. Soc., Coll.*, 2:93−106.

56. *JR*, 3:89, 91.

57. James P. Baxter, ed., *Gorges*, 2:76, 77; Henry Gardiner, *New England's Vindication*, p. 22.

58. *JR*, 3:91.

59. James Rosier, "True Relation," in *Early Voyages*, ed. Henry S. Burrage, p. 391; A. L. Rowse, *The Elizabethans and America*, p. 101.

60. John Smith, *Description of New England*, in *Tracts*, ed. Peter Force, 2:10−11; John Smith, *A Description of New England*, in *Travels and Works of Captain John Smith*, ed. Edward Arber, 1:17, 22, 187−188, 199−200; also in Henry S. Burrage, ed., *Gorges*, pp. 103−125; Edwin C. Rozwenc, "Captain John Smith's Image of America," *W&MQ* 16 (1959): 27−36; Ronald Sanders, *Lost Tribes and Promised Lands* (Boston, 1978), p. 277; George Parker Winship, ed., *Sailors' Narratives*, p. 232.

61. John Smith, *Description of New England*, in *Tracts*, ed. Peter Force, 2:18; Karen Ordahl Kupperman, "English Perceptions of Treachery, 1583−1640: The Case of the American 'Savages,' " *The Historical Journal* 20 (1977): 263−287; Karen Ordahl Kupperman, *Settling with the Indians: The Meeting of English and Indian Cultures in America, 1580−1640* (Totowa, N.J.: Rowman and Littlefield, 1980).

62. John Smith, *Description of New England*, in *Tracts*, ed. Peter Force, 2:26, 29−30.

63. Sir Ferdinando Gorges, "A Briefe Narration of the Originall Undertakings of the Advancement of Plantations into the Parts of America," in *Me. His. Soc., Coll.*, 1st ser., vol. 2, pp. 38, 62; James P. Baxter, ed., *Gorges*, 1:223−224; 2:49; Sydney V. James, ed., *Three Visitors to Early Plymouth* (Plymouth, Mass.: Plymouth Plantation, 1963), pp. 15−16; Howard Mumford Jones, "The Colonial Impulse," p. 151; C. H. Levermore, ed., *Forerunners*, 2:602−603.

64. The following paragraphs on Christopher Levett are drawn from "A Voyage into New England, Begun in 1623, and Ended in 1624," *Me. His. Soc., Coll.*, 2:77−109, and George Parker Winship, ed. *Sailors' Narratives*, pp. 271−284; see

James P. Baxter, *Christopher Levett, of York, The Pioneer Colonist in Casco Bay* (Portland, Me., 1893).

65. John Smith, *Description of New England*, in *Tracts*, ed. Peter Force 2:25, offered to protect the Abenaki from the Micmac. William Wood, *New Englands Prospect*, pp. 60–61, notes how the English taught the Abenaki to swear.

66. Neal Salisbury, *Manitou and Providence*, pp. 50–84; John G. Reid, *Acadia, Maine, and New Scotland: Marginal Colonies in the Seventeenth Century* (Toronto: University of Toronto Press, 1981), pp. 20–33; John Bartlett Brebner, *New England's Outpost, Acadia before the Conquest of Canada*, pp. 21–27; Charles M. Andrews, *The Colonial Period*, 1:313–329.

## 2: THE SACRED AND THE PROFANE

1. Marc Bloch, *Feudal Society*, trans. L. A. Manyon (Chicago: University of Chicago Press, 1961), pp. 123–175, 433–437; Colin Morris, *The Discovery of the Individual: 1050–1200* (New York: Harper and Row, 1972); Marc Bloch, *French Rural History: An Essay on Its Basic Characteristics* (Berkeley and Los Angeles: University of California Press, 1966), pp. 162–164; Alan Macfarlane, *The Origins of English Individualism: The Family, Property, and Social Transition* (Oxford: Basil Blackwell, 1978); Philippe Ariés, *L'Enfant et La Vie Familiale: Sous l'Ancien Régime* (Paris: Librairie Plon, 1960).

2. J. R. Hale, *Renaissance Europe: Individual and Society, 1480–1520* (Berkeley, Los Angeles, London: University of California Press, 1971), pp. 101–137; Henry Osborn Taylor, *The Mediaeval Mind: A History of the Development of Thought and Emotion in the Middle Ages*, 4th ed. (Cambridge, Mass.: Harvard University Press, 1949), 2:260–312; Marc Bloch, *French Rural History*, pp. 198–235; Robert Mandrou, *Introduction to Modern France, 1500–1640: An Essay in Historical Psychology*, trans. R. E. Hallmark (New York: Harper and Row, 1975), pp. 77–138; Lucien Febvre, *Life in Renaissance France*, ed. Marian Rothstein (Cambridge, Mass.: Harvard University Press, 1977); Natalie Zemon Davis, *Society and Culture in Early Modern France* (Stanford, Calif.: Stanford University Press, 1975); Harold A. Innis, *The Bias of Communication* (Toronto: University of Toronto Press, 1951).

3. Robert Mandrou, *Modern France*, pp. 77–79; Georges Duby, *The Early Growth of the European Economy: Warriors and Peasants to the Twelfth Century*, trans. Howard B. Clarke (Ithaca, N.Y.: Cornell University Press, 1974); Henri Pirenne, *Medieval Cities, Their Origins and the Revival of Trade* (Princeton: Princeton University Press, 1952); John U. Nef, *Industry and Government in France and England, 1540–1640* (Ithaca, N.Y.: Cornell University Press, 1957); John Tonkin, *The Church and the Secular Order in Reformation Thought* (New York: Columbia University Press, 1971); Jan de Vries, *The Economy of Europe in an Age of Crisis, 1600–1750* (London: Cambridge University Press, 1976).

4. Carl Bridenbaugh, *Vexed and Troubled Englishmen, 1590–1642* (New York, 1968), p. 143.

5. Francis Bacon, "Of Plantations," in *The Essays or Counsels Civil and Moral of Francis Bacon*, ed. A. S. Gaye (Oxford: Clarendon Press, 1911), p. 107; Natalie Zemon Davis, *Early Modern France*, pp. 124, 137, 154, 258−267; Robert Mandrou, *Modern France*, p. 135; J. R. Hale, *Renaissance Europe*, pp. 174−175; Wallace Notestein, *The English People on the Eve of Colonization, 1603−1630* (New York: Harper and Row, 1954), p. 13. These attitudes endured; see "A Country of Savages," in Eugen Weber, *Peasants into Frenchmen: The Modernization of Rural France, 1870−1914* (Stanford, Calif.: Stanford University Press, 1976), pp. 3−22.

6. Robert Mandrou, *Modern France*, pp. 63−64; Margaret Hodgen, *Early Anthropology in the Sixteenth and Seventeenth Centuries* (Philadelphia: University of Pennsylvania Press, 1964), pp. 214−215; Jeanne Ferté, *La Vie Religieuse dans les Campagnes Parisiennes (1622−1695)* (Paris: Librairie Philosophique J. Vrin, 1962), pp. 197, 199, 275−276, 284−285, 297, 336; John Bossy, "The Counter-Reformation and the People of Catholic Europe," *Past and Present* 47 (1970): 51−70; Keith Thomas, *Religion and the Decline of Magic: Studies in Popular Beliefs in Sixteenth and Seventeenth Century England* (London: Weidenfeld and Nicolson, 1971), p. 666, cites Sir Thomas Browne, *Vulgar Errors*, and John Aubrey, *Remains of Gentilisme and Judaisme*; Natalie Zemon Davis, *Early Modern France*, pp. 229, 233, 246−247, 250, 252, 254−255; Francis Bacon, "Of Superstition," in *Essays*, ed. A. S. Gaye, pp. 62−63.

7. As quoted in Margaret Hodgen, *Early Anthropology*, pp. 73−74.

8. For text and critical assessments see Edward Shurtz and J. H. Hexter, eds., *The Complete Works of St. Thomas More* (New Haven: Yale University Press, 1965); Sir Thomas More, *Utopia*, ed. Robert M. Adams (New York: W. W. Norton, 1975); and see Henry S. Bausum, "Edenic Images of the Western World: A Reappraisal," *The South Atlantic Quarterly* 67 (1968): 672−686.

9. Peter Laslett, *The World We Have Lost* (London: Methuen, 1965).

10. Derek Wilson, *The People and the Book: The Revolutionary Impact of the English Bible, 1380−1611* (London: Anchor Press, 1976); and see Introduction, note 16.

11. C. A. Patrides, *The Grand Design of God: The Literary Form of the Christian View of History* (London: Routledge and Kegan Paul, 1972), pp. 72, 79; N. G. Pauling, "The Employment Problem in Pre-classical English Economic Thought," *Economic Record* 27 (June 1951): 52−65.

12. Boemus (1520), quoted by Margaret T. Hodgen, *Early Anthropology*, pp. 132, 140.

13. Francis Bacon, "Of Superstition," in *Essays*, ed. A. S. Gaye, pp. 62−63. For the relationship between English aversion to heathenism and their reaction to the pope see Howard Mumford Jones, "The Colonial Impulse," p. 131; Michael Hechter, *Internal Colonialism: The Celtic Fringe in British National Development, 1536−1966* (Berkeley, Los Angeles, London: University of California Press, 1975); C. A. Patrides, *The Grand Design of God*, pp. 49, 74; Margaret T. Hodgen, *Early Anthropology*, p. 255; G. G. Coulton, *Medieval Panorama: The English Scene from Conquest to Reformation* (New York: W. W. Norton, 1974), pp. 681−704.

14. Alan Macfarlane, *Witchcraft in Tudor and Stuart England: A Regional and Comparative Study* (London: Routledge and Kegan Paul, 1970); Christopher Hill, *Reformation to Industrial Revolution: A Social and Economic History of Britain, 1530−1780* (London: Weidenfeld and Nicolson, 1967); Keith Thomas, *Religion and the Decline of Magic*; A. L. Rowse, *The Elizabethan Renaissance: The Cultural Achievement*, 2 vols. (London: Macmillan, 1971−72); Christopher Hill, *The World Turned Upside Down: Radical Ideas during the English Revolution* (New York: Viking Press, 1972); D. B. Quinn, *The Elizabethans and the Irish* (Ithaca, N.Y.: Cornell University Press, 1966); J. R. Hale, *Renaissance Europe: Individual and Society, 1480−1520* (Berkeley, Los Angeles, London: University of California Press, 1971); Michael Waltzer, *The Revolution of the Saints: A Study in the Origins of Radical Politics* (New York: Atheneum, 1973); J. H. Elliot, *The Old World and the New, 1492−1650* (Cambridge: Cambridge University Press, 1970).

15. Howard Mumford Jones, *O Strange New World: American Culture: The Formative Years* (New York: Viking Press, 1964), pp. 167, 173; J. H. Rowe, "The Renaissance Foundations of Anthropology," *AA* 67 (1965): 4, observes that ethnological theory and social philosophy were different intellectual traditions in the sixteenth century; Roy Harvey Pearce, "Primitivistic Ideas in the *Faerie Queene*," *The Journal of English and Germanic Philology* 44 (1945): 144; M. E. Strieby, "Scotch Highlanders and American Indians," in *Twenty-seventh Annual Report of the Board of Indian Commissioners, 1895* (Washington, D.C.: Government Printing Office, 1896), pp. 58−64; William Christie Macleod, *The American Indian Frontier* (New York: Alfred A. Knopf, 1928), pp. 152−171; Franklin L. Baumer, "England, the Turk, and the Common Corps of Christendom," *The American Historical Review* 50 (1944): 26−48; W. R. Jones, "The Image of the Barbarian in Medieval Europe," *Comparative Studies in Society and History* 13 (1971): 376−407; Nicholas P. Canny, "The Ideology of English Colonization: From Ireland to America," *W&MQ* 30 (1973): 575−598; Michael Hechter, *Internal Colonialism*; C. A. Patrides, " 'The Bloody and Cruell Turke': the Background of a Renaissance Commonplace," *Studies in the Renaissance* 10 (1963): 126−135; C. A. Patrides, *The Grand Design of God*, pp. 48−49, 71, 107.

16. Margaret Hodgen, *Early Anthropology*, p. 129; A. Irving Hallowell, "The History of Anthropology as an Anthropological Problem" and "The Beginnings of Anthropology in America," both in his *Contributions to Anthropology*, pp. 21−125; Natalie Zemon Davis, *Early Modern France*, pp. 152−187.

17. Christopher Columbus, *The Journal of Christopher Columbus*, trans. Cecil Jane (New York: Clarkson N. Potter, Inc., 1960), pp. 23−24, 52, 76−77, 100−102; Amerigo Vespucci, as quoted in Lee E. Huddleston, *Origins of the American Indians: European Concepts, 1492−1729* (Austin: University of Texas Press, 1967), p. 4. For Europeans' penchant for cultural description in the negative mode, see Margaret Hodgen, *Early Anthropology*, pp. 197−198. Hodgen's remark that Columbus reported on Native Americans with remarkable realism seems extreme (*Early Anthropology*, pp. 19−20). See Robert Berkhofer, *The White Man's Indian: Images of the*

*American Indian from Columbus to the Present* (New York: Alfred A. Knopf, 1978), pp. 4—9, 73—74, for another view; Frederick Turner, *Beyond Geography: The Western Spirit against the Wilderness* (New York: Viking Press, 1980), pp. 118—143.

18. Christopher Columbus, *Journal*, p. 119; Olive Dickason, "The Concept of *l'Homme Sauvage* and Early French Colonialism in the Americas," *Revue Française d'Histoire d'Outre-Mer* 63 (1977): 8, observes that the image of the American Indian as a child of nature, living ideally in a Golden Age "never ceased to haunt the Europeans' mind."

19. Henry Harrisse, *Découverte et Évolution Cartographique de Terre-Neuve et des Pays Circonvoisins, 1497—1501—1769* (London: Henry Stevens, Son and Stiles, 1900), p. 116; H. P. Biggar, *The Precursors of Jacques Cartier, 1497—1534* (Ottawa: Public Archives of Canada, 1911), p. 100; H. P. Biggar, *The Voyages of Jacques Cartier* (Ottawa: Public Archives of Canada, 1924), p. 60; Olive Dickason, "Concept of *l'Homme Sauvage*," pp. 6—7; James P. Howley, *The Beothucks, or Red Indians, the Aboriginal Inhabitants of Newfoundland* (Cambridge: Cambridge University Press, 1915), pp. 5, 7; S. E. Morison, *The European Discovery of America: The Northern Voyages, A.D. 500—1600* (Boston: Little, Brown, 1972), pp. 215—216, 231; Roy Harvey Pearce, "Primitivistic Ideas," p. 149; Bernard G. Hoffman, *Cabot to Cartier* (Toronto: University of Toronto Press, 1961), pp. 116—117.

20. William Wood, *New Englands Prospect* (London, 1634), p. 80. This discussion of English reactions to Indians closely follows Karen O. Kupperman, *Settling with the Indians: The Meeting of English and Indian Cultures in America, 1580—1640* (Totowa, N.J.: Rowman and Littlefield, 1980).

21. Thomas Morton, *New English Canaan*, in *Tracts and Other Papers, Relating Principally to the Origin, Settlement, and Progress of the Colonies in North America, From the Discovery of the Country to the Year 1776*, ed. Peter Force (Gloucester, Mass.: Peter Smith, 1963), 2:40; Roger Williams, *Key to the Indian Language, Rhode Island His. Soc., Coll.*, 1:46, 57, 61.

22. Harry Levin, *The Myth of the Golden Age in the Renaissance* (Bloomington: Indiana University Press, 1969), especially "Some Paradoxes of Utopia," appendix A, pp. 187—192; Henri Baudet, *Paradise on Earth: Some Thoughts on European Images of Non-European Man* (New Haven: Yale University Press, 1965).

23. On early cultural relativism see Olive Dickason, "Concept of *l'Homme Sauvage*," p. 9; Marc Lescarbot, *The History of New France*, ed. H. P. Biggar, 3 vols. (Toronto: Champlain Society, 1907—14), 2:126, 136, 149, 172.

24. Marc Lescarbot, *History of New France*, 1:32—33; 3:77, 79.

25. Ibid., 3:210—211.

26. Ibid., 3:93—94, 264.

27. *JR*, 2:153; 3:128, 151; Marc Lescarbot, *History of New France*, 3:98.

28. Marc Lescarbot, *The History of New France*, 1:174—175, 215, 272.

29. Ibid., 3:216, 255—256.

30. Ibid., 3:152, 216, 256.

31. *JR*, 1:173.

32. *JR*, 2:75−77.

33. *JR*, 2:87.

34. *JR*, 2:7, 237.

35. *JR*, 2:11−13, 49; 3:85, 131, 135.

36. *JR*, 2:9−11, 13.

37. Roger Williams, *Key to Indian Language*, p. 158. William S. Simmons, "Cultural Bias in the New England Puritans' Perceptions of Indians," *W&MQ* 38 (1981): 56−72; William S. Simmons, "Southern New England Shamanism: An Ethnographic Reconstruction," in *Papers of the Seventh Algonquian Conference, 1975*, ed. William Cowan (Ottawa: Carleton University, 1976), pp. 217−256; Frank Shuffleton, "Indian Devils and Pilgrim Fathers: Squanto, Hobomok, and the English Conception of Indian Religion," *New England Quarterly* 49 (1976): 108−116. Chretien LeClercq, *New Relation of Gaspesia, With the Customs and Religion of the Gaspesian Indians*, ed. William F. Ganong (Toronto: Champlain Society, 1910), pp. 142, 216−217.

38. Keith Thomas, *Religion and the Decline of Magic*, pp. 664−665.

39. Chretien LeClercq, *New Relation of Gaspesia*, pp. 125, 233, 234.

40. Ibid., pp. 116−117, 288, 296.

41. Ibid., pp. 142, 216−217.

42. Chretien LeClercq, *New Relation of Gaspesia*, pp. 209, 212, 214, 216; Calvin Martin, "The European Impact on the Culture of a Northeastern Algonquian Tribe: An Ecological Interpretation," *W&MQ* 31 (1974): 15; A. G. Bailey, *The Conflict of European and Eastern Algonkian Cultures, 1504−1700* (Toronto: University of Toronto Press, 1969), p. 139.

43. Chretien LeClercq, *New Relation of Gaspesia*, pp. 210−211.

44. Ibid., pp. 211−213.

45. Ibid., p. 213; Roger Williams, *Key to Indian Language*, p. 117; for the larger cultural differences see A. Irving Hallowell, "Temporal Orientations in Western Civilization and in a Pre-literate Society," *AA* 39 (1937): 647−670.

46. F. G. Speck, *Naskapi: The Savage Hunters of the Labrador Peninsula* (Norman: University of Oklahoma Press, 1935), pp. 56, 234. For a more sensitive discussion see E. T. Adney to Avery Shaw, July 10, 1948, New Brunswick Museum Archives.

47. A. Irving Hallowell, "Ojibwa Ontology," in *Culture in History: Essays in Honor of Paul Radin*, ed. Stanley Diamond (New York: G. P. Putnam's Sons, 1913), pp. 21, 28.

48. A. Irving Hallowell, "Ojibwa Ontology," p. 24; Robert Redfield, *The Primitive World and Its Transformations* (Ithaca, N.Y.: Cornell University Press, 1953), p. 9; and see Wilson D. Wallis and Ruth Sawtell Wallis, *The Malecite Indians of New Brunswick*, Ministry of Northern Affairs and National Resources, bulletin 148, Anthropological series 40 (Ottawa, 1957), p. 27; C. J. Wheeler and A. P. Buchner, "Rock Art: A Metalinguistic Interpretation of the Algonkian Word for Stone," in *Papers of the Sixth Algonquian Conference, 1974*, ed. William Cowan (Ottawa: National Museums of Canada, 1975), pp. 362−371; and see Sam D. Gill, "Prayer as Person:

The Performative Force in Navajo Prayer Acts," *History of Religions* 17 (1977): 143−157; Jonathan Z. Smith, "I Am a Parrot (Red)," *History of Religions* 11 (1971): 391.

49. A. Irving Hallowell, "Ojibwa Ontology," pp. 29, 44−45.

50. Charles G. Leland, *The Algonquin Legends of New England or Myths and Folklore of the Micmac, Passamaquoddy, and Penobscot Tribes* (Boston, 1884), pp. 15−17; F. G. Speck, "Penobscot Transformer Tales, Dictated by Newell Lion," *International Journal of American Linguistics* 1 (1918): 187−244.

51. F. G. Speck, "Penobscot Transformer Tales," pp. 184−194; F. G. Speck, "Penobscot Tales and Religious Beliefs," *JAFL* 48 (1935): 6, 38.

52. For the myth texts from which these details have been drawn, see John D. Prince, *Passamaquoddy Texts*, vol. 10 (New York: Publications of the American Ethnological Society, 1921), pp. 37, 41, 79; Charles G. Leland, *Algonquin Legends*, pp. 29−30, 47−62, 111−120, 183; F. G. Speck, "Penobscot Tales and Religious Beliefs," pp. 8, 10, 40−49; F. G. Speck, Penobscot Transformer Tales," pp. 187−216.

53. John D. Prince, *Passamaquoddy Texts*, p. 31; Charles G. Leland, *Algonquin Legends*, p. 60; A. Irving Hallowell, "Ojibwa Ontology," p. 47; F. G. Speck, *Penobscot Man: The Life History of a Forest Tribe in Maine* (Philadelphia: University of Pennsylvania Press, 1940), p. 47; for historic evidence see J. Saint-Vallier, *Estat present de l'eglise et de la Colonie françoise dans la Nouvelle France* (Paris: Chez Robert Pepie, 1688), p. 42.

54. F. G. Speck, "The Family Hunting Band as the Basis of Algonkian Social Organization," in *Cultural Ecology: Readings on the Canadian Indians and Eskimos*, ed. Bruce Cox (Toronto: McClelland and Stewart, 1973), p. 301; F. G. Speck, "Abenaki Clans—Never!" *AA* 42 (1915): 530; F. G. Speck, *Penobscot Man*, pp. 203, 210; F. G. Speck, "Penobscot Tales and Religious Beliefs," pp. 42−43; for a Passamaquoddy version see Charles G. Leland, *The Algonquin Legends*, pp. 114−119; Anthony F. C. Wallace, "Political Organization and Land Tenure among the Northeastern Indians, 1600−1830," *Southwestern Journal of Anthropology* 13 (1975): 301−321; and for a Maliseet account see F. G. Speck, "Malecite Tales," *JAFL* 30 (1917): 480−481.

55. Wilson D. Wallis and Ruth Sawtell Wallis, *The Malecite*, p. 31; F. G. Speck, "Penobscot Shamanism," *Memoirs of the American Anthropological Association* 6 (1919): 240, 249−253; F. G. Speck, "Game Totems among the Northeastern Algonkians," *AA* 3 (1890): 66; on the shamans' "guardian spirits" see Garrick Mallery, "Fight with the Giant Witch," *AA* 3 (1890): 66; F. G. Speck, *Naskapi*, pp. 53−55.

56. F. G. Speck discusses the shamans' responsibility for causing illness but denies them a significant role in healing (F. G. Speck, "Penobscot Shamanism," p. 259). While many illnesses were treated, as Speck observes, by women herbalists, he also admits that seventeenth-century sources indicate that the shamans were medical specialists. See F. G. Speck, "Penobscot Shamanism," p. 266, and see F. G. Speck,

"Medicine Practices of the Northeastern Algonquians," *Proceedings of the Nineteenth International Congress of Americanists* (Washington, D.C., 1917), pp. 307−313.

57. F. G. Speck, *Naskapi*, p. 122; F. G. Speck, "Penobscot Tales and Religious Beliefs," p. 23; Calvin Martin, "European Impact," p. 13; Chretien LeClercq, *New Relation of Gaspesia*, pp. 176−177, 214.

58. Chretien LeClercq, *New Relation of Gaspesia*, p. 235; *JR*, 3:87, 91.

59. Chretien LeClercq, *New Relation of Gaspesia*, p. 240; A. I. Hallowell, "Some Psychological Characteristics of the Northeastern Indians," in *Man in Northeastern North America*, ed. Frederick Johnson, (Andover, Mass.: Phillips Academy, 1946), p. 206 (emphasis in original).

60. Chretien LeClercq, *New Relation of Gaspesia*, pp. 91, 240.

61. *JR*, 3:95; Thomas Morton, *New English Canaan* (Amsterdam, 1637), p. 57.

62. Kenneth M. Morrison, "Towards a History of Intimate Encounters: Algonkian Folklore, Jesuit Missionaries, and Kiwakwe, the Cannibal Giant," *American Indian Culture and Research Journal* 4 (1979): 51−80; for European analogues see Olive Dickason, "The Concept of *l'Homme Sauvage*," pp. 5−32; Edward Dudley and Maxmillian E. Novak, eds., *The Wild Man Within: An Image in Western Thought from the Renaissance to Romanticism* (Pittsburg: University of Pittsburg Press, 1972); and see Harold G. McGee, "The Windigo Down-East, or the Taming of the Windigo," in *Proceedings of the Second Congress, Canadian Ethnology Society*, ed. Jim Freedman and Jerome H. Barkow (Ottawa: National Museums of Canada, 1975), pp. 110−132; James G. E. Smith, "Notes on the Wiitiko," in *Papers of the Seventh Algonquian Conference, 1975*, ed. William Cowan (Ottawa: Carleton University, 1976), pp. 18−38; Richard J. Preston, "The Wiitiko: Algonquian Knowledge and Whiteman Interest," in *Actes du Huitième Congrès des Algonquinistes*, ed. William Cowan (Ottawa: Carleton University, 1977), pp. 101−106.

63. Chretien LeClercq, *New Relation of Gaspesia*, pp. 112−114.

64. F. G. Speck, *Penobscot Man*, pp. 58, 86, 157−159; Chretien LeClercq, *New Relation of Gaspesia*, pp. 209, 212; Marc Lescarbot, *History of New France*, 2:104; A. G. Bailey, *Conflict of Cultures*, p. 47.

65. *JR*, 2:79; 3:109; Chretien LeClercq, *New Relation of Gaspesia*, p. 246; A. I. Hallowell, "Some Psychological Characteristics," p. 201—quoting *JR*, 3:73.

66. *JR*, 2:125; 3:73, 75; and see *JR*, 1:177; 3:109, 123, 213; Marc Lescarbot, *History of New France*, 3:125.

## 3: SOCIAL DEMONS AND RELIGIOUS DREAMS

1. Alfred W. Crosby, *The Columbian Exchange: Biological and Cultural Consequences of 1492* (Westport, Conn.: Greenwood, 1972); Virginia P. Miller, "Aboriginal Micmac Population: A Review of the Evidence," *Ethnohistory* 23 (1967): 117−127; Sherburne F. Cook, "The Significance of Disease in the Extinction of the New

England Indians," *Human Biology* 45 (1973): 485–508; Alfred W. Crosby, Jr., "Virgin Soil Epidemics as a Factor in the Aboriginal Depopulation in America," *W&MQ* 33 (April 1976): 289–299; Alfred W. Crosby, "God . . . Would Destroy Them and Give Their Country to Another People," *AA* 29 (1978): 38–43; Neal Salisbury, *Manitou and Providence: Indians, Europeans, and the Making of New England, 1500–1643* (New York: Oxford University Press, 1982), pp. 58–59, 101–109.

2. Joseph Nicolar, *The Life and Traditions of the Red Man* (Fredericton, N.B.: St. Anne's Press, 1979), p. 83.

3. Ibid.

4. Ibid., pp. 106–108; Frank G. Speck, "Penobscot Shamanism," *Memoirs of the American Anthropological Association* 6 (1919): 243, 280–283.

5. For the English evidence see Samuel Purchas, "Purchas, his pilgrimes," 2d ed. (London, 1616), in *The Sagadahoc Colony*, ed. Henry O. Thayer (Portland, Me.: The Gorges Society, 1892), p. 88. As early as 1611 the Abenaki shamans told the French that their powers were declining: *JR*, 2:77.

6. Frank G. Speck, "Penobscot Tales and Religious Beliefs," *JAFL* 48 (1935): 5.

7. Neal Salisbury, *Manitou and Providence*, pp. 147–151.

8. James Kendall Hosmer, ed., *Winthrop's Journal 'History of New England,' 1630–1649*, 2 vols. (New York: Charles Scribner's Sons, 1908), 1:69; *Province and Court Records of Maine* (Portland: Maine Historical Society, 1928–), 1:2–4; John Winter to Robert Trelawny, Oct. 4, 1636, *Bax. Mss.*, 3:86; William Willis, *The History of Portland, from 1632 to 1864*, 2 vols. (Hallowell, Me.: Glazier, Masters, 1832), 1:35; Samuel G. Drake, *The Old Indian Chronicle* (Boston: S. G. Drake, 1867), p. 25.

9. Quoted in Joseph Sewall, "The History of Bath," *Me. His. Soc., Coll.*, 1st ser. (Portland, Me.: The Society, 1847), vol. 2, pp. 194–195; Ronald O. MacFarlane, "Indian Relations in New England, 1620–1760: A Study of a Regulated Frontier" (Ph.D. diss., Harvard University, 1933), p. 324.

10. H. P. Biggar, ed., *The Works of Samuel de Champlain*, 6 vols. (Toronto: Champlain Society, 1922–36), 1:314–317; 3:44–46; 5:313; 6:43.

11. Neal Salisbury, *Manitou and Providence*, pp. 147–151; Ruth A. McIntyre, *Debts Hopeful and Desperate: Financing the Plymouth Colony* (Plymouth, Mass.: Plimouth Plantation, 1963), p. 51.

12. *JR*, 12:187–189; A. G. Bailey, *Conflict of European and Eastern Algonkian Cultures, 1504–1700* (Toronto: University of Toronto Press, 1969), p. 27.

13. *JR*, 21:67–71.

14. For background see James P. Ronda, "The Sillery Experiment: A Jesuit-Indian Village in New France, 1637–1663," *American Indian Culture and Research Journal* 3 (1979): 1–18; James P. Ronda, " 'We Are Well As We Are': An Indian Critique of Seventeenth Century Christian Missions," *W&MQ* 34 (1977): 66–82; Cornelius Jaenen, "Amerindian Views of French Culture in the Seventeenth Century," *CHR* 55 (1974): 274–275.

15. *JR*, 25:117–119, 135; 29:65–67.

16. *JR*, 25:119.

17. *JR*, 25:119—121, 135—143.

18. *JR*, 24:183—185; 25:123.

19. *JR*, 25:117.

20. *JR*, 24:61; 28:215; 29:69—71.

21. *JR*, 24:61—63; 28:215.

22. *JR*, 31:207.

23. *JR*, 1:13; 31:187; 24:57; p. 243; E. C. Cummings, "Capuchin and Jesuit Fathers at Pentagoet," *Me. His. Soc., Coll.*, 2d ser., vol. 5 (1894), pp. 161—168; P.-André Sévigny, *Les Abénaquis: Habitat et Migrations ( 17ₑ et 18ₑ siècles)* (Montréal: Les Éditions Bellarmin, 1976), p. 91; Sister Mary Celeste Leger, *The Catholic Indian Missions in Maine ( 1611 — 1820)* (Washington, D.C.: Catholic University of America, 1929), pp. 29—36, 41—42, 90.

24. *JR*, 36:53.

25. *JR*, 36:75—81, 105—107; J. G. Shea, ed., "Journal of an Embassy from Canada to the United Colonies of New England, in 1650," *New York His. Soc., Coll.*, 2d ser., vol. 3 (1857), pp. 303—328.

26. Nomination de M. de Godefroy pour traicter avec les Commissaires de la Nouvelle Angleterre, Juin 20, 1651, *Coll. de Mss.*, 1:128—129; *Bax. Mss.*, 4:433—436; Lettre du Conseil de Quebec aux Commissaires de la Nouvelle Angleterre, Juin 20, 1651, *Coll. de Mss.*, 1:127—128; *NYCD*, 9:5—7; Ronald D. Cohen, "New England and New France, 1632—1651: External Relations and Internal Disagreements among the Puritans," *Essex Institute Historical Collections* 108 (1972): 252—271.

27. *JR*, 36:103; 37:77; 38:39, 48; 40:195—197; 45:203—205; 48:61; 49:139—141; Instructions pour le Sieur de Courcelles au Sujet des Indiens, 1665, *Coll. de Mss.*, 1:175; Lettre du Ministre à M. Talon, Fevrier 11, 1671, *Coll. de Mss.*, 1:207—208, and *NYCD*, 9:70; Micheline Dumont-Johnson, *Apôtres ou Agitateurs: La France Missionnaire en Acadie* (Trois-Rivières: Le Boréal Express, 1970), pp. 23—45. On the Iroquois conflict as a holy war see Joyce Marshall, ed., *Word from New France: The Selected Letters of Marie de l'Incarnation* (Toronto: University of Toronto Press, 1967), pp. 186, 212, 220—221, 228, 255, 257, 271, 308, 312, 318.

28. I have discussed this process of religious change in my "The Mythological Sources of Abenaki Catholicism: A Case Study of the Social History of Power," *Religion* 11 (1981): 235—263.

29. *JR*, 28:203; 29:71; Calvin Martin, "The European Impact on the Culture of a Northeastern Algonquian Tribe: An Ecological Interpretation," *W&MQ* 31 (1974): 17; F. G. Speck, *Naskapi: The Savage Hunters of the Labrador Peninsula* (Norman: University of Oklahoma Press, 1935), p. 224.

30. *JR*, 8:251; 9:9; 31:187.

31. *JR*, 31:185—187.

32. *JR*, 29:85; 31:185—187, 203; John Josselyn, "An Account of Two Voyages to New England," *Mass. His. Soc., Coll.*, 3d ser., vol. 3 (Cambridge, Mass.: The Society, 1933), p. 299, states that shamans avoided the sick under epidemic conditions. See Lucien Campeau's remarks on the Abenaki's recognition of Druillettes's

power: "Gabriel Druillettes," *DCB*, 1:281−282; Calvin Martin, "European Impact," p. 20, states that the "missionary was successful only to the degree that his power exceeded that of the shaman"; Andre Vachon, "L'Eau de Vie dans la Société Indienne," *Canadian Historical Association, Report* (1960), pp. 22−32, agrees. It is striking that Father Jacques Bigot, a later Abenaki missionary, considered that he played a shamanistic role in Abenaki society: *JR*, 63:107. Also see my "Towards A History of Intimate Encounters: Algonkian Folklore, Jesuit Missionaries, and Kiwakwe, the Cannibal Giant," *American Indian Culture and Research Journal* 3 (1979): 51−80.

33. *JR*, 31:193−197.

34. *JR*, 37:251−253; 38:37; F. G. Speck, "Penobscot Shamanism," *Memoirs of the American Anthropological Association* 6 (1919): 240−241; Dr. Peter Paul, a Maliseet linguist, corroborates the accuracy of the *Jesuit Relations* in observing that the term *Nioueskou* means one who is blessed or holy.

35. *JR*, 40:239; Druillettes quickly learned Abenaki but already knew the Montagnais dialect, *JR*, 31:187−193; for estimations of Jesuit facility with Indian languages, see Victor Egon Hanzeli, *Missionary Linguistics in New France: A Study of Seventeenth and Eighteenth Century Descriptions of American Indian Languages* (The Hague: Mouton, 1969), and Frank T. Siebert, "The Penobscot Dictionary Project: Preferences and Problems of Format, Presentation and Entry," *Papers of the Eleventh Algonquian Conference*, ed. William Cowan (Ottawa: Carleton University, 1980), pp. 115−124. It may be that the Kennebec identified "he-who-made-all" with No-chi-gar-neh, the Spirit of the Air. In 1650 the Kennebec sagamore greeted Gabriel Druillettes as follows: "I see now that the great Spirit who commands in the Skies is pleased to regard us with favor, since he sends us back our Patriarch" (*JR*, 37:249).

36. *JR*, 31:199−201.

37. *JR*, 6:83, 183; 7:169, 277−279; 9:75−77, 213; 21:199−201; 31:199−201; 37:255, 257; 38:21.

38. *JR*, 38:27.

39. *JR*, 37:245.

40. *JR*, 7:145−161, 277−279, 285; 9:69−71; 14:139−141; 18:199−201; 27:185−189; 31:197; 37:245, 251; 38:21; 48:53. Calvin Martin, *Keepers of the Game: Indian-Animal Relationships and the Fur Trade* (Berkeley, Los Angeles, London: University of California Press, 1978), pp. 144−149, argues to the contrary that Christianity undermined traditional man-animal relationships among Algonkian peoples.

41. *JR*, 38:21−23; A. G. Bailey, *Conflict of Cultures*, pp. 136−137.

42. *JR*, 37:251, 255.

43. *JR*, 37:251, 255; 38:33−37.

44. *JR*, 33:33−37.

45. G. F. G. Stanley, "The First Indian 'Reserves' in Canada," *Revue d'Histoire de l'Amérique Française* 4 (1950): 178−210.

46. See chapter 4.

47. P.-André Sévigny, *Les Abénaquis*, pp. 117−168; Gordon M. Day, *The*

*Identity of the Saint Francis Indians* (Ottawa: National Museums of Man, Mercury Series, no. 71, 1981).

48. *JR*, 60:233–235.

49. *JR*, 60:237–239.

50. *JR*, 60:239–241.

51. *JR*, 62:256–261; J. Saint-Vallier, *Estat present de l'eglise et de la Colonie françoise dans la Nouvelle France* (Paris: Chez Robert Pepie, 1688), pp. 181–183; Thomas M. Charland, *Histoire des Abénakis d'Odanak (1675–1937)* (Montréal, 1964), pp. 15–25.

52. *JR*, 62:47–49; A. G. Bailey, "The Ordeal of the Eastern Algonkians," in *Culture and Nationality* (Toronto: McClelland and Stewart, 1972), p. 38. On the optimistic French view of the Indians see George R. Healy, "The French Jesuits and the Idea of the Noble Savage," *W&MQ* (3d ser.) 15 (1958): 143–167; on the new leadership at the missions see *JR*, 18:100, 102; 62:111–115, 127; J. Saint-Vallier, *Estat present*, p. 132; Cornelius Jaenen, "The Relations between Church and State in New France, 1647–1685" (Ph.D. diss., University of Ottawa, 1962), p. 459; Robert Conkling, "Legitimacy in Social Change: The Case of the French Missionaries and the Northeastern Algonkian," *Ethnohistory* 21 (1974): 18. Other Frenchmen noted the Abenaki's piety; see Memoire de M. de la Chesnage sur le Canada, 1676, *Coll. de Mss.*, 1:257.

53. *JR*, 1:167; 2:185; Chretien LeClercq, *New Relation of Gaspesia, With the Customs and Religion of the Gaspesian Indians*, ed. William F. Ganong (Toronto: Champlain Society, 1910), pp. 173–174. For a different view see Calvin Martin, *Keepers of the Game*; A. G. Bailey, "Ordeal," pp. 39–40.

54. *JR*, 8:144; 62:43, 135. See generally François-Marc Gagnon, *La Conversion par l'Image: Un aspect de la Mission des Jésuites auprès des Indiens du Canada au XVIIe siècle* (Montréal, 1975); Leon Pouliot, *Étude sur les Relations des Jésuites de la Nouvelle-France, 1632–1672* (Paris: Desclée de Brovwer, 1940), pp. 182–184.

55. *JR*, 62:29, 31–33. For the psychological background see A. I. Hallowell, *Culture and Experience* (Philadelphia, 1955), pp. 266–290.

56. *JR*, 62:37, 43–45, 115, 119.

57. *JR*, 62:33, 35, 39. For folkloric evidence of continuing Jesuit-shaman tensions, see Elsie Clews Parsons, "Micmac Folklore," *JAFL* 38 (1925): 90–91, and Charles G. Leland and John D. Prince, *Kuloskap, the Master* (New York, 1902), pp. 242–243.

58. *JR*, 62:35; A. G. Bailey, "Ordeal," pp. 37–38.

59. *JR*, 31:197; 62:143.

60. Chretien LeClercq, *New Relation*, pp. 244–245, 254–256; Nicholas Denys, *The Description and Natural History of the Coasts of North America (Acadia)*, ed. William F. Ganong (Toronto: Champlain Society, 1908), pp. 443–445; André Vachon, "L'Eau de Vie dans la Société Indienne," *Canadian Historical Association, Report* (1960), pp. 22–32; L'Abbé A. Gosselin, *Vie de Mgr de Laval, Premier Evéque de Quebec et Apôtre du Canada, 1622–1708* (Québec, 1890), 1:279–301; Micheline Dumont-Johnson,

*Apôtres ou Agitateurs*, p. 60; Robert Conkling, "Legitimacy and Conversion in Social Change," p. 6.

61. *JR*, 29:77; 38:35−37; 62:25−27, 35; Joyce Marshall, ed., *Word from New France*, pp. 132, 273−274, 339, 355, 361; *JR*, 62:263−265; W. J. Eccles, *Canada under Louis XIV, 1663−1701* (Toronto: McClelland and Stewart, 1964), pp. 87−89; A. G. Bailey, *Conflict of Cultures*, pp. 70−71.

62. H. P. Biggar, ed., *The Works of Samuel de Champlain*, 3:145−146; 4:321−336. Father Gabriel Sagard, *The Long Journey to the Country of the Hurons*, ed. George M. Wrong (Toronto: Champlain Society, 1939), p. 176. For general background see Sigmund Diamond, "An Experiment in 'Feudalism': French Canada in the Seventeenth Century," *W&MQ* 18 (1961): 3−34; Bruce G. Trigger, "Champlain Judged by His Indian Policy: A Different View of Early Canadian History," *Anthropologica* 13 (1971): 85−114.

63. W. J. Eccles, *The Canadian Frontier, 1534−1760* (New York: Holt, Rinehart, and Winston, 1969), pp. 35−59; W. J. Eccles, *France in America* (New York: Harper and Row, 1972), pp. 29−59; Cornelius Jaenen, "The Relations between Church and State in New France," p. 443; Brian Slattery, "The Land Rights of Indigenous Canadian Peoples, As Affected by the Crown's Acquisition of Their Territories" (Ph.D. diss., Oxford University, 1979), pp. 86−87.

64. Joyce Marshall, ed., *Word from New France*, pp. 131, 336; Cornelius Jaenen, "The Relations between Church and State in New France," pp. 478, 492; *JR*, 33:145; Bruce G. Trigger, "The Jesuits and the Fur Trade," *Ethnohistory* 12 (1965): 39.

65. For irate descriptions of the *coureurs de bois*, see M. Du Chesneau to M. de Seignelay, November 10, 1679, *NYCD*, 9:131−136; M. Du Chesneau to M. de Seignelay, November 13, 1680, *NYCD*, 9:140−145; Count de Frontenac to the King, November 2, 1681, *NYCD*, 9:145−146; Marcel Trudel, "La Rencontre des Cultures," *Revue d'Histoire de l'Amérique Française* 18 (1965): 477−516.

66. M. Colbert to M. Talon, April 5, 1666, *NYCD*, 9:43. Cornelius Jaenen, "Problems of Assimilation in New France, 1603−1645," in *Canadian History before Confederation: Essays and Interpretations*, ed. J. M. Bumsted (Georgetown, Ontario: Irwin-Dorsey, 1972), p. 66.

67. M. Talon to M. Colbert, November, 1666, *NYCD*, 9:55; M. Colbert to M. Talon, April 6, 1667, *NYCD*, 9:59; W. J. Eccles, *Canada under Louis XIV*, p. 87; Cornelius Jaenen, "The Relations between Church and State in New France," pp. 471−472, 475; Marcel Trudel, *The Beginnings of New France*, pp. 156−157.

68. Count de Frontenac to M. Colbert, November 2, 1672, *NYCD*, 9:93; M. Colbert to M. de Frontenac, May 17, 1674, *NYCD*, 9:115; Cornelius Jaenen, "The Relations between Church and State in New France," p. 496. See also W. J. Eccles, *Frontenac: The Courtier Governor* (Toronto: McClelland and Stewart, 1959), pp. 51−74; Jean Delanglez, *Frontenac and the Jesuits* (Chicago: Institute of Jesuit History, 1939).

69. A M. Duchesneau, May 8, 1679, *AC*, ser. B., 8, p. 12; Roy a M. Duchesneau, April 30, 1681, *AC*, ser. B. p. 145; M. de Denonville to M. de Seignelay, and

the latter's answer, August 3, 1685, and November 12, 1685, *NYCD*, 9:277; Memoire du Roy au Sr. Marquis de Denonville, May 31, 1686, *AC*, ser. B. pp. 12, 105 — 106, and *Coll. de Mss.*, 1:363; M. de Denonville to M. de Seignelay, January, 1690, *NYCD*, 9:440 — 443. *JR*, 63:117, 129 — 131; for Louis XIV's view of francization, 31 May, 1686, Ser. B, 12, pp. 105 — 106, 125 — 126.

70. *JR*, 28:29 — 31, 33; 62:49, 123 — 125; Cornelius Jaenen, "Amerindian Views of French Culture," p. 278. The Jesuits were more lenient with newcomers from Maine. In 1685, for example, Jacques Bigot observed: "While I was issuing all the orders against drunkenness, I allowed more diversion and dancing in the mission than I would have permitted at other times; this I did to make them swallow the pill more easily after some orders had been given." *JR*, 63:115; J. Saint-Vallier, *Estat present*, p. 132.

71. Memoire Touchant les Savages Abénaquis de Sillery, 1679, *Coll. de Mss.*, 1:273; M. Du Chesneau to M. de Seignelay, November 13, 1681, *NYCD*, 9:150.

72. Chretien LeClercq, *New Relation*, pp. 116, 119. For the cultural importance of song and dance see Marc Lescarbot, *The History of New France*, ed. H. P. Biggar, 3 vols. (Toronto: Champlain Society, 1907 — 14), 3:181 — 182; Lucien Campeau, *Monumenta Novae Franciae, I, La Première Mission d'Acadie (1602 — 1616)* (Québec: Les Presses de l'Université Laval, 1967), p. 242; G. F. G. Stanley, "The Policy of 'Francisation' as applied to the Indians during the Ancien Regime," *Revue d'Histoire de l'Amérique Française* 3 (1949): 333 — 348; for a contrary view of Jesuits and assimilation see Cornelius J. Jaenen, *Friend and Foe: Aspects of French-Amerindian Cultural Contact in the Sixteenth and Seventeenth Centuries* (Toronto: McClelland and Stewart, 1979).

73. *JR*, 62:43.

74. *JR*, 62:25, 109; 63:61 — 67; J. C. Webster, *Acadia at the End of the Seventeenth Century* (St. John: New Brunswick Museum, 1934), p. 164; A. G. Bailey, *Conflict of Cultures*, p. 31.

75. J. A. Maurault, *Histoire des Abénakis, Depuis 1605 Jusqu'à Nos Jours* (Sorel, Québec, 1866), p. 275.

76. Father Jacques Bigot, for example, remarked that he functioned in a shamanistic role among the Abenaki, *JR*, 63:107; A. G. Bailey, *Conflict of Cultures*, emphasizes the destructive effect of the meeting. Andre Vachon, "L'Eau de Vie," pp. 22 — 32, and Calvin Martin, "European Impact," pp. 20 — 21, assert that the Jesuits' success depended on their undermining the status of the shamans. Martin even asserts that the Micmac apostatized in accepting Christianity and European trade. He amplifies this argument in *Keepers of the Game*. See Shepard Krech III, *Indians, Animals, and the Fur Trade: A Critique of Keepers of the Game* (Athens: University of Georgia Press, 1981).

77. Charles Leland, *The Algonquin Legends* (Boston: Houghton Mifflin, 1884), p. 249.

78. Frank G. Speck, "Montagnais and Naskapi Tales from the Labrador Peninsula," *Journal of American Folklore* 38 (1925): 19 — 21.

79. Frank G. Speck, "Penobscot Tales and Religious Beliefs," pp. 4 — 5, 19, 246,

note 1; John M. Cooper, "The Northern Algonquian Supreme Being," *Primitive Man* 4 (1933): 41–112; William Jones, "The Algonkin Manitou," *JAFL* 28 (1905): 183–190; Paul Radin, "Monotheism among American Indians," in *Teachings from the American Earth*, ed. Dennis Tedlock and Barbara Tedlock (New York: Liveright, 1975), pp. 219–257; Åke Hulkrantz, *The Religions of the American Indians*, trans. Monica Setterwall (Berkeley, Los Angeles, London: University of California Press, 1979), pp. 15–26; Fannie Hardy Eckstorm, *Old John Neptune and Other Indian Shamans* (Portland, Me.: The Southworth-Anthoensen Press, 1945).

80. Frank G. Speck, "Penobscot Tales and Religious Beliefs," p. 9; Jeanne Guillemin, *Urban Renegades: The Cultural Strategy of American Indians* (New York: Columbia University Press, 1975), pp. 102–110, provides a compelling treatment of Gluskap's enduring importance to contemporary Micmac people. For a different point of view see Wilson D. Wallis and Ruth Sawtell Wallis, "Culture Loss and Culture Change among the Micmac of the Canadian Maritime Provinces, 1912–1950," in *The Native Peoples of Atlantic Canada: A Reader in Regional Ethnic Relations*, ed. Harold F. McGee (Toronto: McClelland and Stewart, 1974), p. 142.

81. A. G. Bailey, *Conflict of European and Eastern Algonkian Cultures*, p. 188; Frank G. Speck, "Some Micmac Tales from Cape Breton Island," *JAFL* 28 (1915): 60–61; Frank G. Speck, "Wawenock Myth Texts from Maine," *Forty-third Annual Report of the Bureau of American Ethnology* (Washington, D.C.: Government Printing Office, 1928), pp. 180–181, 186; Joseph Nicolar, *The Life and Traditions of the Red Man*, p. 10; Elsie Clews Parsons, "Micmac Folklore," *JAFL* 38 (1925): 88–89.

82. Joseph Nicolar, *The Life and Traditions of the Red Man*, pp. 27, 30–32; and see Helen Keith Frost, "Two Abenaki Legends," *Journal of American Folklore* 25 (1912): 188–189; Edward Jack, "Maliseet Legends," *JAFL* 8 (1895): 194; Frank G. Speck, "Penobscot Tales and Religious Beliefs," p. 6; Jeanne Guillemin, *Urban Renegades*, p. 109.

## 4: POLITICS OF LAW AND PERSUASION

1. Robert Conkling, "Legitimacy and Conversion in Social Change: The Case of the French Missionaries," *Ethnohistory* 21 (1974): 1–24.

2. John G. Reid, *Maine, Charles II, and Massachusetts: Governmental Relationships in Early Northern New England* (Portland: Maine Historical Society, 1977).

3. For the national and international rivalries affecting the Maine frontier, see John G. Reid, *Acadia, Maine, and New Scotland: Marginal Colonies in the Seventeenth Century* (Toronto: University of Toronto Press, 1981); Richard R. Johnson, *Adjustment to Empire: The New England Colonies, 1675–1715* (Rutgers, N.J.: Rutgers University Press, 1981); George A. Rawlyk, *Nova Scotia's Massachusetts: A Study of Massachusetts–Nova Scotia Relations, 1630 to 1784* (Montreal: McGill-Queen's University Press, 1973); John Bartlett Brebner, *New England's Outpost: Acadia before the Conquest of Canada* (New York: Columbia University Press, 1927). For Massachusetts's Indian

relations see Alden Vaughn, *New England Frontier: Puritans and Indians, 1620–1675*, rev. ed. (New York: W. W. Norton, 1979); Francis Jennings, *The Invasion of America: Indians, Colonialism, and the Cant of Conquest* (Chapel Hill: University of North Carolina Press, 1975); Neal Salisbury, *Manitou and Providence: Indians, Europeans, and the Making of New England* (New York: Oxford University Press, 1982); Gary B. Nash, *Red, White, and Black: The Peoples of Early America*, 2d ed. (Englewood Cliffs, N.J.: Prentice-Hall, Inc., 1982).

4. Neal Salisbury, *Manitou and Providence*, p. 224.

5. See Richard Slotkin, *Regeneration through Violence: The Mythology of the American Frontier, 1600–1860* (Middletown, Conn.: Wesleyan University Press, 1973); Edmund S. Morgan, *The Puritan Family: Religion and Domestic Relations in Seventeenth Century New England* (New York: Harper and Row, 1966); Larzer Ziff, *Puritanism in America: New Culture in a New World* (New York: Viking Press, 1973).

6. The next two paragraphs are based on David Thomas Konig, *Law and Society in Puritan Massachusetts: Essex County, 1629–1692* (Chapel Hill: University of North Carolina Press, 1979).

7. Ronald O. MacFarlane, "Indian Relations in New England, 1620–1760: A Study of a Regulated Frontier" (Ph.D. diss., Harvard University, 1933), pp. 3, 5, 323. For background orientations see Richard R. Beeman, "The New Social History and the Search for 'Community' in Colonial America," *American Quarterly* 29 (1977): 422–442; John M. Murrin, "Review Essay," *History and Theory* 11 (1972): 226–275; Alan Heimert, "Puritanism, the Wilderness, and the Frontier," *New England Quarterly* 26 (1953): 361–381; Michael McGiffert, "American Puritan Studies in the 1960's," *W&MQ* 27 (1970): 36–67; David C. Stineback, "The Status of Puritan-Indian Scholarship," *New England Quarterly* 51 (1978): 80–90; G. E. Thomas, "Puritans, Indians, and the Concept of Race," *New England Quarterly* 48 (1975): 3–27.

8. For the major viewpoints see David Bushnell, "The Treatment of the Indians in Plymouth Colony," *New England Quarterly* 26 (1953): 193–218; Yasuhide Kawashima, "Indians, and the Law in Colonial Massachusetts, 1689–1763" (Ph.D. diss., University of California, Santa Barbara, 1967); Yasuhide Kawashima, "Jurisdiction of the Colonial Courts over the Indian in Massachusetts, 1689–1763," *New England Quarterly* 42 (1969): 532–550; Yasuhide Kawashima, "Legal Origins of the Indian Reservation in Colonial Massachusetts," *American Journal of Legal History* 13 (1969): 42–56; Lyle Koehler, "Red-White Power Relations and 'Justice' in the Courts of Seventeenth-century New England," *American Indian Culture and Research Journal* 3 (1979): 1–32; James P. Ronda, "Red and White at the Bench: Indians and the Law in Plymouth Colony, 1620–1691," *Essex Institute Historical Collections* 90 (1974): 200–215; G. E. Thomas, "Puritans, Indians, and the Concept of Race," *New England Quarterly* 48 (1975): 3–27; Alden Vaughn, *New England Frontier*, pp. 185–210; Kenneth M. Morrison, "The Bias of Colonial Law: English Paranoia and the Abenaki Arena of King Philip's War, 1675–1678," *New England Quarterly* 53 (1980): 363–387.

9. William Hubbard, "A Narrative of the Troubles with the Indians in New-England, from Pascataqua to Pemmaquid," in *The History of the Indian Wars in New England*, ed. S. G. Drake, 2 vols. (Roxbury, Mass., 1865), 2:256—257.

10. Neal Emerson Salisbury, "Conquest of the 'Savage': Puritans, Puritan Missionaries, and Indians, 1620—1680" (Ph.D. diss., University of California, Los Angeles, 1972), p. 120; James Kendall Hosmer, ed., *Winthrop's Journal 'History of New England,' 1630—1649*, 2 vols. (New York: Charles Scribner's Sons, 1908), 2:99; Charles E. Clark, *The Eastern Frontier: The Settlement of Northern New England, 1610—1763* (New York: Alfred A. Knopf, 1970), pp. 13—35; Henry S. Burrage, *The Beginnings of Colonial Maine, 1602—1658* (Portland, Me.: Marks Printing House, 1914), passim; see also the remarks by John Josselyn, *An Account of Two Voyages to New England* (London: Printed for *Giles* Widdows, 1674), pp. 211—212; Cotton Mather, *Frontiers Well-Defended* (Boston, 1707).

11. Although there is no study of New England Algonkian law-ways, several works on other American Indian legal systems suggest the dynamics outlined here which governed the relationship between Abenaki social structure and law. See E. Adamson Hoebel and Karl N. Llewellyn, *The Cheyenne Way: Conflict and Case Law in Primitive Jurisprudence* (Norman: University of Oklahoma Press, 1941); John Phillip Reid, *A Law of Blood: The Primitive Law of the Cherokee Nation* (New York: New York University Press, 1970); John Phillip Reid, *A Better Kind of Hatchet: Law, Trade, and Diplomacy in the Cherokee Nation during the Early Years of European Contact* (University Park: Pennsylvania State University Press, 1976); Rennard Strickland, *Fire and the Spirits: Cherokee Law from Clan to Court* (Norman: University of Oklahoma Press, 1975); Fred Gearing, *Priests and Warriors: Social Structures for Cherokee Politics in the Eighteenth Century* (Menasha, Wisc.: American Anthropological Association Memoir 93, 1962); Paul Bohannan, "The Differing Realms of the Law," in *Law and Warfare*, ed. Paul Bohannan (Garden City, N.Y.: Natural History Press, 1967), pp. 43—56. For the consensual law-ways of the Montagnais and Naskapi, Algonkian peoples culturally related to the Abenaki, see John H. Dowling, "Individual Ownership and the Sharing of Game in Hunting Societies," *AA* 70 (January 1968): 502—507; Julius E. Lips, "Public Opinion and Mutual Assistance among the Montagnais-Naskapi," *AA* 34 (1937): 222—228; F. G. Speck, "Ethical Attributes of the Labrador Indians," *AA* 25 (1933): 559—594.

12. For English reaction to frontier immorality—rather than criminality—as the cause of the Abenaki war, see William Hubbard, "Narrative of the Troubles," 2:94—97, 256—257; Cotton Mather, *Magnalia Christi Americana* (Hartford, Conn., 1920), 2:499—500.

13. Hubbard, "Narrative of the Troubles," 2:91—92.

14. Ibid., 2:135—136.

15. Ibid., 2:149.

16. Ibid., 2:94. For the early settlement of Maine see Wilbur D. Spencer, *Pioneers on Maine Rivers with Lists to 1851* (Portland, Me.: Lakeside Printing Company, 1930), and Charles E. Clark, *The Eastern Frontier*. Historians commonly interpret the Abenaki

war as an extension of Massachusetts's conflict with the Wampanoags. See Douglas E. Leach, *Flintlock and Tomahawk: New England in King Philip's War* (New York: Macmillan, 1958), pp. 94, 161, 199, 215, 248; also revisionist comments by John O. Noble, "King Philip's War in Maine" (M. A. thesis, University of Maine, Orono, 1970); and see Douglas E. Leach, *The Northern Colonial Frontier, 1607 – 1763* (New York: Holt, Rinehart, and Winston, 1966), p. 56; George W. Ellis and John E. Morris, *King Philip's War* (New York: Grafton Press, 1906), pp. 293 – 315, acknowledge that the conflict with the Abenaki was distinct from the southern war and devote an appendix to it. The English also blamed the French for the outbreak in Maine, but Louis XIV actually ordered New France to live peacefully with the English. See Letter du Roy à M. le Comte de Frontenac, April 16, 1676, *Coll. de Mss.*, 1:236. Douglas Leach responds equivocally in "The Question of French Involvement in King Philip's War," *Colonial Society of Massachusetts, Publications*, vol. 38 (1959), pp. 414 – 421, because he does not examine French documents and must therefore rely on English rumors.

17. William Hubbard, "Narrative of the Troubles," 2:149 – 150; Letter Thos. Gardner to Gov. Leverett, September 22, 1675, *Bax. Mss.*, 6:92 – 93; Att A Council, October 16, 1675, *Bax. Mss.*, 6:96 – 97.

18. William Hubbard, "Narrative of the Troubles," 2:153 – 156 (emphasis in original).

19. William Hubbard, "Narrative of the Troubles," 2:155 – 164.

20. See "Francis Card his Declaration of their Beginning," in William Hubbard, "Narrative of the Troubles," 2:192 – 193, 201 – 204, 217 – 222, and *Bax. Mss.*, 6:149 – 151. George W. Ellis and John E. Morris, *King Philip's War*, p. 309, claim that Mogg was carried forcibly to Boston.

21. William Hubbard, "A Narrative of the Troubles," 2:189 – 192, 201, 203 – 204, 217 – 222.

22. Moxes and Indians W. H. and G. recd by Mrs. Hamond, July 1, 1677, *Bax. Mss.*, 6:177 – 179; General Concerns of New York, November, 1677, *CSP*, 10:184.

23. Maj. Genl. Denison and Joseph Dudley to treat with the Indians, July 10, 1677, *Bax. Mss.*, 6:187.

24. Letter A. Brockhollt & others to the Govr & Council, August 18, 1677, *Bax. Mss.*, 6:191 – 193; At a Councell, September 11, 1677, in "Papers Relating to Pemaquid . . .," comp. Franklin B. Hough, *Me. His. Soc., Coll.*, 1st ser.,vol. 5, pp. 18 – 19; September 22, 1677, Order and Directions for the Commander at Pemaquid, *Me. His. Soc. Coll.*, 1st ser., vol. 5, pp. 19 – 23; Edwd. Rawson to Major Walden and Major Pendleton, March 9, 1677/78, *Bax. Mss.*, 6:201; William Durkee Williamson, *The History of the State of Maine*, 2 vols. (Hallowell, 1832), 1:553.

25. *Province and Court Records of Maine*, March 30, 1680, 3:8, 20 – 21, 31, 88 – 89; Proposals for the future, October 15, 1681, *Bax. Mss.*, 6:405 – 407.

26. Edward Cranfield to Thomas Hinckley, February 14, 1683/84, "Hinckley Papers," *Mass. His. Soc., Coll.*, 4th ser., vol. 5, p. 121; Francis Hook to Walter Barefoot, February 11, 1683/84, *CSP*, 11:634; Franklin B. Hough, comp., "Papers

Relating to Pemaquid," pp. 60—61, 62—63; *Province and Court Records of Maine*, February 21, 1683/84, 3:190; Anthony Bracket to Major Davis, February 23, 1683/84, *CSP*, 11:635; Francis Hook to Governor Cranfield, March 11, 1683/84, *CSP*, 11:635.

27. Governor Dongan to Council of New Hampshire, April 11, 1684, in "Papers Relating to Pemaquid," comp. Franklin B. Hough, pp. 93—94; Governor Cranfield to Lords of Trade, May 14, 1684, *CSP*, 11: 633 (emphasis in original); William Durkee Williamson, *History of Maine*, 1:575.

28. Articles between Indians and New Hampshire, *CSP*, 12:89, William Durkee Williamson, *History of Maine*, 1:576; Jeremy Belknap, *The History of New Hampshire*, 3 vols. (Boston, 1812—13), 1:348.

29. Jeremy Belknap, *History of New Hampshire*, 1:196. Letter from Edward Tyng, August 18, 1688, *Bax. Mss.*, 6:419.

30. Letter from Edward Tyng, October 1, 1688, *Bax. Mss.*, 6:436; New Englands Faction Discovered, by C. D., *The Andros Tracts*, ed. W. H. Whitmore, 3 vols. (Boston, 1868—74), 2:206—207.

31. Examinaton of Moses Eyares, October 22, 1688, *Bax. Mss.*, 6:440—441; Deposition, September 4, 1688, *Bax. Mss.*, 6:421—422; Letter from Edward Tyng, September 9, 1688, *Bax. Mss.*, 6:423; Letter from Edward Tyng, September 18, 1688, *Bax. Mss.*, 6:429—430.

32. Letter to Sr E. Andros, September 11, 1688, *Bax. Mss.*, 6:428.

33. Examination of Henry Smith Chyrurgion, October 31, 1688, *Bax. Mss.*, 6:443—447.

34. Ibid.; Letter from Silvanus Davis, September 28, 1688, *Bax. Mss.*, 6:432—433. The standard interpretation of the outbreak of the Abenaki war with Massachusetts derives from Governor Andros's mistaken notion that his attack on Saint Castin's trading post triggered the conflict. See "An Answer to Sr. Edmund Andross's Account of the Forces raised in New England for Defense of the Countrey against the Indians &c. in the Yeare 1688," in *The Andros Tracts*, 3:7. Later versions can be found in Jeremy Belknap, *History of New Hampshire*, 1:197; William Durkee Williamson, *History of Maine*, 1:588—589; Francis Parkman, *Count Frontenac and New France under Louis XIV* (Boston: Little, Brown, 1901), p. 221; Douglas E. Leach, *Northern Colonial Frontier*, p. 110.

35. Larzer Ziff, *Puritanism in America*, pp. 203—228; Richard R. Johnson, *Adjustment to Empire*, pp. 71—135.

36. "The Revolution in New England justified," in *The Andros Tracts*, ed. W. H. Whitmore, 1:109—110.

37. Ibid., p. 110; "A Narrative of the Proceedings of Sir Edmond Androsse and his Complices . . . ," in *Andros Tracts*, ed. W. H. Whitmore, 1:145—146; The Boston Declaration of Grievances, April 18, 1689, in *The Glorious Revolution in America*, ed. Michael G. Hall, Lawrence H. Leder, Michael G. Kammen (Chapel Hill: University of North Carolina Press, 1964), p. 45.

38. "The Revolution in New England justified," p. 101; "Petition of the Inhabitants of Maine," in *Andros Tracts*, ed. W. H. Whitmore, 1:177.

39. Thomas Hutchinson, *History of the Colony and Province of Massachusetts-Bay*, ed. Lawrence Shaw Mayo, 3 vols. (Cambridge, Mass.: Harvard University Press, 1936), 1:315.

40. Edward Randolph to Francis Nicholson, July 29, 1689, *CSP*, 13:109−110; Answer of the Agents of Massachusetts to the Complaints of Sir Edmund Andros, 1688, *Me. His. Soc., Coll.*, 1st ser., vol. 5, p. 395; An Account of the Forces Raised in New England for the Defence of the Country, April, 1689, *Mass. His. Soc., Coll.*, 3d ser., vol. 1, p. 86; Col. Ledgels Memorll touching Trade wth the Indians &c., February, 1692/93, *Bax. Mss.*, 10:1−2; Letter to Mr. John Usher, July 10, 1689, *CSP*, 13:82.

41. See chapter 3, note 63.

42. J. A. Maurault, *Histoire des Abénakis, Depuis 1605 Jusqu'à Nos Jours* (Sorel, Québec, 1866), p. 275.

43. Naomi E. S. Griffiths, *The Acadians: Creation of a People* (Montreal: McGraw-Hill, 1973).

44. Robert La Blant, "La Première Compagnie de Miscou, 1635−1645," *Revue d'Histoire de l'Amérique Française* 17 (1963−64): 363−370; Bernard Bailyn, *The New England Merchants in the Seventeenth Century* (Cambridge, Mass.: Harvard University Press, 1955), pp. 115−116, 128, 145−146; John Bartlet Brebner, *New England's Outpost*, pp. 37−47; Louis-André Vigneras, "Letters of an Acadian Trader, 1674−1676," *New England Quarterly* 13 (1940): 98−110; Jean Daigle, "Nos Amis les Ennemis: Les Marchands Acadiens et le Massachusetts à la fin du $17_e$ siècle," *Les Cahiers de la Société Historique Acadienne* 7 (1976): 162−170.

45. For the development of this rivalry see Max Savelle, *The Origins of American Diplomacy: The International History of Anglo-America, 1492−1763* (New York: Macmillan, 1967), pp. 89−121; Viola F. Barnes, *The Dominion of New England: A Study in British Colonial Policy* (New Haven: Yale University Press, 1923), pp. 212−230; George A. Rawlyk, *Nova Scotia's Massachusetts*, pp. 17−34; John G. Reid, "Styles of Colonization and Social Disorders in Early Acadia and Maine: A Comparative Approach," *Les Cahiers de la Société Historique Acadienne* 7 (1976): 105−117; William I. Roberts, "The Fur Trade of New England in the Seventeenth Century" (Ph.D., diss., University of Pennsylvania, 1958), pp. 114−115; "Hector D'Andigne de Grandfontaine," *DCB*, 2:61−63; Andrew Hill Clark, *Acadia: The Geography of Early Nova Scotia to 1760* (Madison: University of Wisconsin Press, 1968), pp. 56−70.

46. John E. Godfrey, "Jean Vincent, Baron de Saint-Castin," in *Me. His. Soc., Coll.*, 1st ser., vol. 7, pp. 55−56; Pierre Daviault, *Le Baron de Saint-Castin, chéf Abénaquis* (Montréal: Editions de l'A. C-f, 1939), pp. 70−73; *DCB*, 2:4−7; and see Gorham Munson's review essay, "St. Castin: A Legend Revised," *Dalhousie Review* 65 (1965): 338−360.

47. John Smith, *A Description of New England*, in *Tracts and Other Papers*, ed. Peter Force (Washington, D.C., 1837), 2:13.

48. George A. Rawlyk, *Nova Scotia's Massachusetts*, pp. 35−49; John Daigle, "Michel Le Neuf de la Vallière, Seigneur de Beaubassin et Gouverneur d'l'Acadie, 1678−1684" (M.A. thesis, Université de Montréal, 1970); *DCB*, 1:589−591; Mémoire sur l'estat présent de la Coste *de l'Acadie, 1684, AC*, ser. C11D, 1, pp. 399−400; M. Callières to M. De Signelay, 1684, *NYCD*, 9:265—266. For Dongan's role in the overall rivalry see W. J. Eccles, *Canada under Louis XIV*, pp. 148−159, and Douglas E. Leach, *The Northern Colonial Frontier, 1607−1763* (New York: Holt, Rinehart, and Winston, 1966), pp. 106−108; Douglas E. Leach, *Arms for Empire: A Military History of the British Colonies in North America, 1607−1763* (New York: Macmillan, 1973), pp. 72−77.

49. For Breda see Max Savelle, *Origins of American Diplomacy*, pp. 56−57.

50. Castin à Mons. de Denonville, Juillet 2, 1687, *Coll. de Mss.*, 1:399−401; Castin à Mons. de Menneval, September 15, 1687, *Coll. de Mss.*, 1:403; Mémoire de l'Etat des Affaires du Canada, October 27, 1687, *Coll. de Mss.*, 1:405; Mémoire sur l'Acadie par Mons. de Meneval, 1687, *Coll. de Mss.*, 1:412; Résumé d'un Mémoire sur l'Acadie par Mons. de Meneval, December 1, 1687, *Coll. de Mss.*, 1:410−411; Avantage que procurera à l'Estat et au commerce des sujets du Roy, l'éstablissement d'une compagnie à la coste et puis de l'Acadie, 1687, *AC*, C11D, 2−1, p. 319; Lettre du Roy à Mons Le Marquis de Denonville, January 1, 1688, *Coll. de Mss.*, 1:413−414; Mémoire Pour Servir D'Instruction Au Sieur Marquis De Denonville sur les Esclaircissements À Donner Au Sujet Des Contestations qui Sont Entre Les Francois Et des Anglais, 1688, *Coll. de Mss.*, 1:418−419; Lettre du Ministre à Mons de Meneval, April 10, 1688, *Coll. de Mss.*, 1:422; Mémoire pour Servir d'Instruction au Sieur Pasquine, Ingénieur, 1688, *Coll. de Mss.*, 1:421; George A. Rawlyk, *Nova Scotia's Massachusetts*, pp. 51−54; "Louis Alexandre des Friches de Meneval" and "Francois Marie Perrot," *DCB* 2:182−184, 540−542.

51. Lettre de M. de Denonville, October 18, 1688, *Coll. de Mss.*, 1:437.

52. Lettre de Mons. Le Marquis de Denonville au Ministre, October 30, 1688, *Coll. de Mss.*, 1:442.

53. Ibid., 1:442−444.

54. Ibid.

55. Mémoire du Roy au Sr Marquis de Denonville et de Champigny, May 1, 1689, *Coll. de Mss.*, 1:448; George A. Rawlyk, *Nova Scotia's Massachusetts*, pp. 51−84.

56. Résumé des lettres sur les Sauvages Abenaquis, 1689, *Coll. de Mss.*, 1: 468−469.

57. Lettre du Pere Thury, 1689, *Coll. de Mss.*, 1:464−465; Relation du Combat de Cannibas par M. de Thury, 1689, *Coll. de Mss.*, 1:477−481.

58. Relation du Combat de Cannibas par M. de Thury, *Coll. de Mss.*, 1:481. Résumé des lettres sur les Sauvages Abenaquis, 1689, *Coll. de Mss.*, 1:468−469;

Mémoire de Monsieur de Denonville Envoyé à Monsieur le Marquis de Seignelay, *Coll. de Mss.*, 2:2.

59. Résumé des rapports avec les notes du Ministre, 1689, *Coll. de Mss.*, 1: 474–476; January 1690, *AC*, C11A, 11, pp. 315–316, and *NYCD*, 9:440–441; Summary of Intelligence of Canada, 1688–89, *NYCD*, 9:438.

60. Agreement in re Expedition Against Indians, February 5, 1689/90, *Bax. Mss.*, 23:2; Journal of Benj. Bullivant, February 2, 1689/90, *CSP*, 13:264; A Monsieur de Menneval, Juillet 14, 1690, *AC*, Ser. B, 15, p. 409; Louis XIV to Count de Frontenac and M. de Champigny, July 14, 1690, *NYCD*, 9:453; W. J. Eccles, *Canada under Louis XIV*, pp. 169–177.

61. M. de Frontenac, April 30, 1690, *AC*, Ser. F3, 6-1, p. 532; Gustave Lanctot, *A History of Canada*, 3 vols. (Cambridge, Mass.: Harvard University Press, 1963–65), 2:115–116. For Silvanus Davis and a historiographical note on the fall of Fort Loyal see Alice R. Stewart, "Silvanus Davis," *DCB*, 2:172; see also Relation de ce qui s'est passé de plus remarquable en Canada, depuis le départ des vaisseaux, au mois de November, 1689, jusqu'au mois de November, 1690, *Coll. de Mss.*, 1:497–500; Rapport de Monsieur de Champigny, 1690, *Coll. de Mss.*, 2:29; Francis Parkman, *Count Frontenac*, pp. 228–232; Douglas E. Leach, *Arms for Empire*, pp. 88–89.

62. Parolles des Sauvages de la mission de Pentagoet proshe de Pemkuit, January 6, 1691, *Coll. de. Mss.*, 2:34–36; *AC*, Ser. F3, 7–1, pp. 9–14; Réponse de Monsieur le Comte de Frontenac aux Sauvages de Pentagouet, March 8, 1691, *Coll. de Mss.*, 2:38–39; Narrative of the Most remarkable Occurrences in Canada, 1691, *NYCD*, 9:514.

63. Proposition du Sr. de Villebon pour l'Acadie, Février, 1691, *AC*, C11D, 2-2, pp. 405–406; April 7, 1691, *AC*, Ser. B, 16-1, pp. 67–68.

64. Mémoire du Roy aux Srs Comte de Frontenac et de Champigny, *AC*, Ser. B, 16-1, pp. 67–68; Mémoire du Roi, April 7, 1691, *AC*, Ser. B, 16-1, pp. 80, 86; Mémoire pour servir d'Instruction au Sr Villebon, Commandant à l'Acadie, April 7, 1691, *AC*, Ser. B, 16-1, pp. 104–110, and *Coll. de Mss.*, 2:45–47; Mémoire pour servir d'Instruction au Sr Bonnaventure, April 7, 1691, *AC*, Ser. B, 12-1, pp. 98–103.

65. Frontenac to Pontchartrain, May 10, 1691, *NYCD*, 9:495; Champigny au Ministre, May 10, 1691, *NYCD*, 9:498, and *Coll. de Mss.*, 2:57–59; Rapport de M. de Monseignant au Ministre, September 10, 1691, *Coll. de Mss.*, 2:63; Lettre de Monsieur de Frontenac au Ministre, September 15, 1691, *Coll. de Mss.*, 2:85; Ce qu'on fait les Abénaquis de l'Acadie et ceux qui sont à Sillery . . . contre l'Anglois vers la fin de 1691 et en 1692, October 5, 1692, *AC*, Ser., F3, 7-1, pp. 2–8; Lettre de Monsieur de Champigny au Ministre, October 5, 1692, *Coll. de Mss.*, pp. 89–90; Charles E. Banks, *History of York, Maine*, 2 vols. (Boston: Calkins Press, 1931–35), 1:290–291; William Durkee Williamson, *The History of Maine*, 1:628–629.

66. M. de Villebon to Pontchartrain, October 12, 1691, *NYCD*, 9:506; Journal of what has happened in Acadia from October 13th, 1691 to October 25th, 1692, in

*Acadia at the End of the Seventeenth Century: Letters, Journals and Memoirs of Joseph Robineau de Villebon*, ed. J. C. Webster (St. John: The New Brunswick Museum, 1934), p. 33; Mémoire Pour Le Comte de Frontenac Touschant l'Acadie, March 15, 1692, *Coll. de Mss.*, 2:76; Lettre du Roy au Sieur de Villebon, April, 1692, *Coll. de Mss.*, 2:82–83, and *AC*, Ser. B, 16-1, pp. 278–286.

67. S. A. Drake, ed., *The History of King Philip's War* (Exeter, N.H., 1829), pp. 211–214; Phipps to Nottingham, October 12, 1692, *Bax. Mss.*, 10:3–4, and *CSP*, 13:721; J. C. Webster, ed., *Acadia*, p. 42. For accounts of the attack see Cotton Mather, *Decennium Luctuosum*, in *Narratives of the Indian Wars, 1675–1699*, ed. Charles H. Lincoln (New York: Charles Scribner's Sons, 1913), pp. 232–240; Daniel Neal, *The History of New-England*, 2 vols. (London, 1720), 2:484–486; William Durkee Williamson, *History of Maine*, 1:631–633; Edward E. Bourne, *The History of Wells and Kennebunk* (Portland, Me., 1875), pp. 213–216.

68. Memoir on the projected attack on Canada, 1692, *NYCD*, 9:544–545; Mémoire sur l'Acadie et la Nouvelle Angleterre par Monsieur de Lagny, 1692, *Coll. de Mss.*, 2:98–100; Extrait d'un Mémoire par Monsieur Champigny, *Coll. de Mss.*, 2:100–101.

69. A Monsieur le Comte de Frontenac, Février 14, 1693, *AC*, Ser. B, 16-1, pp. 151–156; Mémoire pour servir d'Instruction au Sr de Villebon, Commandant à l'Acadie, Février 14, 1693, *AC*, Ser. B, 16-2, pp. 12–39; *Coll. de Mss.*, 2:106–108; Estat des Présens à Envoyer Aux Chefs Abnaquis à l'Acadie, 1693, *Coll. de Mss.*, 2:111; Estat des Présens à Envoyer aux Sauvages Abenaquis Dans lesquel Les Chefs Auront part, *Coll. de Mss.*, 2:111. See also Estat des munitions et marchandises embarqués en France sur le frégatte 'La Suzanne' en 1693 pour estre portez à l'Acadie, *Coll. de Mss.*, 2:129–130.

70. J. C. Webster, ed., *Acadia*, p. 37.

71. Cotton Mather, *Life of Phips*, pp. 156–157; Truce between Indians and English, July 21, 1693, *Bax. Mss.*, 23:4–5; Govr Phipps to Govr Fletcher, July 26, 1693, *Bax. Mss.*, 23:5–6; The Submission and Agreements of the Eastern Indians, August 11, 1693, *Bax. Mss.*, 10:9–11; February 24, 1693/94, *Acts and Resolves*, February 24, 1693/94, 1:150–151; Letter to Governor Fletcher and Draft of Treaty with Indians at Pemaquid, August 24, 1693, *Bax. Mss.*, 23:6–9; Phips to Nottingham, September 11, 1693, *CSP*, 14:157.

72. Nouvelle de l'Acadie, 1693, *Coll. de Mss.*, 2:127; Narrative of the most remarkable Occurrences in Canada, *NYCD*, 9:570–571.

73. Journal of Events in Acadia from September 15, 1693 to September 2, 1694, in *Acadia*, ed. J. C. Webster, pp. 53–54.

74. Ibid.

75. Unless otherwise noted, the following paragraphs are drawn from Rélation du Voyage faict par le Sieur de Villieu à la teste des Sauvages Abénaquis, Kanibats et Malecoites de l'Acadie pour faire la querre Aux Anglois de Baston, Printemps, 1694, *Coll. de Mss.*, 2:135–143; J. C. Webster, ed., *Acadia*, pp. 55–57.

76. Covenant of Lands with Sir William Phips, by Madokawando, Sagamore of Penobscot, May 9/19, 1694, *Bax. Mss.*, 8:11−15; *York Deeds*, 10:237−238, 257−258.

77. Callière au Ministre, October 19, 1694, *AC*, C11A, 13, pp. 128−129; for English views of these events and the attack of Oyster River see Cotton Mather, *Decennium Luctuosum*, pp. 252−254; Thomas Hutchinson, *History of Massachusetts-Bay*, 2:55, 61−62; Jeremy Belknap, *The History of New Hampshire*, 1:215−221; William Durkee Williamson, *History of Maine*, 1:640; Francis Parkman, *Count Frontenac*, pp. 365−366.

## 5: SEEKING NEUTRALITY

1. The phrase "political priests" is Alvin Morrison's "Dawnland Decisions: Seventeenth-century Wabanaki Leaders and Their Response to the Differential Contact Stimuli in the Overlap Area of New France and New England" (Ph.D. diss., State University of New York, 1974), but his view is widely accepted. For the standard Eurocentric interpretations of the colonial wars, see Francis Parkman, *Count Frontenac and New France under Louis XIV* (Boston, 1884); Douglas E. Leach, *The Northern Colonial Frontier, 1607−1763* (New York: Macmillan, 1958), pp. 109−125; Douglas E. Leach, *Arms for Empire: A Military History of the British Colonies in North America, 1607−1763* (New York: Macmillan, 1973), pp. 80−115; John Bartlet Brebner, *New England's Outpost: Acadia before the Conquest of Canada* (New York: Columbia University Press, 1927), pp. 49−50; W. J. Eccles, *France in America* (New York: Harper and Row, 1972), pp. 90−91; W. J. Eccles, *Canada under Louis XIV, 1663−1701* (Toronto: McClelland and Stewart, 1964), pp. 169−184.

2. For brief accounts of these priests' careers see "Jacques Bigot," "Vincent Bigot," "Sebastien Rale," and "Louis-Pierre Thury," *DCB*, 2:63−65, 542−545, 649. There are various spellings of Racle's name. I follow the autograph letters in the Houghton Manuscripts, Harvard University Library.

3. Relation de ce qui s'est passé de plus remarquable en Canada, depuis le départ des vaisseaux, au mois de Novembre, 1689, jusqu'au mois de Novembre, 1690, *Coll. de Mss.*, 1:528.

4. Letter to Govr Fletcher and Draft Treaty, August 24, 1693, *Bax. Mss.*, 23:6−9; Declaration and Precept by Sir William Phips, August 8, 1694, Mass. Arch., 30:351; Declaration and Precept by Sir William Phips, August 8, 1694, Mass. Arch., 30:351, and *Bax. Mss.*, 23:10−11; see Hutchinson's comments on the hostage policy, Thomas Hutchinson, *History of the Colony and Province of Massachusetts-Bay*, ed. Lawrence Shaw Mayo, 3 vols. (Cambridge, Mass.: Harvard University Press, 1936), 2:61.

5. Declaration and Precept by Sir William Phips, August 8, 1694, *Mass. Arch.*, 30:351; Instruction for Captain John Alden, August 8, 1694, *Bax. Mss.*, 23:9−11.

6. Lettre de Monsieur de Champigny au Ministre, October 24, 1694, *Coll. de Mss.*, 2:162−63; Letter from Governor Stoughton to Governor Fletcher, January 28, 1694/95, *Bax. Mss.*, 23:11−12.

7. Stoughton's Letter of January 21, 1695, in Narrative of the most remarkable Occurrences in Canada, 1694, 1695, *NYCD*, 9:613−614; Answer of the Abenaki Indians to the Letter of the Lieutenant Governor of Boston, *NYCD*, 9:614−615; Reponse à la Lettre de Vice-Gouverneur de Boston par les Sauvages Abénaquis, 1695, *Coll. de Mss.*, 2:196−199.

8. Narrative of the most remarkable Occurrences in Canada, 1694, 1695, *NYCD*, 9:615−616; Letter from John March, March 8, 1694/95, *Bax. Mss.*, 23:12−13; Letter Gov. Stoughton to Gov. Fletcher, March 25, 1695, *Bax. Mss.*, 23:13−14; Samuel Niles, "A Summary Narrative of the Wars in New England with the French and Indians," *Mass. His. Soc. Coll.*, 3d ser., vol. 6, pp. 237−238; see Thomas Hutchinson, *History of Massachusetts-Bay*, 2:66; William Durkee Williamson, *History of Maine*, 1:641−642.

9. Résumé d'une Lettre de Monsieur de Villebon au Ministre, September 19, 1694, *Coll. de Mss.*, 2:158−159; M. de Villebon to M. de Pontchartrain, August 20, 1694, *NYCD*, 9:574−577; Lettre de Monsieur de Champigny au Ministre, October 24, 1964, *Coll. de Mss.*, 2:162−163; Narrative of the most remarkable Occurrences in Canada, 1694, 1695, *NYCD*, 9:616−617.

10. Lettre du R. P. Thury à Monsieur le Comte de Frontenac, September 11, 1694, *Coll. de Mss.*, 2:160−162.

11. Au Sr de Villebon, April 16, 1695, *AC*, Ser. B, 17-2, p. 105.

12. A Mr. de Thury, April 16, 1695, *AC*, ser. B, 17-2, pp. 126−128; *Coll. de Mss.*, 2:174−175; "Acadian Journal, September 17, 1694 to July 12, 1695," in *Acadia*, ed. J. C. Webster, pp. 78−79. On the metropolitan trade policy see "Au Sr de Villebon, April 16, 1695," in *Acadia*, ed. J. C. Webster, pp. 163−169; "Ministre à Frontenac, April 16, 1695," *Coll. de Mss.*, 2:169−170.

13. Mémoire sur l'Acadie par M. Tibierge, October 1, 1695, *Coll. de Mss.*, 2:185−187; Mémoire de la Compagnie de l'Acadie, October 13, 1695, *Coll. de Mss.*, 2:199−201.

14. Narrative of the most remarkable Occurrences in Canada, 1694−1695, *NYCD*, 9:616−617.

15. Narrative of the most remarkable Occurrences in Canada, 1695, *NYCD*, 9:630−631; M. de Frontenac et de Champigny au Ministre, November 10, 1695, *AC*, C11A, 13, p. 331; Frontenac à Lagny, November 2, 1695, *Coll. de Mss.*, 2:187−188; Champigny au Ministre, November 6, 1695, *Coll. de Mss.*, 2:189−190; Mémoire du Roy au Srs Comte de Frontenac et de Champigny, Juin 14, 1695, *AC*, Ser. B, 17-3, pp. 213−215, and *Coll. de Mss.*, 2:182; M. de Frontenac et de Champigny au Ministre, November 10, 1695, *AC*, C11A, 13, pp. 330−331.

16. Narrative of the most remarkable Occurrences in Canada, 1696, *NYCD*, 9:642−643; *Coll. de Mss.*, 2:221−222; *AC*, C11A, 14, pp. 43−45; Cotton Mather,

*Decennium Luctuosum*, p. 261; Samuel Niles, "A Summary Narrative of the Wars in New England," 6:244; Thomas Hutchinson, *History of Massachusetts-Bay*, 2:70; William Durkee Williamson, *History of Maine*, 1:642.

17. Lettre de D'Iberville à M. de Pontchartrain, in *Journal d'une Expedition de D'Iberville*, ed. L'Abbé A. Gosselin (Évreux: Imprimérie de l'Eure, 1900), pp. 75—77; Certain of the late garrison of Pemaquid Fort to Lieutenant-Governor Stoughton, 1696, *CSP*, 15:143—144; Thomas Hutchinson, *History of Massachusetts-Bay*, 2:70; Journal du Voyage que j'ay fait avec M. D'Iberville, Capitaine de Fregate . . . Du 26 juin 1696 jusqu'en May 1697 par l'Abbé Jean Beaudoin, in *Journal d'une Expedition*, ed. L'Abbé A. Gosselin, pp. 34—36; Relation de ce qui s'est passé de plus remarquable en Canada dépuis le départ des vaisseaux jusqu'au commencement de novembre 1696, *AC*, C11A, 14, pp. 91—92, and *NYCD*, 9:658.

18. Journal, Villebon to Pontchartrain, March 2, 1697, in *Acadia*, ed. J. C. Webster, p. 101, and *AC*, C11A, 14, p. 200; Sieur Tibierge à M. le Comte de Frontenac, Aoust 20, 1697, *Coll. de Mss.*, 2:286; Rapport de Monsieur de Champigny, October 16, 1697, *Coll. de Mss.*, 2:287—288; Lt. Gov. Stoughton to Council of Trade, September 30, 1697, *CSP*, 15:624, 625; Lettre du Sieur Deschambeault, September 24, 1697, *AC*, C11D, 3-1, pp. 166—170; Villebon à Ministre, *AC*, C11D, 3-1, p. 200.

19. Journal of Events in Acadia, October, 1696 to October 1, 1697, in *Acadia*, ed. J. C. Webster, pp. 107, 110; Résumé des letters de M. de Champigny au Ministre, October 20, 1697, *Coll. de Mss.*, 2:288.

20. Memorial from Mr. Nelson, July 2, 1697, *Bax. Mss.*, 10:20—21; J. Nelson to Lords of Trade and Plantations, November 2, 1697, *Bax. Mss.*, 10:21—25; Traitté de Paix entre la France et l'Angleterre Conclu à Ryswick, September 20, 1697, *Coll. de Mss.*, 2:227—240.

21. *Acts and Resolves*, 7:600.

22. Bellomont to William Popple, January 8, 1697/98, *CSP*, 26:84; Earl of Bellomont to Count Frontenac, April 22, 1698, *NYCD*, 9:690.

23. Report of Peter Schuyler and Godfrey Dellius of their mission to Frontenac, May, 1698, *CSP*, 16:341—342.

24. Bellomont to the Council of Trade, September 21, 1698, *CSP*, 16:449.

25. Cotton Mather, *Magnalia Christi Americana*, 2 vols. (Hartford, Conn., 1820), 2:511, 517, 531, 538 (emphasis in original).

26. William Bradford, *Of Plymouth Plantation, 1620—1647*, ed. S. E. Morison (Boston: A. A. Knopf, 1963), pp. 336—337.

27. Massachusetts charter quoted in Alexander Young, ed., *Chronicles of the First Planters of the Colony of Massachusetts Bay from 1623 to 1636* (Boston, 1846), p. 142; Cotton Mather, *Magnalia Christi Americana*, 2:577 (emphasis in original).

28. Cotton Mather, *Magnalia Christi Americana*, 2:577 (emphasis in original); A. W. Plumstead, ed., *The Wall and the Garden: Selected Massachusetts Election Sermons, 1670—1775* (Minneapolis: University of Minnesota Press, 1968), p. 134.

29. Cotton Mather, *Frontiers Well-Defended* (Boston, 1707), p. 23 (emphasis in original); Letter John Minot to Col. Stephen Minot, October 4, 1725, *Bax. Mss.*, 10:346; Cotton Mather, *Life of Phips*, p. 163.

30. Cotton Mather, *India Christiana* (Boston, 1721), p. 41; Cotton Mather, *A Monitory, and Hortatory Letter* (Boston, 1700), p. 13; Cotton Mather, *Frontiers Well-Defended*, p. 25; Cotton Mather, *Duodecennium Luctuosum* (Boston, 1714), p. 12 (emphasis in original).

31. Cotton Mather, *Frontiers Well-Defended*, p. 45; Cotton Mather, *A Monitory Letter*, pp. 12−13 (emphasis in original).

32. Cotton Mather, *Magnalia Christi Americana*, 2:306, 509−512, 535, 537, 574 (emphasis in original).

33. Ibid., 2:545−546 (emphasis in original).

34. Ibid., 2:538−540 (emphasis in original).

35. John Nelson and Silvanus Davis to Lord Bellomont, *CSP*, 17:558.

36. Minutes of Council of Massachusetts, November 22, 1699, *CSP*, 17:538, 549; Bellomont to Council of Trade, November 29, 1699, *CSP*, 17:554−555.

37. On the persistent rumors see *CSP*, 18:91−92, 95−97, 123; Storer, Hamond, and Wheelwright to Bellomont, March 27, 1699/1700, *Bax. Mss.*, 10:43−45; Benjamin Sabin to Bellomont, March 27, 1699/1700, *CSP*, 18:182.

38. Proclamation by the Earl of Bellomont, March 14, 1699/1700, *CSP*, 18:182; *Bax. Mss.*, 23:22a−22b.

39. Bellomont to Commissioners of Indian Affairs at Albany, March 21, 1699/1700, *CSP*, 18:184; W. Romer to Earl of Bellomont, April 11, 1700, *CSP*, 18:366−368, and *Bax. Mss.*, 10:45−52.

40. Examination of Suckquaus and Sasquhaan, April 7, 1700, *CSP*, 18:186−187; Robert Livingston to Lord Bellomont, April 8, 1700, *CSP*, 18:185.

41. The Memoriall of William Rayment Lieutenant of the New Detached Company . . . within the County of York, April 13, 1700, *CSP*, 18:183, and *Bax. Mss.*, 10:52−54.

42. Governor & Council of New Hampshire to the King, April, 1700, *CSP*, 18:775; *Bax. Mss.*, 10:54−56; J. W. Hanson, *History of Gardiner, Pittston, and West Gardiner* (Gardiner, Me., 1852); George A. Wheeler, *History of Castine, Penobscot, and Brooksville* (Bangor, Me., 1875), pp. 21−22; Francis Parkman, *A Half-Century of Conflict*, 2 vols. (Boston: Little, Brown, 1905), 1:215; Douglas E. Leach, *Arms for Empire*, p. 182; Philip S. Haffenden, *New England in the English Nation, 1689−1713* (Oxford: Clarendon Press, 1974), pp. 206, 210, 213.

43. Peter Schuyler, Robt Livingston, and Hend Hansen to Lord Bellomont, May 3, 1700, *CSP*, 18:273; S. Sewall to Sir William Ashhurst, May 3, 1700, *Mass. His. Soc., Coll.*, 6th ser., vol. 1, pp. 232−233.

44. Bellomont to the Council of Trade, May 25, 1700, *CSP*, 18:268; Minutes of General Assembly of Massachusetts, May 30, 1700, *CSP*, 18:293−294, 305.

45. Bellomont to the Council of Trade, June 22, 1700, *CSP*, 18:362, 400.

46. Minutes of Council in Assembly of Massachusetts, July 11, 1700, *CSP*,

18:410; Bill for reviving and continuing the act for giving necessary supplies to the Eastern Indians and for regulating trade with them, July 12, 1700, Mass. Arch., 30:462; Remarks . . . upon some Acts past in the General Assembly of Massachusetts Bay, December 15, 1697—March 13, 1699—1700, *CSP*, 18:629.

47. Minutes of Council of Massachusetts Bay, September 5, 1700, *CSP*, 18:517; Lt. Gov. William Stoughton to Council of Trade, December 20, 1700, *CSP*, 18:757; Father Bigot's Letter to George Turfrey, September 24, 1700, *CSP*, 18:538; *Bax. Mss.*, 5:455; Letter to Vincent a Bigot, April 10, 1701, *Bax. Mss.*, 9:109—110.

48. Lord Bellomont's Conference with the Indians at Albany, August 26—September 4, 1700, *CSP*, 18:584—600; Governor Bellomont to Council of Trade, November 28, 1700, *CSP*, 18:676.

49. Lt. Governor Stoughton to Council of Trade and Plantations, June 3, 1700, *CSP*, 19:275. The following paragraphs are based on a report of the conference, June 3, 1701, *Bax. Mss.*, 10:87—95; Vincent Bigot, *Relation de ce Qui s'est passé de plus Remarquable dans la Mission des Abnaquis à L'Acadie, L'Année 1701* (À Manate, 1863), pp. 8—10.

50. Message of Indians, and Answers of Council, December 27, 1701, *Bax. Mss.*, 23:31—35, and Mass. Arch., 30:480—483; Notes of a Conference at New Harbor with the Truckmaster, *Bax. Mss.*, 23:35—37; Minutes of Council of Massachusetts Bay, April 28, 1702, *CSP*, 20:280.

51. An Act re Indian Supplies, July 14, 1699, *Bax. Mss.*, 23:23—26; Minutes of General Assembly of Massachusetts, July 14, July 17, 1699, *CSP*, 17:340, 350; Brouillan to Bellomont, August 8, 1701, *Bax. Mss.*, 10:96—97; Isa Addington to Brouillan, August 22, 1701, *Bax. Mss.*, 10:103—104.

52. Ministre à Monsieur de Villebon, March 26, 1698, *Coll. de Mss.*, 2:295—296; Présents des sauvages de l'Acadie, *AC*, Ser. B, 20, pp. 67—69.

53. Villebon à Ministre, October 3, 1698, *AC*, C11D, 3-1, pp. 363—373.

54. A M. de Thury, March 26, 1698, *AC*, Ser. B. 20, p. 107; Ministre à M. Thury, April 15, 1699, *Coll. de Mss.*, 2:317.

55. This paragraph and the next are based on Parolles des Sauvages Abénakis des quatre villages de l'Acadie, *AC*, F3, 2—2, pp. 377—385; see also Yves Zoltvany, *Philippe de Rigaud de Vaudreuil, Governor of New France, 1703—1725* (Toronto: McClelland and Stewart, 1974), pp. 41—42; Jacques Bigot, *Relation de la Mission Abnaquise de St. François de Sales l'Année 1702* (Nouvelle York, 1865), pp. 21—23.

56. Robert H. Lord, John E. Sexton, and Edward T. Harrington, *The History of the Archdiocese of Boston*, 3 vols. (New York: Sheed and Ward, 1944), 1:56.

57. Mémoire Joint à la lettre de Monsieur de Brouillan, October 6, 1701, *AC*, C11D, 4, part 1, p. 146; Abrégé d'une lettre de Monsieur de Brouillan au Ministre, October 30, 1701, *Coll. de Mss.*, 2:386; Robert H. Lord, John E. Sexton, and Edward T. Harrington, *Archdiocese*, 1:80—81; Ministre à Brouillan, March 15, 1702, *AC*, C11D, 4-2, p. 315.

58. Abrégé d'une lettre de Monsieur de Villebon au Ministre, 1698, *Coll. de Mss.*, 2:305—306; see also Lettre de Villebon au Ministre, October 27, 1699, *Coll. de Mss.*,

2:330. The minister realized that Villebon undercut French relations with the Abenaki, especially by selling them liquor. See Note du Ministre, Villieu au Ministre, October 20, 1700, *Coll. de Mss.*, 2:337; Résumé d'une lettre du Sieur de Villieu au Ministre, October 20, 1700, *Coll. de Mss.*, 2:336; Robert H. Lord, John E. Sexton, and Edward T. Harrington, *Archdiocese of Boston*, 1:81; L'Abbé Casgrain, *Les Sulpiciens et les Prêtes de Missions-Étrangères en Acadie (1676–1762)* (Québec, 1897), pp. 239, 242.

59. M. de Callière à M. de Pontchartrain, November 4, 1702, *AC*, C11A, 20, p. 72, and *NYCD*, 9:738; Lettre de Monsieur Beauharnois au Ministre, November 11, 1702, *Coll. de Mss.*, 2:396. Antoine Gaulin, a Franciscan priest, earlier remarked that the journey was inconvenient and he thus offered an explanation why the Quebec-based Jesuits gradually assumed responsibility for both the Abenaki and the Maliseet missions (L'Abbé Casgrain, *Les Sulpiciens*, pp. 226–227).

60. Governor Dudley's meeting with Abenaki, July, 1702, *CSP*, 20:502–505; Samuel Penhallow, *The History of the Wars of New England with the Eastern Indians* (Cincinnati, 1859), p. 17, asserted that the Abenaki meant to attack the English as the conference closed, although Dudley does not mention any incident.

61. John Wheelwright to Joseph Dudley, August 4, 1702, *Me. His. Soc., Coll.*, 1st ser., vol. 3, pp. 343–344; Dudley to Council of Trade, August 5, 1702, *CSP*, 20:501; Governor Dudley to the Council of Trade, September 17, 1702, *CSP*, 20:592.

62. Minutes of Council, March 31, 1703, *CSP*, 21:308; April 1, 1703, *CSP*, 21:309; April 5, 1703, *CSP*, 21:332–333; April 27, 1703, *CSP*, 21:385; May 1, 1703, *CSP*, 21:396; Gov. Dudley to Council of Trade and Plantations, April 4, 1703, *CSP*, 21:323–324; Cyprian Southack to Dudley, May 10, 1703, *Me. His. Soc., Coll.*, 1st ser., vol. 3, pp. 345–346; *The Campbell News-Letters*, June 7, 1703, in *Historical Digest*, comp. Lyman H. Weeks and Edwin M. Bacon, p. 46.

63. June 30, 1703, *Acts and Resolves*, 8:286–287, also in *Mass. His. Soc., Coll.*, 5th ser., vol. 6, pp. 85–87.

64. Dudley to Lords of Trade, August 5, 1703, *Bax. Mss.*, 9:145; Minutes of Council in Assembly, July 8, 1703, *CSP*, 21:542–543; July 9, 1703, *CSP*, 21:543.

65. August 18, 1703, *Acts and Resolves*, p. 302; Minutes of Council, August 18, 1703, *CSP*, 21:647. "Sieur de Vaudreuil's opinion is," the minister commented, "that the English and the Abenakis must be kept irreconcilable enemies." Abstract of certain parts of a Despatch from Messrs de Vaudreuil and Beauharnois, with Notes by the Minister, November 15, 1703, *NYCD*, 9:755–756; Yves F. Zoltvany, *Philippe de Rigaud de Vaudreuil*, p. 114; Philip S. Haffenden, *New England in the English Nation*, p. 213.

66. Robert H. Lord, John E. Sexton, and Edward T. Harrington, *Archdiocese of Boston*, 1:84; Racle quoted in Beauharnois et Vaudreuil au Ministre, November 15, 1703, *Coll. de Mss.*, 2:405–406, and *AC*, C11A, 21, pp. 13–16, and *NYCD*, 9:756.

67. The priests and the Abenaki "met at Norridgewock and [the Jesuits] told the

Indians that they must look for some other country, for that it was impossible for them to live there." Thomas Church, *The Old French and Indian Wars, from 1689 to 1704*, in Benjamin Church, *The History of the Great Indian War of 1675 and 1676, Commonly Called Philip's War*, ed. Samuel G. Drake (Hartford, 1851), p. 283; Messrs de Vaudreuil to M. de Pontchartrain, November 17, 1703, *NYCD*, 9:762.

68. Abstract of certain parts of a Despatch from Messrs de Vaudreuil and Beauharnois, with Notes by the Minister, November 15, 1703, *NYCD*, 9:756.

69. Parolles des sauvages Abénakis d'amesoquanty, May 12, 1704, *AC*, F3, 2-2, pp. 392−395; Parolles des sauvages Abénakis de Koessek, Juin 13, 1704, *AC* F3, 2-2, pp. 407−410; Reponses des Sauvages de pintaguouet aux parolles de Monsieur de Vaudreuil et de Monsieur de Beauharnois, *AC*, F3, 2-2, pp. 627−628; M. de Vaudreuil to M. le Pontchartrain, November 16, 1704, *NYCD*, 9:758−759; Messrs de Vaudreuil et Beauharnois au Ministre, November 17, 1704, *AC*, C11A, 22, pp. 44−45.

70. Yves F. Zoltvany, *Philippe de Rigaud de Vaudreuil*, pp. 74−76.

71. Dudley to the Council of Trade, February 1, 1705/06, *CSP*, 23:31; Minutes of Council in Assembly, December 2, 1703, *CSP*, 21:852−854, and December 20, 1703, pp. 890−891. See the Reverend Solomon Stoddard's advice to Dudley urging him to use dogs against the Abenaki, October 22, 1703, *Mass. His. Soc., Coll.*, 4th ser., vol. 2, pp. 235−237; Sha'd Walton to Governor Dudley, February 24, *Me. His. Soc., Coll.*, 1st ser., vol. 3, pp. 348−350; Capt. Hilton's Journal, February, 1703/04, *Bax. Mss.*, 9:140−143; His Excllys Speech, April 19, 1704, *Bax. Mss.*, 9:185−186; Dudley to Council of Trade, April 20, 1704, *CSP*, 22:99−100; Thomas Church, *French and Indian Wars*, p. 284; *Boston News-Letter*, March 5, 1705; Samuel Penhallow, *History of the Wars of New England with the Eastern Indians*, p. 38; Robert H. Lord, John E. Sexton, and Edward T. Harrington, *Archdiocese of Boston*, 1:87; Haffenden notes that "hostilities on land had almost ceased" but does not report that the Abenaki were in Canada (Philip S. Haffenden, *New England in the English Nation*, p. 239).

72. *Boston News-Letter*, May, 1706; Dudley to the Council of Trade and Plantations, October 2, 1706, *CSP*, 23:233; Philip S. Haffenden, *New England in the English Nation*, pp. 214−215; John Williams, *The Redeemed Captive Returning to Zion or the Captivity and Deliverance of Rev. John Williams of Deerfield*, reprint of 6th ed. (Springfield, Mass.: H. R. Hunting, 1908), pp. 99, 100, 101. For background see Guy Frégault, *Le XVIII$_e$ Siècle Canadien, Études* (Montréal: Édition H.M.H., 1968), pp. 58−85.

73. M. de Pontchartrain to M. de Vaudreuil, June 6, 1708, *NYCD*, 9:813, and *AC*, ser. B, 29-4, p. 803.

74. M. de Vaudreuil to M. de Pontchartrain, November 12, 1708, *NYCD*, 9:816−819; Subercase à Ministre, December 28, 1708, *AC*, C11D, 6, 260; Dudley to Lords of Trade, March 1, 1708/09, *Bax. Mss.*, 9:263.

75. Sebastien Racle to his brother, 1711, Houghton Mss., n.p.; M. Vaudreuil to M. de Pontchartrain, April 27, 1709, *NYCD*, 9:824; The king sent thirty silver

medals and ten of silver gilt to those Abenaki sachems who were most attached to the
French to encourage them: Mémoire du Roy aux Vaudreuil et Raudot, Mai 10, 1710,
*AC*, Ser. B, 32-1, pp. 95—96.

76. Letter from Capt. Saml Moodey to Gov. Dudley, January 3, 1712/13, *Bax.
Mss.*, 9:315—316.

77. Letter from Capt. Samuel Moodey to Governor, January 6, 1712/13, *Bax.
Mss.*, 9:316—317, and Mass. Arch., 51, p. 257.

78. Letter from Govr. Dudley to Capt. Saml Moodey, January 17, 1712/13, *Bax.
Mss.*, 9:317—319; Lettre du R. P. Rasle à Monsieur le Gouverneur General, September 9, 1713, *Coll. de Mss.*, 2:562.

79. Thomas Hutchinson, *History of Massachusetts-Bay*, 2:150; Treaty of Eastern
Indians, July 11, 1713, *Bax. Mss.*, 23:40—41, 42—43, 44.

80. Treaty of Eastern Indians, July, 1713, *Bax. Mss.*, 23:47—49.


## 6: IDEALS AND ACTUALITIES

1. For the text of the treaty see Francis Gardner Davenport, *European Treaties on the
History of the United States and Its Dependencies*, 4 vols. (Washington, D.C.: Carnegie
Institute of Washington, 1934), 3:197—198.

2. Lettre de M. de Pontchartrain, August 10, 1712, *Min. Aff. Etr.*, 24, part 2,
pp. 173—176.

3. Lettre de M. de Pontchartrain, December 21, 1712, *Min. Aff. Etr.*, 24,
part 2, pp. 138—139.

4. Treaty of Eastern Indians, July 11, 1713, *Bax. Mss.*, 23:39, 40; A Journal of
Commissioners at Portsmouth, July 13, 1713, *Bax. Mss.*, 23:49.

5. At a Council, January 11, 1713/14, *Bax. Mss.*, 23:52—54.

6. Gyles to Shute, December 20, 1718, *Bax. Mss.*, 9:442, 447; Letter from
Joseph Heath & John Minot to Gov. Shute, May 1, 1719, *Bax. Mss.*, 9:447, and
Mass. Arch., 51, p. 317; Mass. Council, in *RSUS*, May 13, 1719, May 17, 1719,
September 11, 1719.

7. At a Council, January 11, 1713/14, *Bax. Mss.*, 23:53.

8. Ibid., 23:57.

9. Indian Conference, July 27—28, *Bax. Mss.*, 23:74, 76.

10. Bannister to Council of Trade, June 6 to December 20, 1717, as cited in
Robert H. Lord, John E. Sexton, and Edward T. Harrington, *History of the Archdiocese
of Boston* (New York: Sheed and Ward, 1944), 1:3.

11. The Council attempted to enforce these regulations. In March 1714 one
Richard Carr was arrested for loading his boat with goods to be traded on the
Penobscot. Mass. Council, in *RSUS*, March 22, 1714; At a Meeting with the
Delegates of the Eastern Indians, July 26, 1714, Mass. Arch., 29, pp. 42, 46.

12. A Conference was held with Five of the Eastern Indians, January 11—13,
1713/14, *Bax. Mss.*, 23:52.

13. Ibid., 23:51−57; Eastern Indians to the Governor For Her May Service, February 7, 1713/14, *Bax. Mss.*, 23:60−61.

14. Gov. Nicholson to Gov. Dudley, December 25, 1714, *CSP*, 28:262; Everett Kimball, *The Public Life of Joseph Dudley: A Study of the Colonial Policy of the Stuarts in New England, 1660−1715* (New York: Longmans, Green, 1900), pp. 130−131.

15. Indian Conference, July 23, 1714, *Bax. Mss.*, 23:70−73.

16. Ibid.

17. Mass. Council, in *RSUS*, December 27, 1714; Governor Nicholson to Governor Dudley, December 25, 1714, *CSP*, 28:262−263; Everett Kimball, *The Public Life of Joseph Dudley*, p. 132.

18. Proprietors Proposals to the Committee appointed by the General Court, February 18, 1714/15, Pejebscot Records in *RSUS*, 1:31, 36; The General Courts Confirmation of our Purchase, May 25, 1715, Pejebscot Records in *RSUS*, 1:31; Robert Earle Moody, "The Maine Frontier, 1607−1763" (Ph.D. diss., Yale University, 1933), p. 357; George A. Wheeler and Henry W. Wheeler, *History of Brunswick, Topsham, and Harpswell* (Boston, 1878), pp. 21−30; Gordon E. Kershaw, *The Kennebeck Proprietors, 1749−1775* (Somersworth: New Hampshire Publishing Co., 1975), pp. 18−19.

19. Proprietors Proposals to the Committee appointed by the General Court, February 18, 1714/15, Pejebscot Records in *RSUS*, 1:36; Colonel Nicholson to Mr. Popple, August 13, 1715, *CSP*, 28:261; By order & in behalf of the Committee, May 27, 1715, Pejebscot Records in *RSUS*, 1:38−39; Mass. Council, in *RSUS*, June 28, 1715; W. C. Ford, ed., *Journals of the House of Representatives of Massachusetts* (Boston: Massachusetts Historical Society, 1919−68), 1:19, 62−63, 97; Petition to the House of Representatives, July 28, 1715, Pejebscot Records, in *RSUS*, 1:48−49; Mass. Council, in *RSUS*, September 16, 1715, December 5, 1715, December 24, 1715, March 10, 1715/1716, May 28, 1716; William Durkee Williamson, *History of the State of Maine* (Hallowell, 1832), 2:89; Indian Conference, June 6, 1716, *Bax. Mss.*, 23:80−82, and Mass. Arch., 29, pp. 53−54. The lieutenant-governor decided that the Abenaki were restless because of "false Reports of a War likely to break out between *Great Britain* and *France*" (W. C. Ford, ed., *House Journals*, 1:82).

20. Mass. Council, in *RSUS*, July 10, 1716; Copy of a Letter from Sabastian Ralle, 1716, in *Documents and Records Relating to the Province of New Hampshire*, ed. Nathaniel Bouton, 40 vols (Concord and Manchester, 1867−1941), 8:753−754; W. C. Ford, ed., *House Journals*, 1:125; James P. Baxter, *Pioneers of New France in New England* (Albany, 1894), p. 68; Robert H. Lord, John E. Sexton, and Edward T. Harrington, *Archdiocese of Boston*, 1:11.

21. Except as otherwise noted, the account of the conference is taken from a contemporary pamphlet entitled "Georgetown on Arrowsick Island August 9th, 1717," in "Indian Treaties," *Me. His. Soc., Coll.*, 1st ser., vol. 3, pp. 361−375.

22. Manuscript Journal of the Reverend Joseph Baxter, Me. His. Soc., Archives, p. 6.

23. October 26, 1717, W. C. Ford, ed., *House Journals*, 1:226 (emphasis in

original); Samuel Sewall, "A Memorial Relating to the Kennebeck Indians," *Me. His. Soc., Coll.*, 1st ser., vol. 3, pp. 351−352 (emphasis in original); Governor Shute to the Council of Trade and Plantations, November 9, 1717, *CSP*, 30:101.

24. Samuel Sewall, "A Memorial Relating to the Kennebec Indians," p. 353.

25. See chapter 3.

26. All quotations from Racle are from Sebastien Racle to his Brother, October 30, 1689 and August 26, 1690, Houghton Manuscripts, n.p.

27. Mémoire sur les Limites de l'Acadie, envoyé de Québec à Mgr le Duc d'Orleans, Régent, par le Père Charlevoix, Jésuite, October 19, 1720, *AC*, C11E, 2, pp. 76−85, nd *NYCD*, 9:879−880; Vaudreuil au Ministre, November 14, 1713, *AC*, C11A, 34, p. 49.

28. P. F. X. de Charlevoix, *History and General Description of New France*, ed. John Gilmary Shea, 6 vols. (New York: Francis P. Harper, 1900), 5:270; Memoir on the Limits of Acadia, October 19, 1720, *NYCD*, 9:879−880.

29. Mémoire du Roi aux Sieurs de Vaudreuil et Begon, June 15, 1716, *Coll. de Mss.*, 3:18; Mémoire du Sieurs de Vaudreuil et Begon, July 15, 1718, *Coll. de Mss.*, 3:28.

30. Rapport de Monsieur de Vaudreuil au Conseil, October 31, 1718, *AC*, C11A, 39, pp. 127−134, and *Coll. de Mss.*, 3:31−32; Manuscript Journal of the Reverend Joseph Baxter, pp. 25−26. Joseph Baxter called the old chiefs "the wise men." Manuscript Journal of the Reverend Joseph Baxter, p. 26; Deposition of Lewis Bane of York, *CSP*, 31:365−366.

31. Some of these letters are preserved in the Mass. His. Soc., Archives. They are also printed in James P. Baxter, *Pioneers of New France*, pp. 85−87, 143−153, 397−404; A Letter from Governor Shute to Ralle the Jesuit, February 21, 1718/19, *Mass. His. Soc., Coll.*, 1st ser., vol. 5, pp. 112−119.

32. On the liquor traffic see W. C. Ford, ed., *House Journals*, May 29, 1718, 2:5, 37; June 12, 1718, p. 34; June 27, 1718, p. 48; October 29, 1718, p. 60; Mass. Council, in *RSUS*, August 6, 1718; Rapport de Monsieur de Vaudreuil au Conseil, October 31, 1718, *Coll. de Mss.*, 3:32; Governor Shute to the Council of Trade and Plantations, September 29, 1718, *CSP*, 30:358; Rapport de M. Begon, November 8, 1718, *AC*, C11A, 39, pp. 144−147; *Coll. de Mss.*, 3:33−34.

33. Rapport de Monsieur de Vaudreuil au Conseil, October 31, 1718, *Coll. de Mss.*, 3:32; Mémoire pour servir à regler les Limites, November 8, 1718, *AC*, C11E, 3, pp. 14−29; Council Deliberations on Vaudreuil's letter of October 31, 1718, March 14, 1719, *AC*, C11A, 124, p. 100; Mémoire du Roy à Messieurs de Marquis de Vaudreuil et Begon, May 23, 1719, *Coll. de Mss.*, 3:40, and *NYCD*, 9:892.

34. Rapport de Monsieur de Vaudreuil et Begon, October 26, 1719, *AC*, C11E, 2, pp. 34−36, and *AC*, C11A, 41, p. 68, and also *Coll. de Mss.*, 3:41−42. The quotations of Racle are from Joseph Heath and John Minot to Governor Shute, May 1, 1719, Mass. Arch., 51, pp. 316−317, and *Bax. Mss.*, 9:446−447. See also their other accounts, Deposition of Lewis Bane, December 2, 1719, and Deposition of John Minot, November 27, 1719, in James P. Baxter, *Pioneers of New France*, pp. 279−

280; Governor Shute to Council of Trade and Plantations, December 7, 1719, *CSP*, 31:282–283. For the official minutes see In re Conference at Falmouth, January 1719/20, Mass. Arch., 29, pp. 57–63, and *Bax. Mss.*, 23:83–87.

35. Rale to Moody, February 7, 1719/1720, in James P. Baxter, *Pioneers of New France*, pp. 96–104. Flynt's Manuscript Commonplace Book in the Massachusetts Historical Society archives also quotes this letter.

36. Mass. Council, in *RSUS*, March 3, 1719/20; W. C. Ford, ed., *House Journals*, July 13, 1720, 2:236; July 19, 1720, p. 247; July 21, 1720, pp. 255–257; July 22, 1720, pp. 257, 259; Belknap Papers, Mass. His. Soc., 61A, pp. 89–90; Williamson found the Abenaki's contention an exhibition of "good sense and a just regard for their rights." William Durkee Williamson, *History of Maine*, 2:105; Mass. Council, in *RSUS*, July 20, 1720.

37. The House voted that John Leighton, sheriff of York County, should accompany the forces to apprehend Racle. If the Abenaki refused to "surrender up the Jesuit," the commanding officer was to take hostages to be held until they did so. W. C. Ford, ed., *House Journals*, November 4, 1720, 2:270–272; November 5, 1720, pp. 272–273, 275.

38. Conference with Indians at Georgetown, November, 1720, Mass. Arch., 29, pp. 65–74, and *Bax. Mss.*, 23:97–108. The conference is also reported in Flynt, Commonplace Book, Mass. His. Soc., Archives, pp. 285–286.

39. This document is misdated under the title Mémoir respecting the Abenaquis of Acadia, 1718, in *NYCD*, 9:878–881. It is properly entitled Mémoire sur les Limites de l'Acadie, envoyé de Québec à Mgr le Duc d'Orleans, Régent, par le Père Charlevoix, Jésuite, October 19, 1720, in *AC*, C11E, 2, pp. 76–85, and in *Coll. de Mss.*, 3:49–54.

40. Memoir respecting the Abenaquis of Acadia, 1718, *NYCD*, 9:879–880.

41. Begon to Rale, June 14, 1721, and Vaudreuil to Rale, September 25, 1721, *JR*, 67:54–65. these were printed in W. C. Ford, ed., *House Journals*, which also includes another letter of Vaudreuil's to Rale, June 15, 1721, 3;189–192.

42. Begon to Rale, June 14, 1721, *JR*, 67:55–57, 59.

43. Letter from Capt Saml Moodey to Governor Shute, June 5, 1721, Mass. Arch., 51, p. 353, and *Bax. Mss.*, 9:462–463; Letter from Capt Samuel Moodey to Governor Shute, June 19, 1721, *Bax. Mss.*, 9:463–464; Letter from Samuel Moody to Governor Shute, July 8, 1721, *Bax. Mss.*, 9:464–465. See Mass. Council, in *RSUS*, January 24, 1720/21, and May 6, 1721, for the order to the Abenaki for Racle's dismissal; Messrs. de Vaudreuil and Begon to Louis XV, October 8, 1721, *NYCD*, 9:904; Letter of the Abenakis to Governor Shute, *AC*, Serie F3, Collection Moreau St. Mery, 2-2, pp. 502–507; James P. Baxter, *Pioneers of New France*, pp. 111–118.

44. Mass. Council, in *RSUS*, July 25, 1721; October 19, 1721; February 9, 1721/22; February 19, 1721/22; *The Boston Gazette*, September 23, 1721; August 28, 1721; Governor Phillipps to the Council of Trade and Plantations, August 16, 1721, *CSP*, 32:388; W. C. Ford, ed., *House Journals*, 3:94, 117, 124, 126,

141−143, 150, 152−153, 156−159, 163; Vaudreuil to Rale, September 25, 1721, *JR*, 67:63, and Mass. Arch., 51, pp. 358−359; Messrs de Vaudreuil and Begon to Louis XV, October 8, 1721, *NYCD*, 9:906; *AC*, C11A, 43, p. 234; *Coll. de Mss.*, 3:61. The king said, it should be noted, that Racle's opposition to the English pleased him. Le Roy aux Sieurs de Vaudreuil et Begon, June 8, 1721, *Coll. de Mss.*, 3:54, and *AC*, Serie F3, Collection Moreau St. Mery, 10, part 1, pp. 170−172. See also Parolle des Abénakis au Roy, October, 1721, *AC*, Serie F3, Collection Moreau St. Mery, 2-2, pp. 499−501; Extrait de quelques lettres de Jésuites Missionaries de Canada, au Père Davaugour Leurs Procurer en france, dépuis la fin d'aoust, jusqu'au commencement de Decembre 1721, *AC*, C11A, 124, pp. 179−180; Rale to Nephew, October 15, 1722, *JR*, 67:109−114; Messrs. de Vandreuil and Begon to the Council of Marine, October 17, 1722, *NYCD*, 9:910; *AC*, C11A, 124, pp. 143−144, 285−286, and *Coll. de Mss.*, 3:85−86; Robert LeBlant, *Une figure légendaire de l'histoire Acadienne: Le Baron de St. Castin* (Dax: Édition P. Pradeu, 1734), pp. 113; James P. Baxter, *Pioneers of New France*, p. 120; *The New England Courant*, February 12, 1721/22.

45. W. C. Ford, ed., *House Journals*, March 7, 1721/22, 3:68; June 22, 1722, 4:42; August 13, 1722, p. 81; Governor Shute to Mr. Popple, June 18, 1722, *CSP*, 33:90−91; *The New England Courant*, June 18, 1722; July 16, 1722; July 30, 1722; *The Boston Gazette*, July 23, 1722; July 30, 1722; Mass. Council, in *RSUS*, July 24, 1722; Mass. Arch., 31, pp. 106−108; Robert Earle Moody, "The Maine Frontier," pp. 348−349; Hutchinson noted that the English "chose to call the proceedings against them a prosecution for rebellion but, if a view be taken of all the transactions between the English and them from the beginning, it will be difficult to say what sort of subjects they were, and it is not certain that they understood they had promised subjection at all": Thomas Hutchinson, *The History of Colony and Province of Massachusetts-Bay*, ed. Lawrence Shaw Mayo, 3 vols. (Cambridge, Mass.: Harvard University Press, 1936), 2:203.

46. Kenneth M. Morrison, "Sebastien Racle and Norridgewock, 1724: The Ecstorm Conspiracy Thesis Reconsidered," *Me. His. Soc., Quarterly* 14 (1974): 76−97; Fannie H. Eckstorm, "The Attack on Norridgewock, 1724," *New England Quarterly* 7 (1934): 541−578; Samuel Sewall, *Diary of Samuel Sewall, Mass. His. Soc., Coll.*, 5th ser. (Boston, 1878−82), 7:342−343; Samuel Penhallow, *The History of the Wars of New England with the Eastern Indians* (Cincinnati, 1859), pp. 104, 111.

47. P. F. X. de Charlevoix, *History of New France*, 5:278−279; Letter from Father de la Chasse, *JR*, 67:233; Lettre de Monsieur le Marquis de Vaudreuil au Ministre, October 25, 1724, *Coll. de Mss.*, 3:109.

48. Father Ralle to another priest, August 12/23, 1724, *CSP*, 34:429−431; James P. Baxter, *Pioneers of New France*, pp. 251−252; *Mass. His. Soc., Coll.*, 2d ser., vol. 8, pp. 245−249; Fannie H. Eckstorm, "The Attack on Norridgewock," p. 566.

49. Fannie H. Eckstorm, "The Attack on Norridgewock," pp. 542−546.

50. M. de Vaudreuil to Lt. Governor Dummer, October 29, 1724, Mass. Arch., 52, pp. 77−84; William B. Trask, ed., *Letter of Colonel Thomas Westbrook and Others*

*Relative to Indian Affairs in Maine, 1722−1726* (Boston: George E. Littlefield, 1901), pp. 80−83, 88−91; Letter Lt. Gov. Dummer to Mons. Vaudreuil, January 19, 1724/25, *Bax. Mss.*, 10:175−178, and Mass. Arch., 52, pp. 106−109; Copie de la Commission donné par le Gouverneur de Baston aux Députés par luy envoyés au Canada, *AC*, F3, Collection Moreau St. Mery, 2-2, pp. 535−536; M. Begon to Count de Maurepas, April 21, 1725, *NYCD*, 9:941−945, and *AC*, C11A, 47, pp. 203−211, and also *Coll. de Mss.*, 3:117−123; Abstract of M. de Vaudreuil's Despatch, August 7, 1725, *NYCD*, 9:947−949; Vaudreuil au Ministre, May 22, 1725, *AC*, C11A, 47, pp. 83−88; Journal of Commissioners to Canada, May 28, 1725, in James P. Baxter, *Pioneers of New France*, pp. 350−353; Abstract of Letters respecting the Abenaquis, April 24, 1725, *NYCD*, 9:945.

51. Dummer to Capt. Bane, April 27, 1725, *Bax. Mss.*, 10:249; Dummer to Wentworth, July 9, 1725, *Bax. Mss.*, 10:305; Dummer to John Stoddard & John Wainwright, July 9, 1725, *Bax. Mss.*, 9:306; Dummer to Armstrong, August 16, 1725, *Bax. Mss.*, 10:322.

52. Rapport de MM. Langeuil et Begon au Ministre, October 31, 1725, *Coll. de Mss.*, 3:125−126, and *NYCD*, 9:955−956; Abstract of Despatches from Canada, October 20, 1727, *NYCD*, 9:990; At a Conference with the Delegates of the Indian Tribes, November 12, 1725, *Bax. Mss.*, 23:188−189.

53. Conference with the Delegates of the Indian Tribes, November 17, 1725, *Bax. Mss.*, 23:194.

54. Ibid., 23:197, 200, 201−202; Lettre de Monsieur de Vaudreuil au Ministre, November 18, 1725, *Coll. de Mss.*, 3:114.

55. Mr. Delafaye to Gov. Burnet, December 6, 1725, *CSP*, 24:473.

56. Indian's Letter, January 28, 1726, *Bax. Mss.*, 23:208−210.

57. Conference with the Eastern Indians, July and August, 1726, *Me. His. Soc., Coll.*, 1st ser., vol. 3, pp. 388−389.

58. Ibid., vol. 3, pp. 392−393, 401; Conference, August 4, 1726, *Bax. Mss.*, 23:204−208.

59. Benjamin Colman, "Some Memoirs for the Continuation of the History of the Troubles of the New-English Colonies, From the Barbarous and Perfidious Indians, Instigated by the more savage and Inhuman French of Canada and Nova Scotia," *Mass. His. Soc., Coll.*, 1st ser., vol. 6, p. 111; W. C. Ford, ed., *House Journals*, 7:143; Wenungenit to Dummer, October 4, 1726, *Bax. Mss.*, 10:365−366; Loron to Dummer, quoted in William Durkee Williamson, *History of Maine*, 2:149; Gyles to Dummer, March 15, 1726/27, *Bax. Mss.*, 23:211; Gyles to Dummer, March 17, 1726/27, *Bax. Mss.*, 10:359−360; Capt. Joseph Heath to Dummer, March 24, 1727, *Bax. Mss.*, 10:367−368; Gyles to Dummer, May 19, 1727, *Bax. Mss.*, 10:391−392; Gyles to Dummer, June 14, 1727, *Bax. Mss.*, 10:403−404; Memorial of a Conference at St. Georges River, June 26−27, 1727, *Bax. Mss.*, 23:213−217. For the text of the conference see Conference with the Eastern Indians at the further Ratification of the Peace, held at Falmouth in Casco-Bay, in July 1727, *Me. His. Soc., Coll.*, 1st ser., vol. 3, pp. 407−447.

60. Traité de Paix Entre les Anglois et les Abénakis, August, 1727, *Coll. de Mss.*, 3:134−135; Lettre du R. P. Lauverjeat à Monsieur le Marquis de Vaudreuil, *Coll. de Mss.*, 3:136; Indian Explanation of the Treaty of Casco Bay, 1727, *NYCD*, 9:966−967.

61. "Loron Sauguaaram," *DCB*, 3:584−585; William Walker, Robert Conkling, and Gregory Buesing, "A Chronological Account of the Wabanaki Confederacy," in *Political Organization of Native North Americans*, ed. Ernest L. Schusky (Washington, D.C.: University Press of America, 1980), pp. 41−84.

# INDEX

Meneval, Louis Alexandre des Friche de, 121
Messamouet (Micmac), 33–35
Methodology, 1–11. See also Ethnohistory
Miantonomo (Narragansett), 59
Micmac: defined, 5; early commercial contact, 14–15, 17, 19; partners with French in fur trade, 24–28; in intertribal trade, 31–34; intertribal war, 36–37, 39; characterized by French, 51–60; social psychology, 66; mythology, 99, 101; in King William's War, 127; in outbreak of Queen Anne's War, 158
Mogg (Kennebec), 110
Mohawk, 112, 124, 147
Montagnais-Naskapi: defined, 5; early commercial contact, 14, 17, 19, 20–21; intertribal war, 21, 34; French expectations because of, 32; animate cognitive orientation, 60, 65; persuade French to bar Abenaki from fur trade, 77; Christian Montagnais forge relations with Kennebec, 78–79; interpret sickness as God's anger, 85; demise of mission at Sillery, 93–94; mythology, 100
Montaigne, Michel, 44
Montmagny, Governor Charles Huault de, 77–78, 80
Moody, Samuel, 161–162, 184
More, Sir Thomas, 45
Morton, Thomas, 50, 66
Mt. Desert Island, 127, 157
Moxus (Kennebec), 112, 126, 157–158
Mythology: guide to Algonkian motivation, 6; critical approaches toward, 7, 8, 10; of civilization, 44; of golden age, 54; seeming irrationality of, 58–59; and sociality, 60–68; and historical causality, 61–62; and social organization, 64–65; explanation of disease, 72–74; and social crisis, 78; criteria used to evaluate priests, 83, 88; and reli-

gious syncretism, 99–101; methodology, 199–200 nn. 10, 11, 13. See also Gluskap; Ethnohistory; Jesuits; Religion; Social Organization; Values

Nahanada (Wawenock), 23–24
Narragansett, 31, 103
Negabamat, Noel (Montagnais), 78
Nelson, John, 147
Newfoundland, 13, 17–19, 37
Nicholson, Francis, 169, 173
Noel, Michel, Jean, and Jacques, 19
Norridgewock: symbol of the embattled northeast, 1–2, 5; people oppose English settlement, 174; attack on, 185–187
Norumbega, 20, 35

Olmechin (Saco), 33–35
Onondagas, 149
Oyster River, 143

Panounias (Micmac), 32–35
Passamaquoddy Abenaki: defined, 5; French settle among, 24; in intertribal war, 32, 34; French traders among, 119; English assert control over their territory, 122; missionaries among, 134
Paul, Dr. Peter, x, 84, 101
Pemaquid, 109, 112, 116–117, 123–124, 127, 130, 138
Penhallow, Samuel, 186
Pennacook, 5, 112–113, 147–148
Penobscot Abenaki: defined, 5; meet Jesuits, 25–26; intertribal war, 34–36; mythology, 101; in War of 1675–1677, 108–110; relations with Acadians, 119–120, 122; in King William's War, 123–124, 125–127, 129, 130–132, 134, 139; resist cultural change, 154–155; move to Canada, 159; factionalism, 179–180; lead in the development of the Abenaki confederacy, 185, 188–190

104; English ideology of, 143–146; religious interpretation of, 152; war as crusade, 185; literature on boundary disputes, 222–223 n. 3. *See also* Dummer's War; Ecology; Indian-Indian relations; King William's War; Queen Anne's War; War of 1675–1678

War of 1675–1677, 88–93, 106–111, 143, 153; literature on, 224–225 n. 16.

Wawenock, 5, 89

Waymouth, George, 22–23, 30, 37
Wells, 126, 158
Wenaganet (Kennebec), 172
Wheelwright, John, 156–157
Williams, Roger, 31, 59
Windigo. *See* Cannibal Giant
Winthrop, John, Jr., 81
Wiwurna (Kennebec), 174–176
Wood, William, 49
Worumbos (Kennebec), 126

York, 126, 143, 148

| | |
|---|---|
| Designer: | Kitty Maryatt |
| Compositor: | Trend Western |
| Printer: | Braun-Brumfield, Inc. |
| Binder: | Braun-Brumfield, Inc. |
| Text: | 12/13 Garamond |
| Display: | Garamond |